THE CHRISTIAN REALISM OF REINHOLD NIEBUHR AND THE POLITICAL THEOLOGY OF JÜRGEN MOLTMANN IN DIALOGUE

The Realism of Hope

Robert Thomas Cornelison

Mellen Research University Press
San Francisco

Library of Congress Cataloging-in-Publication Data

Cornelison, Robert Thomas.
    The Christian realism of Reinhold Niebuhr and the political
theology of Jürgen Moltmann in dialogue : the realism of hope /
Robert Thomas Cornelison.
        p.   cm.
    Includes bibliographical references and index.
    ISBN 0-7734-9805-2
    1. Niebuhr, Reinhold, 1892-1971. 2. Moltmann, Jürgen. 3. Hope-
-Religious aspects--Christianity--History of doctrines--20th
century. 4. Theology, Doctrinal--History--20th century.
5. Sociology, Christian--History of doctrines--20th century.
6. Christianity and politics--History--20th century. 7. Christian
ethics--History--20th century. I. Title.
BX4827.N5C67   1992
261.8'092'2--dc20   92-35175
                                                                       CIP

Editorial Inquiries:

Mellen Research University Press
534 Pacific Avenue
San Francisco
CA 94133

Order Fulfillment:

The Edwin Mellen Press
P.O. Box 450
Lewiston, NY 14092
USA

Printed in the United States of America

CONTENTS

FOREWORD

Reading doctoral dissertations about one's own work is, at best, a difficult business. Misunderstandings become evident, forcing one to question whether one's work was understandable to begin with. This work by Robert T. Cornelison, however, I have read with increasing joy and profit. His comparisons of the Christian Realism of Reinhold Niebuhr and my own Political Theology are always fair and correct. He betrays no negative presuppositions, and eschews undue bias. He attempts to draw out the best in each position while leaving the weaknesses to speak for themselves. He does not merely state the differences, but weighs the different positions against each other in order to explore their advantages and disadvantages. Although he does not spare me my many "weaknesses," I feel that he has understood my position and acknowledged and has praised my "strengths."

In the five chapters of the dissertation, Cornelison advances the comparisons in such a way that the reader can independently give each of the positions further thought, which is precisely the task of a doctoral dissertation. This task has been brilliantly achieved in Cornelison's work. What comes next must be reserved for the further individual works which we should certainly await from this author.

In this forward, I would not like to necessarily extend the dialogue between Christian Realism and Political Theology. Rather, I would like to simply offer some indications for a better mutual understanding of the two movements and also some points of conflict autobiographically.

If I remember correctly, the first theological book which I had ever read was the first volume of Reinhold Niebuhr's *Nature and Destiny of Man*. I found the book in 1947 in the small library in the British Norton Prisoner of War Camp, where a theological school was formed and incarcerated theology professors taught incarcerated students. At that time I certainly did not understand much of Niebuhr's book. I do remember, however, a certain pessimistic attitude toward sin which gripped me as I read and with which I agreed in the especially uncomfortable situation behind barbed wire. At that time I was certainly full of despair, but in faith I was "nevertheless confident," full of hope, full of utopias.

As both Cornelison and the biographers of Reinhold Niebuhr reveal, Niebuhr followed the path which led from an optimism in the Social Gospel Movement to what could be called a tragic sense of life in Christian Realism. In a similar manner, Paul Tillich followed an analogous path from being a religious socialist in Germany to being a philosophical theologian of the "border" after his forced emigration to the United States. These paths and changes were always, if not primarily, determined by the historical context of the events of the times: the flagrant treachery of Marxist socialism in Stalinism and its dictatorship of terror in the Soviet Union, through the arrival of anti-communist fascism and its regime of terror and through the necessity of militarily defending democracy. The politics of Christian Realism were self-evident in the extremely dangerous would crises between the years 1930 and 1960. The Christian Realism which Reinhold Niebuhr promulgated appears to me as a form of "emergency theology" in order to mobilize all of the powers possible against the enemies − Communism and Fascism − and to convince hesitant people through Christian principles. The American Christians were at that time highly influenced by idealism. Therefore the obvious polemic against liberal, social, or pacifist utopianism appears in Niebuhr's writings. Or maybe Niebuhr was really reacting in his polemic against his own, idealistic and utopian heart?

My time was different and I moved in an opposite direction: I experienced years of despair caused by the bitter experiences of war and imprisonment that only Kierkegaard (not Hegel), theology of the cross (not the kingdom of God), and the apocalyptic of *finis mundi* (not the kingdom of

God as *telos historiae*) won my attention. In 1948, I returned to Germany and found the public spirit and many private souls dominated by a conservative syndrome of a German Christian Realism. It was not a new future, but the restoration of the old relationships which became the goal under Chancellor Adenauer and Bishop Dibelius. NO EXPERIMENTS! – was the slogan in those days. Only the end of the fifties and the beginnings of the sixties awakened the courage for the future in politics, culture and theology. I discovered Ernst Bloch and the "Principle of Hope" and released myself from Kierkegaard and the "Principle of Despair." I left behind the snailshell of existential preoccupation with the private self and began with a Political Theology which desired to confront the political world with judgment and the kingdom of God. Naturally, my experiences of the time between 1945 and 1989 influenced my path and the changes in my theology. But it was again the insights of the Christian text and not only a reaction to the contemporary context which motivated me to go from a tragic Realism to the "Theology of Hope" and from the privatistic understanding of faith to a "Political Theology."

In order to reveal the theological basis for my decisions, I must ask: HOW CHRISTIAN IS CHRISTIAN REALISM? I would like to introduce some theses which will raise a few alternatives.

1.   Is it possible to recognize and define SIN in itself, or is it only feasible to confess it before God and only perceive its depths in his offer of grace. If one defines SIN in itself as egoism and self-interest, then the relationship to God plays no role. One is only describing general phenomena and calling it "sin," in order to set it aside as evil. Because one cannot alter these general, human phenomena, they are not only indicted, but also justified: The world is this way, and a Realist deals primarily with egoism and the self-seeking of people. This has nothing to do with the "justification of the sinner," but is merely the justification of the sin itself.

2.   The "realistic" result is then not the pardoning of the sinner, but a call for a strong state power in order to place boundaries on the general sin at hand: egoism and self-seeking. Aren't the emphases that politics is based on conflict of power, and that it belongs to the essence of the state to

use coercion, grounded in a doctrine of original sin without a corresponding idea of the grace of God?

3.   For Christian Realism, being a Christian does not overcome the fact of being a sinner, but instead, leads to a paradoxical existence of "*simul justus et peccator.*" This Lutheran idea is indeed the deepest ground for Niebuhr's emphasis on the ambivalence of human action and on tragic human existence. Paul, however, begins with human experience: "Where sin abounds, grace abounds even more" (Romans 5:20). Luther also broadened the paradoxical condition: "*Peccator in re, justus in spe.*" It thus follows – in my words – that the truly realistic Christian is a person of hope. Precisely because of the realistic attitude toward sin it is possible to understand that the experience of the powerful grace of God leads to the optimism of hope. This is no blind or delusive optimism. Rather, it is an optimism through which one becomes smart through experience and, for God's sake, hopes.

4.   Christian Realism emphasizes the transcendence of God and his JUDGMENT against this sinful world. That is indeed correct. But the judgment of God is always only a precursor of the *kingdom of God*, because, in a prophetic and apocalyptic sense, the justice of God in the world will become the foundation for the new world of God. The judgment of God is, in an eschatological sense, only temporary. The last word is: "See, I make all things new." (Revelation 21:5). The NO of God to injustice, sin, and death, serves, following a biblical interpretation, the YES of God to all creatures whom he has created out of love and therefore will also redeem. One who simply stops with the eschatological understanding of the judgment of God as *finis historiae*, stops too quickly. One needs to go a bit further in order to discover the *telos mundi* in the new creation of all things.

5.   Taking sin seriously cannot displace the trust in the original blessing of the good creation of God nor the hope in the definitive kingdom of God. This theological insight has practical consequences: politics is not in the first place power conflicts and coercion, but is the consensus of humans. It is not because people are sinners that they need the state, but because they are essentially *symbiotic* and social, they therefore create states (J. Althusius). Righteousness is necessary for every state. States which are built upon violence, coercion and German "Real Politik" are built upon sand. They

have no lasting future. Finally, in politics there are not only the positive utopias and enthusiasm, but also negative utopias and death-drives. For example, I do not hold the nuclear threat system with its "mutually assured destruction" as realistic, but rather as a nightmare. In the same way one cannot hold destructive economic systems as realistic when they destroy life instead of protecting it.

In conclusion, there are two different attitudes toward the future. The one always considers the worst case. If the worst occurs, then one was correct; if it does not occur, then one can rejoice. The second always hopes for the best. If it does not occur, then one is disappointed; if it does occur, then one can be happy. I *would rather be disappointed a thousand times, than surrender the hope of a better future. "Where there is no vision, the people will perish"* (Proverbs 29:18). In the past few years we have witnessed changes in Germany and in Europe which no one expected, which no one was prepared for. We had all become realists of the Cold War and had given up the hope for freedom and justice and the new community in Germany and in Europe. The person who predicted ten years ago what has occurred in Europe since 1989 was not only rejected because he was considered to be a utopian, but also because he was a dreamer. The fact remains: that person was the only realist among all the utopians of the status quo.

JÜRGEN MOLTMANN
Tübingen, October 26, 1991

PREFACE

What follows in the body of this work is not merely an interest which I developed and then chose to explore. Rather, it is a passion which has held my interest throughout the last decade. At times during the writing of the work that passion waned and even perhaps almost disappeared. Yet it always returned in novel and even stronger ways.

My interest in Reinhold Niebuhr developed early in my theological career. He, more than any other theologian, made clear to me that theology was not merely ideas which were to be understood as logical propositions, but were ideas which had been forged in the heat of practical controversy and struggle. His two volume opus, *The Nature and Destiny of Man*, still ranks for me as one of the finest treatises on the manifold ways in which theology and politics interact.

Being granted the honor of assisting the Liberation Theologian José Miguez Bonino and the Political Theologian Jürgen Moltmann during the semesters they spent at Emory revealed to me other roles that theology has played and continues to play in the political sphere. Yet it also placed me into a personal and intellectual crisis. While I could appreciate Niebuhr's stringent criticism of the socio-political order, I also could appreciate Miguez Bonino's and Moltmann's soaring hope for that same order. The quest and question for me was how to reach some sort of rapprochement of the two perspectives without misrepresenting either. I am under no illusions that the present work will fully satisfy the Niebuhrians or the Moltmannians who read it. I merely hope that it will perhaps give pause to think through some of the issues raised and thus add to the theological discussion of the relationship of theology and politics.

While the present work reflects a personal quest, its completion is the result of the efforts of many. To my colleagues in the theology program at Emory, a great debt of gratitude is due. Of particular mention in this regard is the abiding help, friendship, and comfort of Hal Knight and Curt Lindquist, along with their families, who not only spent long nights discussing and reading this project, but also provided physical and emotional shelter when most needed.

I also owe my deepest gratitude to the professors who have helped me find and refine my theological perspective. The deep faith and academic rigor of Geffrey B. Kelly prompted my interest in theology. The efforts of Jeremy Miller made it possible for me to attend Emory and to succeed there. The guidance of Ted Runyon throughout my studies in Emory, but especially during the dissertation process, was invaluable. Classes and conversations with Walt Lowe and Don Saliers, along with their gracious help in reading and commenting on drafts of the dissertation and finally evaluating it, have allowed me to grow in theological knowledge and sophistication. The trenchant criticisms of the Niebuhr section of my dissertation by Professor Theodore Weber brought me back into line when I went astray.

Dr. Robert West, editor of The Edwin Mellen Press, and Mr. Douglas Flaming of Mellen Book Design tolerated many changes of mind along with innumerable phone calls. Their assistance in creating the final copy of this work cannot be underestimated.

Of similar importance in the completion of the dissertation was the graciousness of Dr. Friedrich-Wilhelm Witt and the Friedrich Ebert Stiftung, whose grant made it possible for me to study in Tübingen during the 1984-1985 academic year.

Of central importance to the completion of the dissertation was the guidance of its director, Jürgen Moltmann. Professor Moltmann's theological work provided the impetus for the book, while his graciousness and warmth in guiding me throughout the process made its completion possible.

Finally, the patience of those closest to me, my family, provided the unconditional support I needed for for the completion of the dissertation. My parents and brothers sacrificed both emotionally and financially for my many years of education. Foremost among all of those who have aided me during the arduous process of writing the dissertation has been my wife, Tamara. Her love and support kept me going throughout the writing process. Her editing of the various drafts allowed me to concentrate on the issues I wanted to raise.

INTRODUCTION

A. THEME OF THE DISSERTATION

This dissertation concerns itself with a dialogical examination of the political relevance of Christian hope as elucidated in Jürgen Moltmann's Political Theology and Reinhold Niebuhr's Christian Realism. A central claim of Moltmann is that

> Hope alone is to be called realistic, because it alone takes seriously the possibilities with which all reality is fraught. Hope and the kind of thinking that goes with it consequently cannot submit to the reproach of being utopian, for they do not strive after things that have "no place", but after things that have "no place *as yet*" but can acquire one....On the other hand, the celebrated realism of the stark facts...is much more open to the charge of being utopian, for in its eyes there is "no place" for possibilities, for future novelty, and therefore for the historic character of reality.(1)

One of the strongest criticisms of the type of hope which Moltmann espouses is found in the Christian Realism of Reinhold Niebuhr. Instead of focusing on the transformative character of hope, Niebuhr contends that:

> ...the Christian faith and hope will be most creative if we are not too preoccupied with its current relevance and pragmatic efficiency....[It must be a faith] which does not place its main emphasis on hope...but upon a life of soberness and watchfulness, of faith and love--which will appeal to a world in the night of despair as having some gleams of light in it, derived from the 'Light that shineth in darkness.'(2)

By bringing the thought of Niebuhr and Moltmann into dialogue, the dissertation extends a discussion which has engaged Christian thought from the very beginning of the Church: how to relate Christian theology to the political realm. Traditionally, the Christian idea of hope has included two diverse elements:

> a penultimate aspect (based on the apocalyptic and eschatology of the early church and the left-wing of the Reformation) which looks toward the transformation of this world, and an ultimate aspect (grounded in Augustinian and Lutheran thought) which points not to the transformation of this world, but to its dissolution and fulfillment after the Parousia. No theology maintains a strictly one-sided perspective; all attempt to keep the ultimate and penultimate elements of Christian hope in a creative tension.(3)

Both Moltmann and Niebuhr agree that hope is a central theme of the Christian message. For both, the question: "What can we hope for?", seems to embody the essence of the Christian quest for coherence and meaning in life and forms a fundamental element of Christian identity. Disagreements arise between the two theological movements, however, as to the relevance of Christian hope. Moltmann contends that Christian hope is fundamentally transformative and liberative in character. It is related to political decision-making, and rather than being an illusory idealism, is true realism. He holds that:

> The hope of the gospel has a polemic and liberating relation not only to the religions and ideologies of men, but still more to the factual, practical life of men and to the relationships in which this life is lived.(4)

Niebuhr, on the other hand, feels that an emphasis on the politically transformative character of Christian hope is really irrelevant to political decision-making because it actually leads to unrealistic expectations for political change and progress. Hope, in Niebuhr's view, too easily succumbs to the idealism which distorts the true power relationships inherent in politics.(5)

These diverse viewpoints concerning the relevance of Christian hope can be understood as the fundamental point of disagreement in the current debate between Christian Realism and Political Theology. The debate began as an outgrowth of an heated exchange of views entitled "Liberation

Theology and Christian Realism," published in *Christianity and Crisis* in 1973. In this exchange Thomas Sanders, flying the banner of Christian Realism, accused Liberation Theology of being "soft utopianism", that is, of being a theology based on a misguided optimism producing illusory hope for a qualitatively better world. This perspective, in Sanders' view, results in irresponsible political decisions.(6) Rubem Alves, in support of Liberation Theology, accepted the appellation of soft-utopianism, stating that its transformative focus is truer to Biblical sources than Niebuhr's realism. In fact, in Alves' view, Niebuhr's realism was nothing more than American ideology cloaked in religious garb.(7)

The subsequent extension of the debate to include Political Theology was based on the recognition by the Christian Realists of a similar soft-utopianism in the thought of J.B. Metz and Jürgen Moltmann. Ruurd Veldhuis, for example, in comparing the thought of Moltmann and Niebuhr, contends that Moltmann's utopianism, derived from his emphasis on the transformative nature of Christian hope, leads to political ambiguity and therefore political uselessness.(8) Dennis McCann includes Political Theology in his criticism of Liberation Theology and Chin Shiba, evaluating both Moltmann and Niebuhr, finds the former to be "formal and abstract", and guilty of "bypassing [the] unavoidable task of patient discernment" in political analysis. Shiba finds Niebuhr's emphasis on the ambiguity of politics as more suitable to political decision-making.(9) Apart from a brief article written by J.M. Lochman concerning the biblical realism of Political Theology, there has been no direct response to these criticisms.(10)

The thesis of this work is that neither Moltmann's nor Niebuhr's perspective on hope, taken individually, does full justice to the political relevance of the Christian message of hope. By bringing the two perspectives into dialogue, it is possible to do justice to both the critical and transformative aspects of Christian hope. Toward this end, this work examines and evaluates Niebuhr's Christian Realism and Moltmann's Political Theology in light of their theological understandings of the God-world relationship, history, anthropology and ethics, with an eye toward developing a more complete understanding of the relevance of Christian hope to the political situation.

B. METHODOLOGICAL CONSIDERATIONS

The book is decidedly theological in nature, examining the theological conceptualizations and symbolizations which undergird the ethical thought of both.(11) Foundational to the dissertation is the insight that the ethical stances adopted by Christian Realism and Political Theology are intimately connected with theological presuppositions which must be carried over relatively intact into any discussion of the ethical merits of either position. One cannot reduce Political Theology to its futurist eschatology, its trinitarian perspective or its understanding of suffering. Similarly, one cannot reduce Christian Realism merely to its idea of sin, or its discussion of power, or its understanding of the social world. Instead one must look at the specific constellation of theological conceptualizations upon which each movement bases its ethical thought. This examination tries to lay bare the links between the theology and ethical stance of each.

While a critical examination of the debate between Christian Realism and Political Theology is necessary, certain methodological difficulties present themselves in a comparison of these two theological movements. Each movement developed in different time periods with different issues. Moltmann's theology is decidedly German in character, developing out of and responding to a German context. Niebuhr's theology was developed out of an American perspective in response to American problems. Furthermore, Moltmann and Niebuhr give priority to different elements of their thought, thus a direct comparison of the two is a difficult, if not misguided, effort. For Moltmann, history, not anthropology, is fundamental. For Niebuhr, however, anthropology is central; it informs his subsequent thought. A direct cross-comparison of the perspective of Political Theology and Christian Realism would lead to misconceptions about the theologies of each. Consequently, any comparisons between the two must be undertaken in such a way that the different emphases of each theology can be accepted and taken into account.

The key for cross-examining these two movements can be found in the specific points of conflict in the theologies of each. Many of the elements of Moltmann's theology which enable him to speak of the relevance of hope are precisely those elements which form the basis for Niebuhr's disavowal of the relevance of Christian hope.

Foremost among the different emphases is the relationship of God and world. This issue, in a sense, subsumes the others. Political Theology and Christian Realism reach different conclusions as to the relationship between God and the world.(12) Moltmann primarily emphasizes the "temporal" transcendence of God over the world. In this perspective the distinction between God and world is fluid and creative. God and world interpenetrate each other. God is *in* the world and the world is *in* God.(13) In this view, God's activity in the world provides for the possibility of the transformation of socio-political structures and relationships.

For Niebuhr, this perspective suggests a surrender to Liberal Theology. Niebuhr primarily emphasizes the "vertical" transcendence of God over the world and draws a precise distinction between God and world.(14) Consequently, the activity of God in the world does not provide as much of a basis for social transformation in Niebuhr's thought as it does in Moltmann's.

A second theological element which impacts on the shape of Moltmann's political ethic is the relationship of history to its end. Here the conflict between Christian Realism and Political Theology lies in differing views of historical perfection.

Moltmann develops a PROMISE/ FULFILLMENT model of history in which history is not only the locus of the disclosure of meaning, but is the arena in which the promises of God are given expression and brought to fulfillment. The fulfillment of history, in Moltmann's view, takes place at the end of history, but occurs proleptically within the dynamic movement of history itself.(15) This perspective implies that history is more open to positive historical change than Niebuhr supposed. Niebuhr, on the other hand, develops a DISCLOSURE/ FULFILLMENT model of history in which the coherence of history remains fragmentary until its end (in the sense of a *finis*). Consequently, for Niebuhr a sharp distinction must be drawn between the disclosure of meaning in history and its fulfillment outside of history.(16)

The final theological element examined in the dissertation is anthropology. The issue here centers on the possibilities of the openness of human nature to change. Moltmann's anthropology emphasizes the openness of human existence to change and transformation. For Moltmann, human nature is primarily historical; that is, it is formed in the process of living a human life. Sin, in this view, is primarily historically conditioned and therefore open to transformation within history.(17)

Niebuhr's anthropology, in contrast, is based on an understanding of human existence as an uncertain balance between elements of freedom and finitude which produces both the possibility for creativity and the possibility for a fall into sin. The creative aspects of human existence allow for the transcendence of given circumstances, while anxiety can become the source of inescapable human sinfulness which taints all human progress. While Niebuhr does allow for some transformation of the human situation, he holds that essential human nature is unchangeable and thus limits both the form and degree of transformation possible in the world.(18)

In this work, Niebuhr's perspective on each of these issues will be examined first, and each will be followed directly by Moltmann's view. The strengths and weaknesses of both theologians' positions will then be examined.

This work will also focus on two related features of the ethical thought of each: the nature and function of utopia and the necessity of understanding politics in relationship to order. The "utopian" vision of Political Theology contends that Christian Realism lacks the critical discernment of the real possibilities for positive political transformation because it does not take into account the mutability of human nature and historical existence and the possibility of novelty and transformation in the world.(19)

The "realist" vision, on the other hand, emphasizes the need to understand the underlying power realities of any political structures. Christian Realism contends that Political Theology falls into the idealism of "soft-utopianism" which does not take full account of the power relationships inherent in political reality and thus lacks the capability for critical discernment among possible political decisions, all of which contain some elements of sinfulness and self-seeking.(20) The question of discernment, as Niebuhr views it, includes a refutation of idealistic/moralistic hopes for building a more rational society.(21)

C. FORMAT OF THE BOOK

The book is divided into six chapters. Chapter One provides the historical contexts of Political Theology and Christian Realism as a means of grounding the discussion of the theology and political perspective of each. Chapters Two, Three and Four examine aspects of each of the theologies which provide the foundation for their political thought and also best distinguish the position of one from the other: the God-world relationship, history and its end, and anthropology. Chapter Five brings together the theologies of the two movements through an examination of the ethical implications of the thought of each in regard to the issues of utopianism and of the relation of theology to the social order.

The conclusion Chapter Six, provides pointers for a rapprochement of the two perspectives in such a way that many of the weaknesses of each position taken individually may be avoided.

Notes to the Introduction

1. J. Moltmann, Theology of Hope (NY: Harper and Row, 1967) 25 (Hereafter, *TH*).

2. Reinhold Niebuhr, "The Theme of Evanston", *Religion in Life*, XXIII/3, 1954, pp. 334-340. It is recognized that Christian Realism is not limited to the work of Reinhold Niebuhr, and that Political Theology is not limited to the work of Moltmann. The restrictions of the dissertation format, however, prevent us from examining all scholars associated with each of these theological movements (e.g., John C. Bennett and Paul Ramsey on the side of Realism, and J.B. Metz, Dorothee Soelle and J.M. Lochman on the side of Political Theology.) The choice of Niebuhr and Moltmann as dialogue partners in this dissertation is a considered one, however. Niebuhr and Moltmann have produced the most developed and comprehensive perspective on Christian Realism and Political Theology, respectively. Consequently, their thought will be considered "representative" of those positions in this work. When capitalized, the term "Political Theology," refers to the specific theological movement presented by Metz and Moltmann, *et al.* When not capitalized, it refers to the general relationship of theology and politics given in the context where it appears.

3. Cf. Reinhold Niebuhr "Walter Rauschenbusch in Historical Perspective", *Religion in Life* 27/4 (Autumn, 1958) 527-536: "We have to hazard our ventures into the culture of our day and hope that we will not make too many mistakes. We must hazard them particularly when the problem of social responsibility is at stake. For the Christian faith is not otherworldly, it always commits us in a responsible relation to the community and bids us to establish justice." and J. Moltmann, "Political Theology and Political Hermeneutic of the Gospel", *On Human Dignity* (Phila.: Fortress, 1984) 97-112 (hereafter, OHD): "A Church which engages in this mode of [practical] theology may no longer ask abstractly about the relation of Church and politics, as if these were two separate things which must be brought together; rather this church must begin with a critical awareness of its own political existence and its actual social functions." Part of the reason for the difference of opinion regarding the relevance of Christian hope has been the ambiguous nature of the New Testament discourse on the subject. The New Testament betrays two general perspectives on hope. On the one hand, there is a predominantly "other-worldly" understanding of hope which emphasized that the object of Christian hope is not the transformation of the world, but is in the hope for the end of the world (and its history). Such a perspective sees little relevance of Christian hope to the socio-political world.

On the other hand, there is a strand of New Testament discourse, based on apocalyptic expectation, which views Christian hope as primarily "this-worldly". Understood in this manner, hope takes on socio-political relevance as an impetus for transformation and liberation. Cf. B. Hebblethwaite, *The Christian Hope*. (Grand Rapids, Mich.: Eerdmans, 1984).

4. *TH*, 330.

5. Reinhold Niebuhr, *Nature and Destiny of Man*, volume I (NY: Scribner's, 1941). (hereafter, NDM,I)

6. Thomas Sanders, "The Theology of Liberation: Christian Utopianism", *Christianity and Crisis* 33, 1973. pp. 167-73.

7. Rubem Alves, "Christian Realism: Ideology of the Establishment", *Christianity and Crisis* 33, 1973. pp. 173-76.

8. R. Veldhuis, *Realism versus Utopianism* (Assen, Netherlands: Van Gorcum, 1975) 157.

9. D. McCann, *Christian Realism and Liberation Theology* (Maryknoll, NY: Orbis, 1982). C. Shiba, *Transcendence and the Political*, (PhD. Diss., Princeton Theological Seminary, 1983) p. 326.

10. J. M. Lochman, "The Problem of Realism in R. Niebuhr's Theology", *Scottish Journal of Theology*, 11, 1958, pp. 253-264.

11. This narrow focus on theology is demanded because much of the recent theological thought which claims for itself a basis in the thought of Niebuhr and Moltmann neglects maintaining any sort of conceptual link with the theological underpinnings of their work. In a recent paper delivered at Emory University, for example, Delwin Brown claimed that there are no substantive differences between Niebuhrian Christian Realism and liberation theology relative to the possibility for social transformation. In order to make this claim, however, Brown had to reinterpret many of Niebuhr's basic theological claims in a Whiteheadian process perspective. Cf. D. Brown, "Some Notes on the Nature and Destiny of Sin, or How a Niebuhrian Process Theology of Liberation is Possible", in *Theology, Politics and Peace*, Theodore Runyon, ed., (Maryknoll, NY: Orbis, 1989), pp. 155-166. Similarly, Ruurd Veldhuis, in a recent book comparing Moltmann and Niebuhr on the issues of realism and utopianism, gives short shrift to the theological presuppositions of the ethical thought of each, in an attempt to define what differences there were in their respective ethical perspective.(R. Veldhuis, *Realism and Utopianism* (Assen, Netherlands: Van Gorcum, 1975). The neglect of, or the violence done to the theological foundations laid by Niebuhr and Moltmann by many contemporary theological attempts render invalid the claim that such attempts are "Niebuhrian" or "Moltmannian".

12.   Cf. J. Gustafson, "Theology in the Service of Ethics: An Interpretation of Reinhold Niebuhr's Theological Ethics", in R. Harris (ed.), *Reinhold Niebuhr and the Issues of Our Times* (Grand Rapids: Eerdmans, 1986, pp. 24-45 and J. Niewiadomski, *Die Zweideutigkeit von Gott und Welt in J. Moltmanns Theologien* (Innsbruck: Tyrolia Verlag, 1982).

13.   Cf. J. Moltmann, *God in Creation* (NY: Harper and Row, 1986) 13. (hereafter, *GC*).

14.   NDM,I, Chapter 6.

15.   Cf. *TH*, Chapter 2.

16.   Cf. Reinhold Niebuhr, *Faith and History* (NY: Scribner's, 1949) Chap. XIV (hereafter, FH) and D. W. Rutledge, "The Salvation of History: History and the End in Reinhold Niebuhr", *Perspectives in Religious Studies*, vol. 8, 1981, 122-133.

17.   Cf. J. Moltmann, *Man*, tr. J. Sturdy (Phila.: Fortress, 1974) 57: "The hope for the future which the Christian faith holds is not the 'solution to the riddle of history' in a unity of the being of man, nature and God, but a new creation of man in his world, in which the contradictions of the present are raised to a new and lasting response to God.

18.   Cf. *Nature and Destiny of Man*, vol. I (NY: Scribner's, 1941) 251: "Since he [the human being] is involved in the contingencies and necessities of the natural process on one hand and since, on the other, he stands outside them and foresees their caprices and perils, he is anxious. In his anxiety he seeks to transmute his finiteness into infinity, his weakness into strength, his dependence into independence."

19.   J. Moltmann, "What is 'New' in Christianity: The Category *Novum* in Christian Theology," in *Religion Revolution and the Future* (NY: Scribners, 1969) 3-18. (hereafter, *RRF*)

20.   R. Veldhuis, *Realism vs. Utopianism*, p. 158.

21.   This is the basis for much of Niebuhr's critique of the progressive aspects the modern concept of history. Cf. NDM, I, Chap. 2 and 4.

CHAPTER I

THE CONTEXT OF CHRISTIAN REALISM
AND POLITICAL THEOLOGY

If theology, as Paul Tillich states in his theory of correlation, always operates between two poles, the truth of the Christian message and the temporal situation in which the truth is received, then theology and the context within which it is written reflexively condition each other: the context of theology always influences the content of the theology itself, and the theology produced similarly influences its context.(1) For Christian Realism and Political Theology the link between the theology produced and the context within which it was written was viewed as an inherent part of the theological enterprise itself.(2) Niebuhr took great pains to elucidate how the absolute love ethic expressed in the scriptural command to love one's neighbor and one's enemy related to the various situations which arose during the half century in which he wrote. In a similar fashion, Moltmann emphasized the necessity of maintaining not only the identity of the Christian message, but also the relevance of that message to the concrete situation of its hearers.(3)

This chapter presents the *contexts* of Christian Realism and Political Theology as foundations for their respective thought. This examination will be painted in broad strokes, introducing themes which will be examined in greater detail later in the work.

I.   1.1: *Christian Realism*

One of the sure signs of the relevance of a theological enterprise is its longevity.   The Christian Realism of Reinhold Niebuhr is one such enterprise.   Niebuhr's theological career spanned the better part of the twentieth century.   He theology has been relevant to situations ranging from the horrors of two world wars to the Viet Nam Conflict.   While constantly changing contexts caused him occasionally to shift emphasis, his thought has remained essentially consistent throughout the years.

Christian Realism developed in the period of rapid industrialization and urbanization of the United States in the late nineteenth and early twentieth centuries.   The growth of industry sparked a new attitude toward history and the role of the person within it.   New industry promised a rapidly growing economy and an increased standard of living.   Henry Ford's factories and assembly lines provided employment not only for their own workers, but also for those involved in auxiliary industries.   Industrialization needed capital, and banks and other lending institutions flourished.   The construction industry boomed, trying to keep pace with the need for new factories and homes for those who flocked to the cities in an attempt to find work.

Ideologically, the *Weltanschauung* of this period was that of secularized progress.(4)   The work of the Enlightenment to remove the religious presuppositions of knowledge was effectively furthered in the nineteenth and early twentieth centuries.   The possibilities for the advancement of the human race which, in earlier times were attributed to God, were now placed within the realm of possibility of autonomous human reason.(5)

Scientific discovery also added fuel to the idea of progress.   Darwin's development of a theory of evolution provided a biological basis for the progress of the human species.   Sociologists such as Herbert Spencer utilized Darwin's fundamental idea of evolution to postulate the ideas of social evolution.(6)

Theologically, this period was marked by two perspectives which took dissimilar views toward the possibilities of human progress.   The traditional theology of the time, Christian Orthodoxy, increasingly criticized the results of the new technology and industrialization. In its place it offered a turn toward inward spiritual goodness in which an individual's relationship to God superseded a social and political emphasis.(7)

A second theological enterprise, the Social Gospel, maintained a critical stance toward the idea of "progressive" industrialization, as did Orthodoxy, but differed from Orthodoxy in that it understood the focus of Christianity to be both socially critical and socially constructive. It did not demand retreat from the world into an interior holiness, but demanded social involvement and transformation.

The main proponent of the Social Gospel was Walter Rauschenbusch. According to Rauschenbusch, Christianity had its basis in the historical Jesus as the founder of a divine, ethical kingdom on earth. With this focus, Christianity embodied a *social* ideal which called for the transformation of the world into a divinely-ordained community:

> The problem of the social gospel is how the divine life can get control of human society. The social gospel is concerned about the progressive social incarnation of God.(8)

The social basis of Christianity, in Rauschenbusch's view, revealed the need for a reconstruction of theology which would embody the social nature of human sin and redemption. Rauschenbusch found the fundaments for this theology in the social admonitions of the prophets (especially Amos and Micah), in the love ethic of Jesus, and later in the kingdom of God and eschatology.

Reading the prophets revealed to Rauschenbusch the structural and personal nature and consequences of human sin and the demand that the Church involve itself in the struggle for social justice. Amos' injunctions against all nations, in particular, proved archetypical for Rauschenbusch as a general critique of societal injustice.(9)

Rauschenbusch contended that the answer to the problem of producing a just society lay in the successive working-out of the love ethic developed by Jesus. Since human existence was for Rauschenbusch fundamentally social, human sin was also conceived of by him as socially conditioned. Sinfulness could therefore be curtailed through the development of countervailing love.(10)

The third pillar upon which the Social Gospel's theology was built was the eschatological conception of the kingdom of God as a future event which was being progressively realized in history. The centrality of the concept of the kingdom of God in Rauschenbusch's thought is developed in his *Theology for the Social Gospel*. According to Rauschenbusch:

1.   The Kingdom of God must be placed at the center of theology, not at the end.
2.   The Kingdom of God idea contained the revolutionary force of Christianity.
3.   The Kingdom of God is both present and future: the kingdom is in the process of being realized in the world.(11)

From this brief sketch, it becomes evident that the socially *critical* aspect of the Social Gospel lies not only in its understanding of the judgment of God against all nations as revealed by the prophets, but also in the distance between the present degree of the realization of the love ethic of Jesus and the total fulfillment of that ethic in the kingdom of God:

> No theories about the future of the Kingdom of God are likely to be valuable or true which paralyze or postpone redemptive action on our part....It is for us to see the Kingdom of God as always coming, always pressing in on the present, always big with possibility, and always inviting immediate action....By accepting it as a task, we experience it as a gift.(12)

The *progressive* aspect of the kingdom lies in its developmental perspective: the kingdom is being realized in the world today through the practice of love and justice among humans:

> The Kingdom of God is humanity organized according to the will of God....[Since] love is the supreme law of Christ, the Kingdom of God implies a progressive reign of love in human affairs.(13)

The Social Gospel maintained its dominance of the American theological effort into the third and fourth decades of the twentieth century.

At that time, one of its own children, Reinhold Niebuhr, was to become one of its greatest critics and was to change the shape of American theology.

Reinhold Niebuhr's earliest theological efforts can be understood as well within the Social Gospel tradition. Like Rauschenbusch, Niebuhr was searching for a means of maintaining a critical attitude toward social conditions, while still holding on to an idealism that would lead beyond despair. As late as 1931, Niebuhr shared, with reservations, the optimistic perspective that it was possible to overcome many of the injustices of the world through educating people to the ideals of Christian love and brotherhood and by applying those ideals as fully as possible in one's life. In Niebuhr's earliest writings we find that

> real morality cannot come from without, but must come from within, from entirely changed hearts and ideals, and only one thing can change man's heart, the Gospel of Jesus Christ.(14)

During the immediate post-World War I period, Niebuhr remarked

> Yet, finally, Europe's salvation must be achieved by more thoroughgoing forces than any political policy. Europe must overcome its hate and learn the divine art of forgiveness....Europe must learn that you can only forgive an enemy by doing the foolish thing and trusting him beyond his deserts, whereupon, as every experience proves, he will justify your faith beyond its expectations.(15)

And when asked about the direction that Christian education should take, Niebuhr responded that

> The universe is not so much what it is, but what it is becoming. Really and spiritually deal with human beings not according to what you see in them in the present moment but according to the possibilities in them, and of course there are always tremendous possibilities in them that have not been realized.(16)

Even though the Niebuhr of this first stage remained within the Social Gospel tradition, he held certain reservations which would eventually lead him to abandon this perspective and forge a new path. This hesitancy toward fully accepting the Social Gospel theology can be seen in Niebuhr's 1927 book, *Does Civilization Need Religion?* In this book, Niebuhr became more cognizant of the difficulties in transforming the world by bringing it into congruence with the will of God. He began to note an inertia in the world.(17) In a move that would become basic for his later thought, he began to understand the tragic nature of the world's intransigence to rational or religious pleas for brotherhood.(18) He also began to question the Social Gospel's one-sidedly optimistic, romantic, perfectionistic anthropology.

The events of the next few years further altered Niebuhr's theological and political opinions. The hopes for an open, better future, as expressed in the increased optimism of industrial American society and in the Social Gospel, soon came crashing down. The Depression revealed the inadequacy of uncontrolled capitalism in the United States: the industrialists had indeed become rich, but the workers had become ever more impoverished. The optimistic view of so-called "progress" which had been embodied in the hope of this age could be maintained only when one was blind to the misery it created.

These facts, along with his own experiences as the pastor of Bethel Church in Detroit, revealed to Niebuhr that the prevailing theologies (Orthodoxy and Social Gospel) needed replacement. To Niebuhr, Orthodoxy relinquished the social relevance of Christianity by retreating into personalistic religion which lacked social effectiveness.(19) In regard to the Social Gospel, Niebuhr was of two minds. On the one hand, Niebuhr was impressed by Rauschenbusch's insistence on the social relevance of Christianity. Rauschenbusch's understanding of the socio-economic basis of political reality as a struggle of power against power was lauded by Niebuhr as "the voice of realism."(20) Yet, the Social Gospel had defects which Niebuhr thought rendered it useless in the struggle for social justice. The Social Gospel revealed its character as a Liberal Theology by seemingly becoming too completely allied with the culture within which it found itself.(21) The Kingdom of God which was promised by Rauschenbusch had come to be identified with the ideal society that modern, American culture had hoped to gain through its evolutionary development.(22)

As we saw above, Rauschenbusch held that the human being and history betrayed a possibility for perfectibility and progress which could be brought into existence if the material conditions of the human situation which hindered such development (e.g., corruption, evil institutions) were destroyed and replaced by more just arrangements. For Rauschenbusch, the impetus behind such development was to be found in a more stringent application of the love ethic presented by Jesus in the Gospels. The more the ethic of love became progressively effective in society, the more just social relations would become.(23) Niebuhr, however, felt that such a transformation of society betrayed undue optimism based on an illusion of progress which did not "even faintly surmise the tragedies of the day."(24) For Niebuhr, the direct application of Jesus' love ethic to social structures was an impossibility because it was too rigorous. It demanded perfect obedience and did not recognize the ambiguity inherent in political decision-making.(25) For in all political decisions it is not a question of choosing an absolute good over an absolute evil, but of deciding on a course of action which has both good and evil consequences. Furthermore, the Social Gospel's belief that the cooperation necessary to create or maintain justice in society could be established through non coercive means is a fallacy which hides the economic and political power relations which undergird society itself.(26) A political decision therefore demands "an inevitable compromise between its ideal and the brute facts of life" and recognition of the truth of St. Paul's well-known confession: "the good that I would do, I do not do; and the evil I would not, that I do."(27)

Niebuhr's disenchantment with the liberalism of the Social Gospel movement led him into the second stage of his thought. Niebuhr felt the need for a reconstruction of Christian theology in such a way that Christianity could maintain its social relevance, yet not succumb to the dangers of becoming a religion which identified itself too closely with its surround culture. Niebuhr concluded that Christian theology had to be combined with a much more radical politics than liberalism could provide. And although Niebuhr was never fully comfortable within its bounds, he took a brief foray into Christian Marxism during the 1930's. During this time, the socialist experiment in the Soviet Union had captured the imagination of the age. American intellectuals began to view socialism as a mean of coming to grips with the ills which plagued society. For Niebuhr, Marxism seemed relevant practically to the search for justice in a way that the Social Gospel and capitalism were not.(28) For the Niebuhr of this period, Marxism provided a realistic interpretation of the power realities which lay at the heart of the socio-political world and thus could prove fruitful in developing strategies for the promotion of justice.(29)   In Marxism he found much with which to agree. Marxism encompassed a healthy moral cynicism.(30)   It had an inherent egalitarianism.(31) He felt that the Marxist analysis of the worker's plight was more correct than that held by liberalism and that it provided a means of resistance to an unjust social system.(32)   He believed that capitalism would fall under its own weight.(33)

For Niebuhr, Communism also seemed to play an important geopolitical role. During this period, Niebuhr felt that political reality was primarily inertial in character. Inequality and disproportion of power and wealth were so endemic to the social structure of the time that nothing short of fanaticism of the left could provide the impetus to change.(34)

The replacement of the Social Gospel by a Marxist interpretation allowed Niebuhr to link the two elements which to him always seemed elusive: a moral cynicism which demanded a realistic approach to politics and gave some insight into the "demonic force in human life" and a healthy idealism which gave the oppressed a vision and a goal. Marxism, to Niebuhr, provided hope for the future similar to that which was embodied in the Social Gospel, but without the surrender to modern culture with which the Social Gospel had been afflicted.

Niebuhr, however, was not totally taken over by Marxism. He saw weaknesses in the Marxist program which, as it would happen, history proved to be traditional Marxism's downfall. The primary weakness that Niebuhr saw in Marxism was its naturalism. Since it located the telos of human striving in history in the overcoming of class conflict and capitalism and in the eventual vindication of the proletariat, Marxism lacked an ultimate perspective on historic and relative moral achievements.(35) Consequently, it tended to identify the interest of the proletariat with absolute truth. In effect, Marxism applied its cynicism to all but itself.

The result of this omission was that Marxism betrayed a utopian tendency which, in Niebuhr's view, would lead to disillusionment.(36) The question of "what happens after the revolution," a question which will occupy much of Niebuhr's polemic against Marxism in his next stage, is here only a nagging doubt.

At this point in Niebuhr's development, these weaknesses of Marxism were not fatal ones. The Marxist interpretation of reality was correct; it just needed a transcendent perspective from which to judge not only others, but also itself. For Niebuhr, this was the genius of *Christian* Marxism. Christian Marxism recognized that all of creation, Marxist and capitalist, owner and proletariat alike, were under the judgment of God. There can be no ideal in history, for this is to identify too closely transcendence and immanence, God and nature.(37)

The second shift in Niebuhr's perspective was the most dramatic. The early Niebuhr had found much in common between Christianity and Marxism. In a sense, both were directed to the same goal on different, but similar tracks. It was a quite different Niebuhr, who in 1953 defined communism as "an organized evil which spreads terror and cruelty throughout the world and confronts us everywhere with faceless men who are immune to every form of moral and political suasion."(38)

The reasons for this shift are not easy to delineate. Certain factors can, however, be evinced. From a political perspective, Niebuhr became dismayed at the developing totalitarianism of the Soviet form of Marxism under Stalin. The socialist experiment in the Soviet Union had produced an oppressive society and a belabored economy. The bright future which had been limned for the Soviet Union became the dark horror of pogroms, of natural and politically induced famine, of an intractable ruling class and of a sluggish economy. The seeming failure of parliamentary socialism in Britain and elsewhere disillusioned Niebuhr about the efficacy of the socialist political program.(39) Rather than remain within the Marxist camp, Niebuhr came to understand the New Deal democracy as a more viable means of dealing with economic and political injustice.(40) And by the time of his writing of *The Children of Light and the Children of Darkness*, Niebuhr had found American democracy, in general, superior to all other schemes for fighting injustice.(41)

Other practical concerns caused Niebuhr to become disillusioned with Marxism. In the period directly preceding World War II, Niebuhr was uncomfortable with the acquiescence of the socialistically organized and controlled unions to Soviet wishes.(42) And the growing Anti-Communism in America directly following the war only strengthened Niebuhr's increasing distrust of socialistic remedies for injustice.

On the theoretical side, the perfectionist strain in Marxism, to Niebuhr's mind, began to look more and more like a fatal flaw. The grounds for Niebuhr's ultimate theoretical disavowal of Marxism lay first and foremost in Niebuhr's understanding of anthropology. Marxism tended, in Niebuhr's view, to disregard the egoistic and selfish elements of human nature. It located the cause of social injustice not in proclivities of the human individual, but in class conflict and in unjust social arrangements.

By the time of his writing of The Gifford Lectures, *The Nature and Destiny of Man*, Niebuhr was convinced that this perspective was based on a naive view of human nature. For Niebuhr, human egoism was the result of the human constitution, itself. Reordering of social arrangements could only ameliorate many of the conflicts arising from this egoism, it could not overcome them. Thus Marxism, in its insistence on the "external" causes of human misery, consequently lost its political relevance because it based its political thought on a faulty view of human nature.(43)

Niebuhr also took issue with the "secularized eschatology" of Marxism. Marxism, at least in its Leninist formulation, contained an inherent historical determinism directed to the perfection of human society. The current, unjust economic system, capitalism, would soon crumble and be replaced by the equalitarian socialist system in which all class conflict would be abolished and in which equality of all social groups would reign. In this new society, the proletariat would take a leading role, not only in the revolution itself, but also in impartially ruling after the revolution. To Niebuhr, this was a tenuously optimistic view (because of human egoism) which ran the risk of having the ideology and interest of the rulers (in this case the proletariat) identified with the general will of the people. In the case of the Soviet Union, the combination of economic and political power in the same group had led to a tyranny which surpassed even that of capitalist owners.(44)

Niebuhr's theological turn during this period can be understood as the development of an American Neo-orthodoxy based on the transcendence of

God. Niebuhr's study of the behavior of individuals and groups and their relationships (which provided the basis for his 1932 book *Moral Man and Immoral Society*) revealed to him the intransigence of human egotism and self-concern. Any hope for human brotherhood or the abolishment of class conflict had therefore to be a transcendent hope a hope which cannot be fulfilled within history through human action.(45) As we saw above, for Niebuhr the hopes of the Social Gospel for perfect justice had their roots in an understanding of God as overly immanent to the world. This immanence of God in the world did maintain the relevance of God to the "horizontal" plane of history, but the "vertical" distinction between a God who was "wholly other," and humanity, which was sinful and presumptuous, a distinction which allowed for God's judgment of the social world, was lost.

The transcendence of God and the transcendent hopes which it produced became for Niebuhr a call to a realistic perspective in politics. Since the human being is irrevocably sinful and for the most part totally in opposition to God, a progressive view of culture or politics is not only misguided but also dangerous because it obfuscates the power conflicts which are inherent in any social or political relationship.

Niebuhr did not merely recast the theology of Karl Barth, the other Neo-orthodox theologian who stressed the transcendence of God. In fact, Niebuhr had strongly criticized Barth's theology for not having the conceptual weapons for discerning the difficulties which were inherent in Marxism. Following the Soviet invasion of Hungary, no statement from Barth was forthcoming. Niebuhr could not remain silent, however, and fired off a letter to Barth questioning his silence on this issue.(46) For Niebuhr, Barth's silence was the result of more than a political miscalculation; it was much more the result of a mistake in his theology. While Barth in his early works did stress the sinfulness of humanity, and used the transcendence of God as a point of criticism of all temporal structures, his later works included eschatological elements which in Niebuhr's view undermined the political relevance of Barth's theology. For Niebuhr, Barth's theology included an enthusiastic element which let a progressive view of society creep back into his theology, and which prompted him to remain silent on the subject of Hungary.(47)

During the late 1950's and early 1960's, the Cold War intensified. By 1962, it nearly escalated into a nuclear war during the Cuban Missile Crisis. Niebuhr's anti-Communism became only dimmer during this period. President Kennedy's realistic appraisal of the political situation and the tough line Kennedy took on Soviet incursions into the Caribbean were applauded by Niebuhr as a sensible and valid political response of power against power. Optimism about the intentions of the Soviet Union, in Niebuhr's view, would have led to disastrous consequences for the safety and security of the United States and the world.(48)

It was during this last period, stretching roughly from the early 1940's until Niebuhr's death, that the disparate elements of Niebuhr's thought which had developed through the three preceding decades congealed into what we currently know as Christian Realism. The tenets of Niebuhr's mature position can be summarized under the following:

1. Any political theory must admit the sinfulness of humanity and not expect any easy solution to world problems through altruism or through optimistic expectations of real consensus between opposing groups or governments. Instead, one must always expect opponents and friends alike to act in their own self-interest.(49) At the same time, we should not surrender to naked self-interest as a means of determining the morality of a certain course of action. The ideal of love as sacrifice and obedience demands that we search for the "impossible possibility" of overcoming self-interest in order to become other-directed.

2. All political relations are power relations. There is no government which rules without coercion. Rational suasion may be partially effective, but in the end will disappoint. At the same time, coercion is not to be regarded as the ultimate method of politics. In the search for justice, rational suasion, optimistic expectations and the appeal to moral principles all play a major role.

3. Often, the best we can hope for in domestic or international relations is a balance-of-power. At the same time, a balance-of-power is not an end in itself. Rather, justice is the ultimate end of politics.

Christian Realism has not diminished in its importance for American theology and politics. Consistently throughout the last decade, the call for realism in political affairs has far outweighed the call for a more optimistic approach.(50)

I. 1.2: *Political Theology*

Although Jürgen Moltmann's Political Theology is most closely associated with the theological efforts of the past two decades, it is firmly rooted in the cultural and theological history of Germany in the twentieth century.

Directly prior to World War I, Germany had dominated much of the cultural life of Europe. The Prussians were still basking in the afterglow of their victory in the Franco-Prussian War. Politically, Germany had been united into a true monarchy under Kaiser Wilhelm and Bismarck. The landed aristocracy had not yet succumbed to the disruptive pressures of industrial society.

This positive attitude toward culture was reflected in German theology. The theological landscape of this time was dominated by ideas strongly influenced by Albrecht Ritschl and his followers. Ritschl, in a response to the supernaturalism of the Lutheran Pietists and other Orthodox Christians, attempted to bring Christian faith into correspondence with modern consciousness. His primary tool was historical criticism. For Ritschl, statements concerning Christ and his importance were not to be determined through metaphysical constructs, but through historical criticism. The fundamental principle which undergirded Ritschl's belief in the power of historical criticism to reveal the nature and importance of Jesus was his Kantian conviction that we cannot know God in himself, but we can know God through the effects that he has on us.(51) Since God is known only through his effects, modern culture and especially the Christian community becomes the locus for finding God.(52) Consequently, following the lead of Schleiermacher almost a century before, theology focused on the religiosity of the human being. Christian anthropology in the form of an examination of religious consciousness became the means of determining the content of the Christian message.(53)

Along with this change in consciousness, came an accommodation to modern society. More and more, the focus on the importance of history led to a recognition of the possibilities of progress in the world. More and more, the kingdom of God was identified with discernible movements in history, and the historical portrait of Jesus began to resemble modern man.(54) Even more, a sense of optimism was replacing the strong sense of sin inherent in Christian Orthodoxy.(55)

With the advent of World War I, this view of optimism and accommodation crumbled. The immensity of the War and the extent of its bloodshed belied a teleological view of the progress of the human community as delineated in Liberal Theology. The bankruptcy of Liberal Theology became most evident to a theologian such as Karl Barth, however, when ninety–three German intellectuals, including Adolf von Harnack, signed a manifesto in support of the war policy of the Kaiser. With this manifesto, the accommodation of theology to the dominant German culture, had become complete.

The theological response to Liberal Theology, Neo-orthodoxy, adopted both transcendentalist and personalist methodologies. On its transcendentalist side, Neo-orthodoxy emphasized the "otherness" and aseity of God. In 1921, as the foremost theologian of this transcendentalist group, Karl Barth defined his method as being limited to "a recognition of what Kierkegaard called the 'infinite qualitative distinction' between time and eternity."(56) This absolute distinction between God and world demanded a focus on revelation from outside of the world, and thus the world was desacralized.(57) From this perspective, contemporary culture was not supported, but was brought into a state of crisis. Religion as an appendage and legitimator of culture must be contrasted with the genuine grace of God.(58)

With the rise of the Hitler regime in Germany during the thirties, Barth's Neo-orthodoxy took on a more Christocentric emphasis. Where earlier, Barth had used the "otherness" of God against all human claims to glory or self-righteousness, against the totalitarianism of the Hitler government, Barth counterposed the sovereign lordship of Christ. Christ's absolute lordship subordinated all other lordship claims, especially those made by the Hitler government which took on totalitarian characteristics.(59)

The personalist side of Neo-orthodoxy also emphasized the otherness of God, but did so in a manner quite different from the transcendentalists. Like Barth, Rudolf Bultmann, the main proponent of the personalist perspective, recognized that the God who is other maintains an aseity which is uncompromised by the will and activities of humans. At the same time, however, this God enters into a personal relationship with the human. Thus for Bultmann, the crisis which characterizes human existence is not the divine "NO" to all human striving, but is the call to decision.(60) For Bultmann this call has anthropological significance. The Word of God was not merely the self-revelation of God, as it is with Barth, but was also the key to an individual's self-understanding.(61) The call to decision is thus the call to authentic selfhood, the call to realize those qualities which are inherent in being human, but are often avoided or misappropriated.

The imperatives placed upon Neo-orthodoxy during the war years demanded a theology which focused on resolving contemporary difficulties. It was a theology of crisis, in that the problems the Church had to face reached crisis proportions. Consequently, this form of theology primarily emphasized the activity of God in the present, while neglecting the importance of God's activity for the future.(62)

Postwar events, however, changed this means of understanding God.

After the collapse of the Hitler totalitarian state in Germany, feelings of hopelessness pervaded German consciousness. The German land and industries had been leveled by the incessant Allied bombing toward the end of the war. After World War I, Germany had experimented with a democratic government, the ill-fated Weimar Republic. The economic realities of having to pay exorbitant reparations, of runaway inflation and of a worldwide depression, coupled with the political neutering of the German government by the Allies, proved too much for the fragile Weimar government to withstand.

The situation after World War II was somewhat different, however. Instead of leveling economy-crushing reparations and creating an emasculated government in Germany, the western Allies worked hand-in-hand with the Germans in order to rebuild a new Germany. Money and assistance poured into Germany through the Marshall Plan. The Currency Reform Act of 1948 shored up an inflation-ridden German Mark. Germany was slowly reintegrated into the European community, and in 1949 the Federal Republic of Germany adopted a democratic constitution and a strong parliamentary government which was recognized both from within West Germany and in the eyes of much of the rest of the world as the legitimate representative voice of the West German people. Germany was poised for an entry into a new future in which the past could be left behind, but not forgotten.

Neo-orthodoxy, either in its Barthian or Bultmannian form, held sway for more than two decades. By the 1960's, however, forces were to come into play which called their basic insights into question. In this era, "complacency with the present" was replaced by "the look toward the future."(63) The student revolts in German universities called for a reform of the overall educational system of Germany. The incipient women's movement not only sought new ways of reordering the relationships between men and women, but also strove to find a new identity for women in a male-dominated society. In the political realm, the Social Democrats had regained power and hoped to reshape the German government along the lines of a social state. These disparate elements were conjoined by a general distrust of "the way things were" and by a look toward the possibilities which could be attained in the horizon of the future.

In a world where progress again seemed possible, Neo-orthodoxy seemed out of place. Furthermore, the ethic derived from both the transcendentalist and personalist sides of Neo-orthodoxy did not seem responsive to the times. Barth's Christocentric theology, developed in response to the Nazi threat to the authority of the Church, emphasized the independence of the Church over and against the state. It responded well to external threat to the autonomy of the Church to proclaim its message.(64) By the 1960's however, the threat to the autonomy of the Church had been gone for twenty years. The Church had become part of the social, political and cultural fabric of Germany itself. The problems of the sixties, poverty, discrimination, oppression, were in a real sense not external problems but were caused by the structure of society itself. In fact, for many at this time, the Church was part of the problem in that it was not critical enough of its own role in furthering oppression.(65) Claims of Christ's lordship of the type offered by Barth did not help to resolve these problems because they were seen primarily as conservative claims for the Church's authority, as the Church tended to identify itself with Christ.

On the personalist side, Bultmann's emphasis on the I-Thou encounter between God and human tended to privatize religion. The focus of religion became the personal encounter. Religion dealt primarily with the private realm; it had very little inherent social commitment. Bultmann's hermeneutic emphasized the demythologizing of biblical texts in order to extract from their existential meaning. For Bultmann, the biblical texts were written in primarily mythological language which was no longer capable of being understood by, much less being meaningful for, contemporary human beings. Myth therefore needed "translation" into a form that could convey the true meaning inherent in the texts themselves in such a way that they would be intelligible to people living in the modern age.(66) Bultmann felt that the true meaning of the biblical texts lay in their existential content: their call to decision for authentic or inauthentic existence.(67) Although this call to decision was considered by Bultmann to have secondary political implications, it was primarily an individual and personal call:

> It is the word of God which...calls him to God, who is beyond the world and beyond scientific thinking. At the same time, it calls man to his true self. For the self of man, his inner life, his personal existence is also beyond the visible world and rational thinking. The word of God addresses man in his personal existence and thereby it gives him freedom from the world....(68)

Later in the same work, Bultmann underlines the personal character of his hermeneutic in the striking statement

> Man's life is moved by the search for God because it is always moved, consciously or unconsciously, by the question about his own personal existence. The question about God and the question about myself are identical.(69)

By identifying the question of God with the question about oneself, religion tended to become a personal, private matter. It dealt with one's personal existence, with one's authenticity or inauthenticity. Historical and religious reflection was to provide self-understanding. Consequently, political questions necessarily receded into the background. Religion no longer had as a primary responsibility the outlining of political behavior.

A major implication of this view is that the privatistic perspective of religion creates a bifurcation between private and public spheres. Since religious values are limited to shaping individual, private morality, they are then deemed inappropriate for direct application to the political sphere. In politics, then, a second set of criteria is necessary for decision-making. Public morality thus becomes discontinuous with private morality.(70)

Again, the Church seemed powerless to resolve the problems of the day, and perhaps even aided their survival.(71) Several factors converged to give shape to a new theological emphasis on the political relevance of the Christian message. The interest in social change brought the philosophy of Marx to the forefront of sociological theory in Germany as an alternative to the more traditional theories in vogue at the time. The Critical Theorists of the Frankfurt School, and especially Ernst Bloch, who was intellectually and personally related to this group, had the most influence on the subsequent development of theology. Bloch's emphasis on hope, on openness to the future and on the liberative elements associated with Jewish-Christian messianism and eschatology, set the parameters for much of the theological inquiry undertaken during this period.(72)

A new interest in Marxist thought also influenced the theology of the period.(73) The interest of some Christian scholars in a rapprochement with Marxism reached its peak in the Christian-Marxist dialogues of 1966-1968. These debates not only raised questions about the political role of Christianity in the world, about the religious role of Marxism in the world, and about the relationship of religion to society, but also raised the issues of theodicy, or the viability of theistic formulations of God and of the traditional notions of transcendence, all themes which were later to be dealt with in length by Political Theology.(74)

Advances in biblical hermeneutics and history of traditions also added fuel to this futurist theology. Bultmann's existential hermeneutic placed anthropology firmly into the center of theology. The work of Ernst Käsemann and others called much of Bultmann's hermeneutic into question. Käsemann contended that apocalyptic, not anthropology, was the "mother of all theology."(75) Consequently, the hermeneutical program of the type proposed by Bultmann was not true to the original impetus behind the Gospels. The impetus was cosmological and set within the horizon of the future, not anthropological and set within the horizon of the individual in the present.

The Political Theology of Jürgen Moltmann can be understood as a critical corrective to the aforementioned theological and cultural emphases.(76) On the one hand, it is a response to the personalism and transcendentalism of Neo-orthodoxy, against which Moltmann places a strident eschatological interpretation of history and a social understanding of the human person.(77) On the other hand, Political Theology is a condemnation of the apathy of (primarily) the middle class to the suffering around it. Against this apathy, Moltmann develops an ideology-critical *Vernunft* in the tradition of the so-called "Second Enlightenment."(78)

The term "political theology," Moltmann contends, has been in use at least since Roman times. The Stoics divided theology into three distinct typologies: natural, mythical, and political (*genus physikon, genus mythiken,* and *genus politiken*). Natural theology was primarily metaphysical, drawing relationships between the realm of nature and the divine world. This type of theology was best suited for academia. Mythical theology was poetic theology, best suited for the theater. Political theology was reserved for dealings with the state gods, and thus was best suited for the public practice of ritual and cult surrounding those gods.(79) In many respects political theology was deemed most important, because the state gods were responsible for the welfare of the state, which in turn protected the welfare of individual citizens. Political theology, therefore, functioned to support and legitimate the state gods and the nations they ruled.

When Christianity was granted status as a *religio licita* by the Emperor Constantine, and ultimately became the political religion of Rome under the

Emperor Theodosius, it fulfilled a legitimating role within the Empire. As the Empire spread throughout Europe and its colonies, Christianity traveled with it, and eventually became the political religion of the West and East.

In the twentieth century, theology in Germany also performed a legitimating function in regard to the state. In a programmatic monograph published in 1922, Carl Schmitt, a theoretician of the Nazi dictatorship, declared that "all meaningful concepts of modern state doctrine are secularized theological concepts."(80)   In Schmitt's view, this meant that theology was to be the subservient handmaiden to the state.   It was to legitimate state government and was to be used as a means of unifying citizens under state rules.(81)

From Moltmann's perspective, Christianity is reduced to functioning as a political religion if its theology is conducive to the maintenance of the status quo. Moltmann understands two related theological elements to be involved in fostering the legitimating function of theology; the development of a monarchical monotheism and the loss of the crucified God at the center of Christian theology.(82)

The eschatological, utopian message of the Christian proclamation disallows such a unity of religion and state.   Following E. Petersen, Moltmann understands the conception of a political monotheism to be seminal for the development of imperial rule both within and outside of the Church. The idea of ONE GOD--ONE CHURCH provided the theoretical underpinnings for the development of monarchical rule: ONE EMPEROR--ONE EMPIRE.(83)

A trinitarian understanding of God, however, destroys the religious legitimation of political monotheism:

> It is only when the doctrine of the trinity vanquishes the monotheistic notion of the great universal monarch in heaven, and his divine patriarchs in the world, that earthly rulers, dictators and tyrants cease to find any justifying religious archetypes any more.(84)

Since the trinitarian God consists of the unity and diversity of the Father, Son, and Spirit, it is impossible to develop an idea of a universal, omnipotent monarch from such a diversity.(85) Divine power is shared power, not power isolated in one individual.

Such an understanding also demands that God not be recognized only in those who have power, but also in those who are powerless. The Son, the God who was crucified in weakness and abandonment, becomes the justification and sanctification for those who are outcasts and powerless.(86)

The doctrine of the trinity is thus for Moltmann a response to the idolatry of granting earthly rules ultimate divine powers and rights. It is in his trinitarian understanding of the "Crucified God," however, that his critique of political religion becomes most pointed.

For Moltmann, the justification of the existing political structure by Christianity is only possible by forgetting the political nature of Christ's death.(87) Therefore, he delineates the political consequences of the Cross over and against all forms of political religion. The starting point for Moltmann is the fact that Christ suffered and was crucified by Roman authorities because he was a political threat. Christ was no zealot, but his eschatological message of freedom undercut all pretensions of a religious state.(88) For Moltmann, therefore, Political Theology is not to support the status quo through its message, but is to become critical of it.

Christians, to the degree that they recognize God in the Crucified One, can no longer relate God to the mighty. Rather, the powerless best represent God.(89) Since Christ was killed in the name of religio-political authority, an authority "from above," justification of any political structures "from above" no longer should be convincing to humans.(90) Since Christianity's confessed Lord is also the Crucified One, human lordship must pattern itself after him. In such a perspective, God becomes identified with the lowly and oppressed, with those who suffer and those who are disenfranchised. In this way, Christianity grounded in the Crucified One must remain "iconoclastic." It must always act to destroy the political idolatry of making partial, penultimate political structures into absolute authorities.(91) Political Theology therefore remains critical of all political structures and programs. It does not allow its concepts and images to be used to legitimate any regime. Rather it calls regimes into question.

The second way that theology supports an existing social structure is by relegating religious insights to the merely personal realm of existence. In this perspective theology was considered to be "a-political" or merely personal belief which had no socio-political import.(92) For Moltmann, foremost among those who hold such a perspective were Martin Luther and those who were his conceptual descendants.

As is commonly known, Luther distinguishes between two realms, sacred and profane. Moltmann sees the benefit of such an interpretation in its polemical attitude. When viewed in such a manner, the two realms doctrine allows neither caesaro-papism nor a clerical theology. It disallows the sacralization of politics.(93)

Moltmann, however, sees inherent dangers in such a view. While Luther and his followers maintained some connection between the two realms, subsequent theologians have interpreted the doctrine in dualistic ways, cleaving the two realms. This produced the transformation of the doctrine into an apology for the Protestant world. While Luther developed the doctrine to disentangle the religious and political worlds, subsequent theologies have interpreted it is such a way that it became a theory of two different dimensions of the world: church and state. In this way, state authority and the power which attended it were left to be autonomous and absolute.(94)

Over and against these a-political interpretations of Christian theology, Moltmann brought political insights into his theology proper. For Moltmann, this move was necessary because human existence is becoming ever more political. In effect, then, the human being is actually a *zoon politikon*.(95) Politics is becoming the context and the means through which people express the possibilities and potentialities of their lives. From the perspective of theology, then, asking about God's relationship to the world means that politics provides the context within which such relationship must be discussed.(96) Theology, to the degree that it reflects this universal eschatological horizon in its discourse, must speak concurrently about God and the world, heaven and earth, divine and human. The political dimension of theology thus emerges from the universal horizon of eschatology itself.(97)

Three stages of development can be delineated in Political Theology.(98) The earliest stage of Political Theology counterposed a future-oriented eschatology over and against what it considered to be the focus of Neo-orthodoxy on the present. Karl Barth's well known statement in his *Römerbrief*, "Any theology which is not completely and unreservedly eschatological, has nothing whatsoever to do with Christ"(99) became the springboard for bringing the future oriented eschatology back into the center of theology. Other theologians also picked up on this new interest in eschatology.(100) Instead of being understood exclusively as the "last things," and thereupon being relegated to its traditional position at the end of dogmatic treatments, eschatology became the context within which theology was to be understood.

This stage began roughly in 1964 with the publication of Moltmann's *Theology of Hope: On the Ground and Implications of a Christian Eschatology*. As the subtitle reveals, Political Theology is an attempt to provide the foundations for a Christian theology based in eschatology. Beginning with the centrality of the Promise to Christian literature, Moltmann contends that God's being is primarily future.(101) History, as the interim between the Promise and its fulfillment, has meaning only in relation to its future goal, the eschatological kingdom.(102) History, itself, is open ended, allowing and desiring the *Novum*, the completely new.(103)

Over and against Barth's transcendental eschatology, the futurist eschatology of Political Theology emphasizes the mutual involvement of God and the world. From Moltmann's perspective, Barth's transcendentalism cannot be supported biblically, for the God who is "transcendent to all ages" cannot be represented as the self-same God intimately involved in history, the God of Abraham and David, the God who leads the people out of Egypt.(104)

Bultmann's personalist understanding of religion as a means of self-understanding also comes under sharp attack from Moltmann's pen. According to Moltmann, Bultmann's theology understands "the future" as the self-fulfillment of the human being, and thus contains a hidden correlation between God and the human self. The Bible, however, speaks not of the opening up of what makes the human being authentic, but of the opening up of history and human destiny in its social, political and religious spheres.(105) Against Bultmann's personalism, Moltmann places a futurist eschatology which is intrinsically social in nature. Eschatology is not a sterile, academic discussion of the "End-things" in Moltmann's hands; rather it is always a correlation between what God promises and the degree that society hinders or facilitates the fulfillment of that promise.(106) Thus, the futurist eschatology of Political Theology contains an "eschatological reservation" which provides not only a criticism of all penultimate structures in society, but also a goal for society to attain.(107) It necessitates a "political hermeneutic" which lays bare the socially critical and liberative elements of the Christian message.(108) This political hermeneutic combines insights of form criticism, historical criticism and a Marxist hermeneutic.

Traditional form criticism begins with the present form of a text and then inquires about the pre-literary context from which it was written. Thus, form criticism attempts to tell us from whom and from where certain texts developed.(109)

In his political hermeneutic, Moltmann adopts a general form critical presupposition: hermeneutics involves moving from an existing text to the *Sitz-im-Leben* of that text. Moltmann goes beyond traditional form criticism, however, by asking what the concrete experience of those who wrote the text was.(110) In this sense, the biblical texts are understood as life-expressions (Lebensauesserungen) of the writers and therefore present us with a reflection of their life experiences and contexts.(111)

Drawing clues from Marx, Moltmann understands these life expressions to be expressions of "real affliction" and a *protest* against real affliction.(112) Thus the form critical analysis of texts needs to take us back to the concrete situations which created the texts and also to understand the texts as responses to those situations.

Moving back from the text to the concrete situation which produced it, however, does not complete Moltmann's hermeneutical inquiry. Form criticism only leads the way to historical criticism. Moltmann adds an Enlightenment understanding of historical criticism to his basic form critical insights as a means of developing revolutionary, liberative freedom:

> At the beginning of modern times, historical criticism was directly bound up with revolutionary criticism. It began by unmasking the authoritarian myths of the contemporary powers of church and state. Then in the name of comprehensive and many-faceted truth, it turned its attention to the scriptures in order to understand the Church's claim to authority.(113)

For Moltmann, historical criticism of the Enlightenment provided an "inheritance of freedom" in that history no longer binds one to a tradition, but rather means the liberation from the burdens of one's past; historical criticism "serves to expose one's own experience and one's own creative power to the future."(114)

This Enlightenment "inheritance of freedom" demanded that hermeneutics be restructured in such a way that the texts being examined revealed their liberative content. Whereas for Bultmann the hermeneutical issue was how past texts could be made intelligible and relevant to modern people, the hermeneutical question for Political Theology became

> ...how the past can be brought into the consciousness of the present so that the freedom of the present for the future can be maintained or increased without being limited by the prejudices of tradition or subordinated to an ideology of history.(115)

Moltmann's political hermeneutics does not, however, remain on the level of revealing suffering and protest. Instead, Moltmann combines a political hermeneutic with an eschatological hermeneutic which emphasizes freedom and emancipation from affliction and suffering. For Moltmann, the horizon of concern of the gospels is a horizon of freedom which is fueled by an understanding of history as a promissory history, as an interim between the Promise made to Moses, and its fulfillment in the Eschaton. When understood in this manner, hermeneutics becomes the attempt to relate the horizon of concern of the Bible (freedom) with the present personal, social and political conditions of humans in the world. Consequently, a political/eschatological hermeneutics is not only critical of the present in light of the future, but also reveals the freedom of the future which is open to humans.

This emphasis on liberation in the Christian texts thus produces an "option for the oppressed."(116) It is toward this group that the texts are primarily directed. And it is this group which understands these texts best.

Moltmann refined this understanding of hermeneutics through recourse to Marx's "Eleventh Thesis on Feuerbach." Moltmann contends that the purpose of hermeneutics is not merely to interpret the world, but to change it. In other words, hermeneutics is "an effort to realize what is announced historically under present circumstances."(117) Consequently, the purpose behind any interpretation of biblical texts is to bring to light the critical-liberative elements inherent in the Christian kerygma.

This function of theology does not call for the identification of Christian theology with political ethics or with the politicizing of religion. Instead it "designates the field, the milieu, the environment and the medium in which theology should be articulated today."(118)

Although this turn to a futurist eschatology at the center of theology was welcomed in the theological community and related well to the contemporary feelings of the Church, there were still inherent weaknesses in that approach to theology. While Political Theology did reconstruct theology is such a way that it had social significance, it was never quite clear about what the relationship between theology and ethics really was.(119) To many, Political Theology was merely a shifting of the place of theology from one which supported the state, to one which was critical of the state.(120) These weaknesses led to the second stage of Political Theology.

The second stage of Political Theology was marked by a conscious effort to incorporate the sociology of knowledge into theology.(121) In effect, Moltmann attempted to create a critical theory of theology, a theology which was self-reflective, conscious of its origins and aware of its "target" those to whom the theology was addressed.(122) This was done in order to make theology aware of the political effects of its message. What Moltmann attempts to do in his Political Theology, therefore is to create

> ...a critical theory in which knowledge-guiding interests and the practical effects of this knowledge is revealed and reflected in men...It is turning from the theory of things to a reflection on the use and the effects of things.(123)

In order to accomplish this, Moltmann found the need to delineate the relationship between theology (theory) and human activity (praxis) in a more direct manner. For Moltmann, the difficulty in discerning the relationship between theory and praxis is the difficult of maintaining a balance between the *identity* of Christianity and its *relevance*.(124) By phrasing the question in this manner, Moltmann undercuts previous ways of combining Christian proclamation and behavior in the world by raising the question of how theological statements are verified.(125)

For Moltmann, the identity of Christianity is regulated by the Christian text. Over and against all forms of accommodation to modern society, Christian identity is defined and limited by the content of the Gospel of Jesus and his message.(126) Christian theology loses its identity when it too closely identifies itself with the culture which surrounds it. At the same time, Christianity becomes irrelevant if it maintains its identity to the detriment of its involvement in the world.(127) For Moltmann, what was needed was a way to relate the Christian message to the contemporary situation without endangering Christian identity or relevance.

Here Moltmann is fighting on two fronts. From his perspective, the *metaphysical* method of verification, which held that the truth of theological statements is determined according to logical consistency, emphasizes the primacy of theory over praxis, and results in a sterile *orthodoxy* which is irrelevant to the world.(128) Theory becomes primary while praxis becomes secondary, and Christian identify is maintained at the expense of Christian relevance.

At the same time, certain Christian groups overemphasized the relevance of the Christian message to the detriment of the identity forming function. The most egregious falsehood surfaced with the theologians of the Ritschlian school. The Liberal Theologians of the nineteenth century, in the attempt to bring theology into accord with the "modern" *Weltanschauung*, reshaped the identity of the Christian message in such a way that it became a reflection of bourgeois attitude.(129)

In an attempt to reconcile these two perspectives, Moltmann adopts the idea of *orthopraxis* as the true mode of verification of theology.(130) For Moltmann, theory (theology) can only be verified through the practice that it produces. However, unlike Liberation Theologians, who, using similar terminology, contend that theology is a critical reflection on praxis, Moltmann holds that there must be a dialectical approach to theory and praxis.(131) Theory is not derived from praxis, but neither is praxis the mere application of theory. Instead, theology (theory) is informed by Christian praxis, but also informs Christian praxis itself. Consequently, theology is verified both by its correlation to Christian praxis, and also by the praxis it produces. In this way, Political Theology is a "functional criticism of the social, political and psychological functions of religion and church.(132) Theology must, according to Moltmann, evaluate how its discourse functions politically. It must evaluate whether or not its discourse aids or hinders the quest for freedom and justice. Consequently, theology becomes the theory of historical praxis.(133) For Moltmann, therefore, any theology which wants to be responsible

> ...must consider self-critically the psychological and political implications of its words, images, and symbols.(134)

Moltmann's ideology critique further implied an *institutional critique* of the Church. From Moltmann's perspective, the causes of the misery of human beings should not be sought in the inner attitudes of people, but in the institutions which give society and the people within it their form. Consequently, according to Political Theology, the Church is more than its theology and ideology; it is a concrete institution with political effect in the world. Political Theology thus demands that theology take into account its concrete practice which is embodied in the Church as institution:

> Implied moreover, is that theology must be self-critical concerning the efficacy of the Church's institutions. We should pose not only this question: 'What is the linguistic meaning of our speaking about God', but further ask what public effect it has in a given situation to speak of God (or to remain silent).(135)

With the clarification of the eschatological perspective in the first stage, and the elucidation of how it relates to praxis in the second stage, Political Theology, and Moltmann in particular, then turned toward a reformation of dogmatic statements in light of the insights of the previous stages.(136)   While not indifferent to dogma, the first two stages of the development of Political Theology concerned themselves mostly with defining its theological terrain in opposition to other theological perspectives.   In its third stage, Political Theology moved on to reconstructing theological doctrines from its own particular perspective.

In the early 1980's, Moltmann began what he called "a series of systematic contributions to theology."(137) The purpose of this series is not to present a theological systematic or dogmatic theology, but through the issues they raise and through the presentation of Moltmann's own perspective, to act as an impetus to further discussion and reformulation by the theological community-at-large.(138) Thus far, two "contributions" have been forthcoming, *The Trinity and the Kingdom* which represents a social doctrine of the trinity, and *God in Creation*, which presents an ecological doctrine of creation.(139)

The foregoing contextual analysis of Christian Realism and Political Theology provides insights into the question of why the respective theology of each movement developed as it did. The following three chapters examine how Niebuhr and Moltmann develop their respective theologies.

Notes to Chapter 1

1. *Systematic Theology, I* (Chicago: University of Chicago, 19) 3.

2. In this sense, both Niebuhr and Moltmann are attempting to develop "practical" theologies.

3. *The Crucified God*, (NY: Harper and Row, 1974), Chapter 1.

4. E. J. Hobsbawn, *The Age of Revolution: 1789-1848*, (NY: Mentor, 1952), pp. 277-289.

5. This idea of secular progress is best represented in Voltaire's *Age of Louis XIV:* "We may believe that reason and industry will always progress more and more; that the useful arts will be improved; that of the evils which have afflicted men, prejudices which are not their least scourge, will gradually disappear among all those who govern nations; and that philosophy, universally diffused, will give some consolation to human nature for the calamities which it will experience in all ages." For an overview of the role of the ideology of progress in this period, see J. Bury, *The Ideas of Progress*, (NY: Dover, 1932).

6. Spencer held that the constancy of human nature is a fallacy, and therefore new forms of social structures are not only possible, but are mandatory. The transitoriness of human nature led him to believe that human perfectibility was possible. Cf. Bury, *The Idea of Progress*, (NY: Dover, 1932).

7. PSA, 114; J. Dillenberger, C. Welch, *Protestant Christianity*, (NY: Scribner's, 1954) 235ff.

8. W. Rauschenbusch, *A Theology for the Social Gospel*, (Nashville: Abingdon, 1978), p. 149.

9. *Ibid.*, 106-7, 110.

10. *Ibid.*, 21, 98, 108, 164, 165, a.o.

11. *Ibid.*, 131-135.

12. *Ibid.*, 141.

13. *Ibid.*, 142.

14. J. Chrystal, (ed.), *Young Reinhold Niebuhr: His Early Writings*, (NY: Pilgrim, 1977) 42.

15. *Ibid.*, 135-136. Cf., also, 238.

32

17.	DCNR, 9, 81, 119.

18.	*Ibid.*, 205, 175-176. He also began to question the Social Gospel's one-sidedly optimistic anthropology. Cf. DCNR, 74, 104, 126.

19.	ICE, 2.

20.	ICE, 105.

21.	ICE, 2, 5, 6.

22.	ICE, 9; MMIS, 78, 79; DCNR, 208.

23.	Rauschenbusch, *Social Gospel*, p. 98.

24.	DCNR, 205; MMIS, 233. This theme of tragedy became the basis for Niebuhr's later book, BT.

25.	ICE, 71f., 87.

26.	ICE, 106, 114.

27.	This became a central theme in Niebuhr's ethics. Cf. DCNR, 64; PSA, 9; NDM, I 248-260; ICE, 44.

28.	ICE, 10; MMIS, 163, 165.

29.	ICE, 110-11, 75; MMIS, 146-50, 163, 165, 177. Cf. J. Bennett, "Reinhold Niebuhr's Social Ethic," in RN, pp. 99-142.

30.	MMIS, 145-6, 149; ICE, 10.

31.	MMIS, 155f., 160.

32.	MMIS, 144-5; ICE, 11.

33.	MMIS, 156-157.

34.	*Ibid.*, 222.

35.	ICE, 10.

36.	*Ibid.*, 11. Even worse, this led to moral complacency. Cf. ICE, 12.

37.	This is also the general thrust of ICE: an ideal is politically relevant only to the degree that it remains ideal, that is, beyond attainment in history. Cf., ICE, Chapter 4.

38.	CRPP, 34.

39. MMIS, 224f.

40. Cf. A. Schlesinger, Jr., "Reinhold Niebuhr's Role in Political Thought." in RN, p. 207.

41. CLCD, 69.

42. Cf. R. Fox, *Reinhold Niebuhr: A Biography*, (NY: Pantheon, 1986), pp. 197-198.

43. NDM, I, 35, 43-49, 93, 195-196; IAH, 20-21; CLCD, 32.

44. Cf. CLCD, 32.

45. As we saw above, for Niebuhr, the hopes of the Social Gospel for perfect justice had their roots in an understanding of God as overly immanent in the World. This immanence did maintain the relevance of God to the "horizontal" plane of human history, but neglected the "vertical" distinction between God and world, a distinction which allowed for God's judgement over history.

46. "Barth on Hungary: An Exchange." *Christian Century*, 74/15 (April 10, 1957), pp. 454-55.

47. *Ibid.*, p. 455.

48. "President Kennedy's Cuban Venture." *Christianity and Crisis*, 21/8 (May 15, 1961), pp. 69-70; "Cuba: Avoiding the Holocaust." *Christianity and Crisis*, 22/20 (November 26, 1962), pp. 204-5.

49. Gordon Harland, *The Thought of Reinhold Niebuhr.* (NY: Oxford, 1960), p. 180.

50. In most recent times, Jimmy Carter, the President who attempted to maintain the most optimistic attitude toward the Soviet Union, turned to a position which more closely resembled that of Christian Realism after the invasion of Afghanistan by Soviet forces in 1979.

51. Cf. A. Ritschl, *The Christian Doctrine of Justification and Reconciliation, III*, pp. 212ff.

52. *Ibid.*, 2-3.

53. Thus for Schleiermacher, the essence of Christianity lay in the "feeling of absolute dependence" before God. Cf. *The Christian Faith*; for Harnack, the truth of the Christian message lay in the "ennoblement of the human soul" and in the relationship of the human to God as Father. Cf. *What is Christianity?* (Gloucester, MA: Peter Smith, 1978) 63.

34

54. For example, in 1887 Ritschl gave a famous lecture in which he defended the Bismarckian state as related to the kingdom of God. Cf. J Kent, *The End of the Line?* (Phila.: Fortress, 1982) p. 91. Harnack also supported the state when he signed the petition in support of the Wilhelmite government at the dawn of World War I.

55. Cf. C. Dawson, *Progress and Religion*, (NY: Doubleday, 1960).

56. K. Barth, *Epistle to the Romans*, (London: Oxford,) 10.

57. *Ibid.*, 36: "God is the unknown God, and precisely because he is unknown, he bestows life and breath on all things. Therefore, the power of God can be detected neither in the world of nature nor in the souls of men."

58. *Ibid.*, 39, 230, 231, 236. Humans are thus deemed righteous not from their own actions but only through their justification by God (*justitia forensis*). Cf. *Romans*, 93, 107.

59. The Barmen Declaration, which Barth and other theologians drafted in May 1934, expressed this absoluteness of the lordship of Christ in no uncertain terms. Cf. W. Burgmueller, *Die Barmer Theologische Erklärung*, (Neukirchen: Neukirchner, 1983), p. 34.

60. R. Bultmann, *Jesus and the Word*. (NY: Scribners, 1958) p. 52.

61. R. Bultmann, *Existence and Faith*, Tr. S. Ogden. (NY: Meridian, 1960), pp. 59, 263.

62. Cf. TH, 40f.

63. Evinced in this regard is the popularity of A. Toffler's *Future Shock*, (NY: Pan, 1970) and R. Heibroner's *An Inquiry into the Human Prospect*.

64. K. Barth, *Community, State and Church*, (Gloucester, MA: Peter Smith, 1974).

65. This view of the Church is best supported by the ideology critique applied to it by Moltmann and others. According to this critique, theology in its Neo-orthodox forms had become "a-political" and therefore supported the status quo. Cf. TH, 45-69 and 95-102.

66. Cf. R. Bultmann, "New Testament and Mythology," *Kerygma and Myth*, ed. H. Bartsch, tr. R. Fuller. (London: SPCK, 1954) pp. 1-44.

67. *Ibid.*, p. 3.

68. R. Bultmann, *Jesus Christ and Mythology*. (NY: Scribners, 1958), p. 40.

69. *Ibid.*, p. 53.

70.   There is also a third object of Moltmann's criticism of the a-political role of theology: Barth's understanding of the transcendent God. According to Moltmann, Barth's transcendentalist perspective, at least in its dialectical phase, focuses on the complete self-revelation of God in the cross and resurrection of Christ. The consequence of this view, however, is that the resurrection ...would not point beyond itself to something still outstanding that is to be hoped for and awaited...(TH, 58). Understood in this way, Barth's theology removes the political impetus from theology because it understands God to be equally immediate to all ages of history and thus the future of the world brings no new activity of God. God has acted in Christ, and the future which proceeds from Christ is only the development of that action. Such a theology sees Christ not as the Lord of History moving it onward and transforming it politically, but as the transcendent in the present, the beyond in the things of this world. (TH, 314).

71.   Cf. Metz, *Faith in History and Society*, (NY: Seabury, 1981).

72.   Cf. Metz's paean to Bloch in *Unterbrechungen*. (Gutersloh: Gerd Mohn, 1981), pp. 58-69.

73.   S. Widenhofer, *Politische Theologie*, (Stuttgart: W. Kohlhammer, 1976), p. 37.

74.   Cf. J. M. Lochmann, *Encountering Marx*, (Phila.: Fortress, 1971) and J. Moltmann, "Chancen für eine kritische Solidarität von Christen und Marxisten," in *UZ*, pp. 26-44.

75.   E. Käsemann, *New Testament Questions of Today*, (Phila: Fortress, 1969), pp. 108-137.

76.   For a brief history of Political Theology, see Widenhofer, *Politische Theologie* and R. Chopp, *The Praxis of Suffering*, (NY: Orbis, 1986)

77.   Cf. Chopp, *Praxis*, 39.

78.   The "First Enlightenment" refers to the development of autonomous reason. It was a demythologization and a secularization of knowledge. The "Second Enlightenment" refers to the critique of autonomous reason by Marx and others. It was primarily ideology critique combined with the sociology of knowledge. Cf. M. Horkheimer, T. Adorno, *The Dialectic of Enlightenment*, (Boston: Beacon, 1972).

79.   CCR, 18; CG, 332.

80.   C. Schmitt, *Politische Theologie*. Berlin: Duncker and Humblot, 1979) 49.

81.   *Ibid.*, 11.

82.   CCR, 24-33; CG, 17, 19, a.o.

83. TK, 194-195.

84. *Ibid.*, 197.

85. *Ibid.*, 197.

86. *Ibid.*, 197.

87. CG, Chapter 2.

88. CCR, 34.

89. CCR, 35; CF, 34; TK, 197.

90. CCR, 35; CF, 34; TK, 197.

91. *Ibid.*, 45.

92. *Ibid.*, 19.

93. OHD, 70.

94. This became most evident for Moltmann when the Lutheran Church could not find a source in its two-kingdoms doctrine for countering Hitler. Cf. OHD, 750.

95. RRF, 218; HP, 109.

96. RRF, 218; Cf. Meeks, *Origins of the Theology of Hope.* (Philadelphia: Fortress, 1974) pp. 130-131.

97. RRF, 202; TH, 325; Cf. C. Braaten and R. Jenson, *The Futurist Option.* (NY: Newman, 1970) for an overview of this perspective.

98. Cf. Widenhofer, *Politische Theologie*, for what follows.

99. K. Barth, *Epistle to the Romans*, (NY: Oxford, 1980), p. 314.

100. Cf. W. Pannenberg, *Theology of the Kingdom of God*, (Philadelphia: Fortress, 1969), 101; FC, 16, 30; TH, 43, 77, 86.

101. FC, 16, 30; TH, 43, 77, 86.

102. TH, 93, 103, 104, 108, 189, 205.

103. FC, 9-10, 29-30; TH, 108; HP, 180; RRF, 3-28.

104. TH, 39-40, 45- 51, 55-56.

105. *Ibid.*, 61, 65.

106. TH, 15-21.

107. TH, 21, 106, 269; Cf. Chopp, *Praxis*, 40.

108. OHD, 97-112; "Toward a Political Hermeneutic of the Gospel" *Union Seminary Quarterly Review*, 23/4. (Summer, 1968), pp. 303-323.

109. Cf. E. McKnight, *What is Form Criticism*. (Philadelphia: Fortress, 1969) for a general discussion.

110. J. Moltmann, *Politische Theologie/Politische Etik*. (Munich: Kaiser-Gruenewald, 1984) p. 12.

111. *Ibid.*, 12.

112. Moltmann, "Toward...", pp. 312-13.

113. *Ibid.*, 303.

114. *Ibid.*, 304.

115. *Ibid.*, 305.

116. This "option for the oppressed" is described in PS, 79-80. For Niebuhr's critique see IAH, 162-164.

117. PS, 312.

118. J. Moltmann, "Political Theology," *Theology Today*, 28 (April 1971) p. 8.

119. Cf. J. Gustafson, *Ethics from a Theocentric Perspective*, (Chicago: University of Chicago, 1981) p. 47.

120. Cf. H. Maier, "Politische Theologie?" *Stimmen der Zeit*, 183/2 (1968), pp. 73-91.

121. Cf. CG, 5-6.

122. CG, 10-11, 12; OHD, 98.

123. UZ, 135.

124. CG, Chapter 1.

125. *Ibid.*, 17.

126. *Ibid.*, 19.

127. *Ibid.*, 12.

128. *Ibid.*, 10-11.

129. For an overview of this perspective see J. Livingston, *Modern Christian Thought: From the Enlightenment to Vatican II.*, (NY: Macmillan, 1971) pp. 245-270.

130. CG, 11.

131. OHD, 107-108.

132. *Ibid.*, 98.

133. UZ, 154; OHD, 8.

134. CCR, 18.

135. *Ibid.*, 18.

136. Chopp, *Praxis*, neglects this important constructive, dogmatic side to Moltmann's work.

137. TK, xi.

138. *Ibid.*, xii.

139. Other works in this series will include: anthropology, Christology and eschatology.

CHAPTER II

THE GOD/WORLD RELATIONSHIP IN

CHRISTIAN REALISM AND POLITICAL THEOLOGY

2.1: *The Place of the God/World Relationship in Christian Realism and Political Theology*

A theological perspective on the world differs from all others in one important aspect: in a theological worldview the world is not self-referential, but is defined only in regard to a primary relationship which grants meaning to all other relationships, the relationship between *God and world* (creation). Thus, in theological discourse, the relationship between God and world takes on hermeneutical priority because it is understood to be the framework within which all other discourse operates.(1)

This is even more the case in Christian Realism and Political Theology. Since both theologies emphasize the political relevance of the Christian message, the God/world relationship becomes primary for them. The anthropologies, theological histories and the ethics of both are grounded in their understandings of the relationship between God and world.

In general terms, the relationship between God and world can be explained in terms of God's *immanence* in the world, or of God's *transcendence* over the world, or of some sort of combination of the two. In its extreme manifestation, emphasis on the immanence of God results in a pantheism, an identification of God and world, while an overemphasis on transcendence results in a deism or a dualism between God and world.

Neither of these extremes applies to the thought of Niebuhr and Moltmann. Both theologians combine elements of immanence and transcendence in their perceptions of the relationship of God and world. For both theologians, the relationship of God and world forms the basis for their respective theologies. But it is the unique manner in which each treats this relationship that provides different emphases and directions in their thought. At this juncture Niebuhr's and Moltmann's perspectives on the God-world relationship will be examined in detail.

2.2: *God and World in Christian Realism*

In his usual dialectical style, Niebuhr contended that Christian revelation equally emphasizes the transcendence of God over creation, and also God's intimate relationship to it. This dialectical approach gave Niebuhr leverage over and against perspectives which tended to emphasize one side of the dialectic over the other. Against those who viewed creation to be essentially evil, Niebuhr proclaimed the intimacy of God to the world.

The aspect of Niebuhr's dialectic which emphasized the intimacy of God and world was derived from a Hebraic understanding of the relationship of God and world as a drama.(2) This drama often takes the form of a battle or conflict between the will of God and the will of humans.(3) And the judgment of God will always be executed in history.(4) Consequently, God is not an unmoved mover, but is engaged in history.(5)

While this "horizontal" relationship of God and world did play a role in Niebuhr's thought, because most of his thought in his Christian Realism period was directed toward the danger of liberalism and idealism, the preponderance of his writing emphasized the distinction between God and world. Against Liberal Theology and the idealist temptation to find God in the world, Niebuhr placed the "vertical" transcendence of God.

As was stated in the previous chapter, Niebuhr's Christian Realism was a response to what he considered to be the overemphasis of the Social Gospel on the immanence of God.(6) Niebuhr felt that the Social Gospel too readily identified the kingdom of God with historical progress and identified God too closely with the world.(7)

I would like to suggest that Niebuhr, in response to this immanentism, counterposes a understanding of the vertical relationship of God and world, while down-playing the horizontal elements of that relationship. Niebuhr emphasizes the "otherness" and aseity of God. God remains *Deus absconditus* even in God's own revelation.(8) God's freedom over and against his creatures is absolute and final.(9) God is thus related to his creatures in a vertical sense, as a king is to his subjects.(10)

A major component of Niebuhr's view was his emphasis on the *sovereignty* of God over the world. Sovereignty is understood by Niebuhr in one sense as the authority of God, the Creator, over his creation.(11) It emphasizes the dependence and contingency of humans in relation to God. For Niebuhr, the whole meaning of history resides in the disclosure of the sovereignty of God.(12)

When Niebuhr speaks of the sovereignty of God, he most often contrasts it with the idolatry of humans. The sovereignty and majesty of God, as Creator, must be recognized by humans as a limitation of their own sovereignty. Egoism, however, causes humans to regard the limited sovereignty which they possess to be equal to God's.(13) They grant their own sovereignty an ultimate stature which is reserved only for God. Consequently, for Niebuhr, human pretensions of sovereignty are expressed as idolatry.(14) For Niebuhr, the fatal flaw in Liberal Theology was that its emphasis on the majesty inherent in the world defied the majesty of God.(15)

As a consequence of this idolatry, God can only vindicate his sovereignty through judgment. In this perspective, history must be interpreted primarily as judgment. Consequently, the human being is placed under a certain moral obligation, under the judgment of God, for failing to recognize his or her own limits.(16)

Niebuhr's understanding of the relationship between God and world thus emphasizes their *discontinuity*. While it may be stated that the human being has a similitude to God in certain ways (as, for example, the idea of the Image of God portrays), (17) against the Liberal Theology of his time Niebuhr wanted to emphasize the distinction of God and world over the similarities between the two.

This emphasis on discontinuity between God and the world took on a phenomenological sense for Niebuhr. While Niebuhr did contend that some causality is located outside of nature,(18) in much of his thought, one gets the sense that creation is a realm of immanent causal connections between historical events with little room for intervention from supernatural sources. Niebuhr examined this aspect of creation in his discussion of myth. In distinguishing between the function of scientific discourse and mythical discourse in the modern world, Niebuhr understood the truth of myth to be the revelation of the depth dimension of human existence. Myth revealed the meaning of human existence which scientific theorizing neglected or was incapable of seeing.(19) What Niebuhr considered untruthful about myth, however, was that myth assigned causality of historical events to supernatural sources:

> The part of mythology which is derived from pre-scientific thought, which does not understand the causal relations in the natural and historical world, must naturally be sacrificed in a scientific age.(20)

Furthermore,

> since every natural phenomenon can be explained in terms of a preceding one the myth becomes useless when science discovers the chain of causality.(21)

It would seem that Niebuhr, in his discussion of myth contended that the *meaning* of reality cannot be found within reality itself, but the *facts* of reality must be explained from within the bounds of human history and activity. In such a view, the meaning of the world is continuous with God, but the eternal is phenomenologically discontinuous with the temporal. Although the events of the world do seem to be causally self-referential, the *meaning* of those events transcends the historical and is only found in God:

> Insofar as man is a limited creature his forms of social organization are *determined* by *natural* compulsions.(22)

The disjunction between God and world can also be understood from Niebuhr's explanation of God's grace operating in the world. According to Niebuhr, God has resources of love, wisdom and power which are available to humans and which enable them to become what they truly ought to be.(23) The human being did not lay hold of these resources through any sort of mystical emanation from the divine (as Niebuhr understood the Catholic perspective to be saying) but apprehended them through faith.(24) Faith in this sense is the understanding of the limitations of human possibilities (in Niebuhr's terms, the feeling of being judged) which creates in the human being a new self because "if it is possible to become aware of the limits of human possibilities by faith, it must also be possible to lay hold of the resources of God by faith."(25)

It is, however, in the recognition of the transcendence of God that the human being has the possibility of becoming a new person:

> For if we understand the possibilities of life from beyond ourselves, this understanding has some potentialities of fulfilling the meaning of life. It breaks the egoistical and self-centered forms of fulfillment, by which the wholesome development of man is always arrested and corrupted.(26)

For Niebuhr, then, God's transcendence is understood in terms of a confrontation between the will of God and the will of the human. When this is apprehended in faith, this confrontation becomes judgment and causes a person to recognize his or her inability to find complete fulfillment in the created world. It breaks the vicious circle of self-centeredness by revealing the source of fulfillment to be outside of the self. Once this fact is apprehended, the person's purpose and intention are set in the direction of Christ as norm. Because the source of this apprehension is God, Christ's perfection is "imputed" to man from without.

In his understanding of the Atonement, Niebuhr did attempt to link the wisdom which one gains through grace with actual power of God.(27) In Niebuhr's view, the Atonement is the revelation of divine forgiveness and mercy offered by God in Christ. As such, the Atonement imparts a knowledge of sin to humans. It points out the depth of human sin which resulted in the death of Christ. It also discloses the misguided attempts of humans to complete themselves through granting ultimate meaning to the penultimate.

At the same time, however, Niebuhr insists that grace is not just knowledge of sin, but also the power to overcome it. If the individual inwardly appropriates the truth of God's mercy and forgiveness, then the moods of hope and despair would be overcome, and the individual would be actually freed to live in serenity and creativity.(28) Niebuhr does not want to fall into an understanding of grace in which God imparts wisdom, but not power, to humanity. In his dialectical style, Niebuhr attempts to maintain the validity of both. Toward this end, Niebuhr posits a "point of contact" between God and world in the individual conscience. In Niebuhr's view, since the human being always feels somewhat uneasy about sinning, God's grace must impinge upon human consciousness in a way that the human being becomes aware of his or her sinfulness. This "point of contact" between God's grace and human existence thus makes sin at least partially the responsibility of the human will.

Similarly, Niebuhr's doctrine of revelation also presupposes the disjunction between God and world. For Niebuhr, revelation falls into three categories: personal, historical and creational revelation. Personal revelation is the recognition in the consciousness of the person that his or her life touches a reality which is deeper and higher than the natural world. Niebuhr defined this recognition as "conscience", the recognition that there is a Being other than ourselves who makes demands on us and judges us.(29)

Historical revelation is built upon personal revelation. According to Niebuhr, historical revelation is part and parcel of God's relationship to human beings in the world. It is the record of those events in history in which faith discerns the self-disclosure of God. What it discerns are actions of God which clarify the confrontation of people by God in the realm of the personal and individual moral life.(30)

The link between personal and historical revelation is thus the "existential content" of historical revelation. The "great acts of God in history" are important to the degree that they function as calls to decision and repentance. In light of this, Niebuhr understands revelation to be an I-Thou encounter between God and humanity. The human being encounters God as the "Other" who cannot be understood until he speaks to us. This relationship reveals the character of God primarily as judgment, mercy and forgiveness.(31)

The third type of revelation, creational revelation, is based on the idea of God as creator of the world and the world as revelatory of God. For Niebuhr, the world is not the revelation of God in the sense of a natural theology. Rather, God is revealed as the dimension of depth in the world. God can be known from the world, yet still maintains his transcendence from the world.(32)

2.3: *The God-World Relationship in Political Theology*

Moltmann also maintains a dialectical approach to the relationship of God and world, although of a different sort than does Niebuhr. While Niebuhr's dialectic is primarily a vertical-horizontal one, dialectically relating the vertical transcendence of God to the world and also the immanence of God to the world, Moltmann's dialectic is a temporal one, dialectically relating the future of God with the future, present and past of the world. The heart of Moltmann's dialectic is found in his eschatological perspective.

For Moltmann, eschatology is at the center of Christian proclamation. It centrally concerns itself with hope for the future:

> Christian hope cannot cling rigidly to the past....Rather it is itself summoned and empowered to creative transformation of reality, for it has hope for the whole reality.(33)

This directedness toward the future means that eschatology does not deal directly with present reality "as it is" but only "as it is in light of its future".(34) The content of that future is revealed by the Promise revealed in the Old Testament and validated by the death and resurrection of Christ. In this sense the future of Jesus Christ becomes indicative and predicative of the future of humanity.(35) Through Christ, therefore, world history and God's history becomes intertwined.

From a futurist eschatological perspective God is the "God of hope" whose essence is primarily future.(36) As the God of Hope, God relates to the world neither from above the world, nor from within the world, but always from ahead of the world:

> The God spoken of here is no intra-worldly or extra-worldly God, but the 'God of hope'...a God with 'future as his essential nature'...as is made known in Exodus and in Israelite prophecy, the God whom we therefore cannot really have in us or over us but always only before us, who encounters us in his promises for the future...(37)

Understood in this eschatological manner, God stands over against the world. The promised future contradicts experienced reality because the future promised points out the discrepancies between what is already present in reality and what is promised for reality:

> Peace with God means conflict with the world for the goad of the promised future stabs inexorably into the flesh of every unfulfilled present.(38)

This eschatological understanding of the relationship between God and world means for Moltmann that the primary Christian response is one of hope. Hope does not focus on the past, but operates in light of the promised future to search out and manifest that future.(39) Because there is a discrepancy between experienced reality and promised reality, those who hope can no longer tolerate reality as it is experienced. Rather, they yearn for the fulfillment which has been promised.(40) With the loss of the eschatological perspective hope also is lost. Only with the loss of both eschatology and hope is Christianity able to synthesize itself with the world without remainder.(41)

While this side of the dialectic plays a significant role in Moltmann's thought, the preponderance of Moltmann's perspective focuses on the other side of the dialectic: the convergence of God and world. This perspective emphasizes the intimate relatedness of God with the world. God and world are interdependent. In some way God's activity has an effect on his creation, while the activity of the world has an effect on Godself.(42)

Moltmann adopts this perspective as the starting point for his theology in general:

> We shall start from the assumption that the relationship between God and the world has a reciprocal character, because this relationship must be seen as a living one....If the relationships which make up life are reciprocal, then even God cannot be thought of simply in his significance for the world and for human history. The world and human history must also be perceived in their significance for God.(43)

Understanding the God-world relationship in such a manner, Moltmann emphasizes the integral qualities of both partners in the God-world relationship. The relationship is not unidirectional, with God active and the world passive (God as subject with the world as object). Rather God and world both are subjects in the relationship; the relationship is reciprocal.(44)

This understanding of the reciprocal relationship between God and world, rather than emphasizing the discontinuity of God and world, as was the case in Christian Realism, emphasizes the continuities between God and world.

> God does not simply confront his creation as Creator. He is not merely, as the incarnate One, the representative and advocate for men and women....In the Spirit...the whole world will become God's home.(45) In making the world his home, God also takes part in the destiny of the world:

> ...Through the presence of his own being, God also participates in the destiny of his own creation. Through the Spirit he suffers with the suffering of his creatures. In the Spirit he experiences their annihilations.(46)

This perspective, therefore, emphasizes over and against Niebuhr's primary view of the "vertical" relationship between God and world, a "horizontal" relationship which emphasizes the inter-relatedness of the history of God with human history. It is the doctrine of the trinity which provides Moltmann with a means of explaining this inter-relatedness.

Following traditional theological explanation, Moltmann understands the trinity in two forms: the immanent trinity which emphasizes the intra-trinitarian relationship and the economic trinity, which emphasizes the relationship of the trinity to world. While usually theology has drawn distinctions between these two operations of the trinity, Moltmann emphasizes the continuities between immanent and economic operations.(47) The relationship between persons in the immanent trinity is reflected in the relationship between the economic trinity and the world. The order of the history of salvation therefore corresponds to the order of origin within the trinity.

For Moltmann, the relationship between persons of the trinity is not primarily a *substantial* one, (understood as the relationship between divine substances) but is an *historical* one in which the relationship between divine persons develops, changes and is transformed over time.(48) If Christ is truly the second person of the trinity, then history has entered into the trinity to the degree that the history of Christ is truly the history of God.(49) Understood in this manner, the trinitarian history of God is not an object to be examined, but is a history to be experienced by us in the world. Through the Holy Spirit the history of Christ with God and the history of God with Christ becomes the history of God with us and our history with God.(50) In this way, the operations of the immanent trinity are understood as one and the same as the operations of the economic trinity.(51)

The trinitarian doctrine of creation does not begin with the antithesis between God and the world. Rather it begins with an immanent tension within God himself. According to Moltmann, the doctrine of the trinity allows each person of the trinity to have a specific and special relationship to the world. The Father creates the world *ex nihilo* in conjunction with the Son and Spirit, but does not relate himself directly with the world. The Son was sent by the Father through the power of the Spirit into the world, and thus became part of the world itself. The Spirit, sent by the Father and the Son, enlivens the world by taking up its dwelling within the world. Consequently, the doctrine combines both the idea that God is different from the world in that he created it, and that God is present in the world and manifests God's being in it.(52)

Paradigmatic for Moltmann is the unity within diversity which a trinitarian understanding of God presents. The unity of persons in the trinity points to the fundamentally self-relational character of God. The intra-trinitarian relationship is in this sense understood as the relationship of God to himself.(53) It is the sharing of a common divine substance which is identical in all three persons.(54)

This understanding of a substantial unity between persons of the trinity does not say quite enough about the trinity, however. For Moltmann, talk of a substantial unity between members of the trinity results in a rigid, one-sided view of God. Substantial unity presents a common divine nature, but does not allow for a relationship between persons (a *personal* relationship) within the trinity. Such a perspective would render the trinity lifeless.(55) Emphasis on the different experiences of the persons of the trinity, while stressing the personal aspects of the trinity, would ultimately end in a tritheism which would destroy any idea of the unity of God. In an attempt to maintain the unity within diversity of God, Moltmann turned to an understanding of divine *perichoresis*.

The idea of divine perichoresis emphasizes the closeness of relations, the mutual penetration and indwelling of divine persons of the trinity which share a common substance.(56) Precisely in the personal characteristics that distinguish them, the Father, Son and Spirit dwell in one another. In a perichoretic understanding of trinitarian unity, "the very thing that divides them becomes that which binds them together."(57)

This understanding of divine perichoresis has a dual function in Moltmann's thought. On the one hand, it provides for an historical understanding of the trinity. The divine persons are related to each other in that they share not only a mutual substance, but also a mutual history. The activity of the Father has an effect on the activity of the Son and the Spirit. The activity of the Son has an effect on the activity of the Father and the Spirit. And the activity of the Spirit has an effect on the activity of the Father and Son.(58)

On the other hand, the divine perichoresis allows for an understanding of the openness of the trinity, not only among persons of the immanent trinity, but also between God and the world. Central to the understanding of the openness of the trinity for Moltmann is the correspondence of the immanent trinity with the economic trinity. As noted above, for Moltmann, the intra-trinitarian activity corresponds to the extra-trinitarian (economic) activity of God. Since the relationship among persons of the trinity is marked by a mutual indwelling and penetration in the divine perichoresis, the same qualities of relationship are present between God and the world. In other words, the perichoretic unity of the trinity is open: it is perceived in salvation history and reflected in salvation history.(59)

The trinitarian history of the Son plays a pivotal role for Moltmann in this correspondence because one link between intra-trinitarian history and human history is formed by the incarnation of the Son in the world. By entering the world, the Son opens up the intra-trinitarian history to the world.(60) The fellowship between Father and Son which was originally restricted to the intra-trinitarian perichoresis enters the world and becomes so all-embracing that it now encompasses not only men and women, but all of creation.(61)

For Moltmann, the eschatological history of Christ, the lordship of Christ, the eschatological coronation of Christ as Lord toward which Christ's history points, when understood in a trinitarian way, means that his history is also open to humans because the trinity is open to humans. In his indwelling, God participates in human destiny.(62) At the same time, however, human destiny is taken up by Christ, through the Spirit, into the trinity itself and God becomes our "home".

> The trinity means the history of God, which in human terms is love and liberation....If Christian belief thinks in trinitarian terms, it says that forsaken men are already taken up by Christ's forsakenness into the divine history and that we 'live in God'.(63)

In this perspective, through the eschatological rule of Christ we participate in the trinitarian process of God's history. By participating in God's history, we experience liberation in the present.(64) Through the openness of Christ's future our future is also opened.

Understood in this manner, the world is not a reflection of the present being of the divine triunity, or of the present perichoretic relationship between persons in the trinity. Rather, it is an anticipation of the fullness of the union between God and world which will be consummated at the Eschaton.(65)

Moltmann deepens this understanding of the openness of God to the world through his understanding of the relationship of the "trinity in the sending" and the "trinity in the origin". From Moltmann's perspective, the traditional doctrine of the trinity was understood first from the perspective of the sending of Christ to the world, and then only secondarily from the perspective of the immanent relations of the trinity. In this sense, the economic trinity, understood from the perspective of the mission of Christ to the world (the trinity in the sending), opens up for us the immanent trinity (the trinity in the origin).(66) The *missio ad extra* reveals the *missio ad intra*, and the *missio ad intra* is the foundation of the *missio ad extra*.(67) Understood in this manner, the immanent trinity is marked by an inherent openness because the primary relationship between members of the trinity is understood not in terms of a closed relationship between the three persons of the trinity, but in the openness of the trinity in the "sending" of the Son to the world. The essence of the immanent trinity is thus a communicative one in which God communicates himself to the world. In this perspective, then, the immanent trinity is directed toward its relationship to the world: The Son is the one sent to the world; The Father is the one who sends the Son to the world; The Son is sent to the world through the power of the Spirit.(68)

The understanding of perichoresis in the trinity is not limited by Moltmann to the openness of God to the world. Rather, the mutual indwelling of the three persons of the trinity is open to the indwelling of God in the world:

> All relationships which are analogous to God reflect the primal reciprocal indwelling and interpenetration of the trinitarian perichoresis: God *in* the world and the world *in* God.(69)

Since Moltmann emphasizes the presence of God *in* the world, more so than the presence of God *to* the world (as was the case with Niebuhr) the world as the "home" of God becomes the recipient of God's grace in a transformative manner. God's grace does not merely preserve the world, but also transforms and renews the world.

> ...God always creates through and in the power of his Spirit, and that the presence of his Spirit therefore conditions the potentialities and realities of his creation....The Spirit is poured out on all that exists, and the Spirit preserves it, makes it live and renews it.(70)

For Moltmann, it is thus the Spirit which is the primary actor in this regard. It is through the Spirit that God's presence is made manifest in the world. It is through the potentialities of the Spirit that God is present to the world. The intra-worldly movements and activities are taken up into the movements and activities of the Spirit and are given new life:

> God the Spirit is also the Spirit of the universe, its total cohesion, its structure, its information, its energy....The evolutions and catastrophes of the universe are also the movements and experiences of the Spirit.(71)

Because the Spirit forms the structure and energy of the universe, the powers of the Spirit possess humans and free them from the powers of the world which enslave them.(72) The Spirit allows humans to live without reserve because their future is opened to and through the power of God.(73) Because the patterns and powers of the world are formed and energized through the presence of the Spirit, people are given a degree of personal liberty and the opportunity to change their lives.(74) Thus, the presence of the Spirit energizes life, and gives it hope because it has taken the world into relationship with God and made world history into God's history. In such a way, in the Spirit the world will be transfigured, transformed into God's world.(75)

Based on the intimate relation of God and world, the world is perceived by Moltmann as both *sacrament* and *stage* for God's activity. Since the Trinity is open to the world, and in some sense dwells in the world, the world is able to reflect and point to the trinitarian history of God. Thus the world is "...reality qualified by God's word and made the bearer of his presence."(76) Nature contains *vestigia Dei* and thus reflects the trinity and the coming reign of God.(77) History becomes the "sacrament" of God in that its horizon has been enlarged by inclusion into the horizon of the future of Christ and is thus able to reflect the divine history.(78) History becomes the "mirror" for the future which is to come in God.(79) Both Church and world become revelations and powers of Christ and his future.(80)

The world understood as the stage of God's activity, means that the world is the place where God interprets himself. It is where God reveals himself and his history. It is not, however, merely the passive locus and receiver of God's revelation. Rather, men and women not only look on at the drama, but also participate in it. They are actors as well as audience.(81)

The strong emphasis on the presence of God in the world in Moltmann's theology affects the manner in which he understands the transcendence and sovereignty of God. We had seen above that Niebuhr emphasized the "over-againstness" of God's sovereignty. God's freedom was not limited by the world, but the world's freedom was limited by God. Moltmann, on the other hand, emphasizes the transcendence of God, not in a way that limits the world, but in a way in which God limits himself to allow for the world. In doing so, God's freedom *over* the world becomes the source of human freedom *in* the world.(82)

Moltmann bases his understanding of the transcendence of God to the world on the freedom of God to create the world *ex nihilo*. For Moltmann, the creation of the world began first as a decision on the part of God to create something different from himself. The world was thus called into existence by the free will of God.(83)

If God is omnipresent, however, in order to create something other than himself, God had to limit himself to "make room" for that which he created. Moltmann finds the kabbalistic doctrine of the *Zimsum*, developed by Isaac Luria, to be a helpful means of understanding this concept.(84) According to Luria, in creating the world, God, who is co-extensive with all space, "contracted" into himself, leaving space for creation to be "other" than God. In this sense, God stands over and against his creation. Moltmann contends that, interpreted through the doctrine of the trinity, the space that God provides through self-contraction is space within the trinitarian relationship itself.(85) Consequently, the space that God provided for creation to be "other" than himself is in actuality space within God himself.

In this perspective, God's transcendence is dialectically related to creation in that God is "other" than the world by contracting into himself, yet is at the same time intimately related to the world in that the space he provided was within the trinitarian relationship itself. When perceived in this manner, creation cannot be misunderstood as an emanation from God which results in a pantheism. The world is created out of the decision and act of God's self-communication, not by the emanation of divine essence.(86) At the same time, the world is not identified with God. Rather, the world is "other" than God, but within the primal relationship among trinitarian persons. It is not a pantheistic perspective because in this view, everything is not God, everything is *in* God.(87)

God's transcendence to the world is also understood by Moltmann in a *temporal* sense. In Moltmann's eschatological perspective, the complete presence of the world in God (when God becomes all-in-all) will occur in the future, at the Eschaton. Consequently, God's presence in and to the world in the present is always partial in relationship to the presence of God which is to come.(88) Understood in this manner, the world is an anticipation of what is to come in the future. At the same time, however, the complete presence of God in the future stands in opposition to the partial anticipation of that future in the present. God is not equally present in the world in all time periods. Consequently, God always remains partially "other" than the world until the consummation of his presence in the world at the eschaton.

With this understanding of God's transcendence, the idea of God's sovereignty also takes on a relational character. In Moltmann's perspective, much of Christian tradition has developed a view of the sovereignty of God from a consistent monotheism. In such a perspective, the single divine Lord is defined through the power he has over his "property", creation.(89) In adopting a trinitarian model of God's sovereignty, however, Moltmann emphasizes the power of God not *over* and *against* the world, but *in* and *for* the world. God's sovereignty is not almighty power, but almighty love.(90) Self-limiting, kenosis and love are the marks of God's governance of the world.(91) God rules through liberating people by opening up their history to the power of God.(92) The lordship of the Son is the active suffering which opens new possibilities for humans.(93)

2.4: *Evaluation*:

As should be clear from the foregoing, Niebuhr presents us with a perspective which primarily emphasizes the disjunction of God and world, while Moltmann presents us with a perspective which mainly stresses the conjunction of God and world. At this point in our discussion, the strengths and weaknesses of each perspective will be examined.

The strength of Niebuhr's perspective lies in its critical stance in regard to those cultural and theological forces which attempted to draw too many parallels between God and the world. The thrust of Niebuhr's understanding of the discontinuity and disjunction of God and world was based on his understanding of the perils of Liberal Theology. For Niebuhr, Liberal Theology too closely identified God and world. It confused the majesty of the world with the majesty of God. By emphasizing the discontinuity of God to the world, Niebuhr avoided giving humankind any grounds for an "easy conscience" or for a progressive view of history. By understanding God to be in a "vertical", relationship to the world, Niebuhr was able to maintain the sovereignty and majesty of God despite the claims of sovereignty and majesty by modern culture

At the same time, however, while Niebuhr contended that he was attempting to maintain both the transcendence and immanence of God in relation to the world, his emphasis on the transcendence of God far outweighed his emphasis on God's intimacy with the world.(94) Consequently, Niebuhr stressed the disjunction of God and the world rather than their conjunction. This disjunction is such that the realm of God and the realm of creation are considered not only distinct and separate, but also exhibit a "closedness" to one another: there is little interplay between the two realms. This is best exhibited in Niebuhr's conception of grace.

Although Niebuhr contends that grace is a power open and available to humankind, he provides few examples of how this grace is operative in the world in any real way, and gives no means for this grace to come within the use of human power. Since Niebuhr contended that grace is a form of power in the world, one expects to find some evidence of God's activity in the world in Niebuhr's theology.(95) Niebuhr, however, did not go beyond positing the power of God in the world. Instead, one finds a "gnosticizing" of grace. For Niebuhr, once a person recognized that he or she had held fallacious conceptions of God and of the world, the recognition of this fact would prompt some sort of metanoia in the sense of turning away from previous erroneous conceptions to newer, more correct conceptions and to a new way of life.(96) At times, Niebuhr seemed to be saying that divine grace acts to bring about this metanoia, but even then the activity of grace is understood in a psychological manner:

> The self is shattered whenever it is confronted by the power and holiness of God and becomes genuinely conscious of the real source and center of all life.(97)

It would seem that Niebuhr falls into the rationalist idealism which he is trying to avoid. If grace from the transcendent God were nothing more than a means of creating the recognition of human limitations and human pretension, then grace is operative primarily in a cognitive sense. Grace does not change the concrete reality within which humankind operates, but only changes the meaning which is granted to that reality. Thus defined, grace reveals to humankind the folly of its ambitious pretension, but does not enable humankind to act in consequence of that recognition. Niebuhr did contend that God's grace completes the structures of *meaning* which were only fragmentary within history.(98) But he did not understand God's grace to be operative in changing the actual living, historical *situation* within which people lead their lives.(99)

Niebuhr's difficulty with accepting a doctrine of the grace of God which is active in the world stemmed from his desire to assure that Christian theology maintained a strong sense of moral responsibility. If God's grace were understood as the single source of a new life, then Christianity would fall into a determinism which would vitiate any sense of human responsibility.(100) This is precisely the difficulty Niebuhr had with the thought of Luther and Barth. Luther's insistence on the "total depravity" of the human being placed all responsibility for altering the human situation upon God. Barth's determinism betrays the same weakness. If human advancement has its source solely in the grace of God, then the human being loses any sense of responsibility for his or her actions.(101)

Niebuhr attempted to avoid the gnosticizing of grace in his explanation of the relationship between wisdom and power in God's grace. Thus he went to great pains to explain how grace was not only wisdom, but also power.(102) Niebuhr, however, defined "power" in different terms when he spoke of God's power, than he did, for example, when he talked about power in the social world. In reference to the social world, Niebuhr understood power in concrete terms as the ability for self-determination, for realizing one's will and for the attainment of one's goals.(103) In his treatment of power in God's grace, however, Niebuhr never went beyond an understanding of grace as "psychological" power. Power in this sense is not concrete but abstract. The interior appropriation of God's forgiveness and mercy brought about a change of attitude and behavior:

> The affirmation that in Christ there is a new beginning, that a "new age" has been initiated in the history of mankind, means that the wisdom of faith which apprehends the true meaning of

life also contains within it the repentance which is the presumption of the renewal of life.(104)

From this passage, it becomes evident that the understanding of being judged by God demanded a response of obedience and repentance. In no way, however, did Niebuhr explain this power of God as a coercive force against the powers of the world. In no way did it change the relationship between those who have power in the world and those who lack it. God's power remains abstract and uninfluential. The serenity and creativity promised by Niebuhr to be the result of God's grace operating in the world, prove to be either illusions or delusions when viewed in light of the concrete domination of the powerful over the powerless in the political sphere. In traditional terms, God's grace operates to sanctify the human being (bring the human being to a new level of existence within the world) but does not act to enable the human being to make that grace manifest in the world. Although Niebuhr does refer to God's providence in the world, he qualifies it to the extent that providence cannot be understood as interrupting free human causality and activity. According to Niebuhr:

> God's providence does not operate in such a way that...the freedom of man is annulled or imperiled and God appears to be an angry despot of the historical drama who creates meanings by special providence, that is, by interference with the natural causalities and coherences which always furnish the foundation upon which human freedom erects the various pinnacles of history.(105)

If the effect of God's grace is a new insight or a new consciousness, not a concrete change in human life, God becomes reduced to a principle of transcendence which "impinges" on the world, not a personal God who acts in the world. The world is effectively closed off from God, and God seemingly remains aloof from it. God's grace does not penetrate the world in any concrete way.

Thus, as D. McCann points out, for Niebuhr "redemption consists more in learning to see things in a new way than in possessing some sort of supernatural power."(106) T. Minemma reaches a similar conclusion that Niebuhr is really docetic in outlook, contending that his understandings of faith and Christ are symbols abstracted from history.(107) E. Brunner questions whether or not there is any "reality" behind the symbols that Niebuhr uses.(108)

Niebuhr's understanding of the Atonement further emphasizes this "cognitive" aspect of God's grace. Rather than emphasize the "real" character of the sacrifice of Christ on the cross as a "real" forgiveness of sins and a "real" atonement, Niebuhr stressed that the cross of Christ brought to light "..the *idea* of a potent but yet suffering divine ideal which is defeated by the world but gains its victory in defeat..."(109)

Niebuhr's treatment of the Holy Spirit also supports the contention that he considered the world closed to God. Traditionally, Christianity has understood the primary means of God's operation in the world to be through the Holy Spirit. As has been often stated, one of the greatest flaws in Niebuhr's theology is his lack of a viable doctrine of the Spirit.(110) This omission, it can be contended, is not an accidental one, nor an oversight in Niebuhr's thought, but is necessary for maintaining his understanding of the relationship of God and the world. Given Niebuhr's understanding of the inviolability of immanent causality in the natural and historical world, and his conception of grace operating in a psychological, abstract way, there is little need for a doctrine of the Holy Spirit. In fact, the omission of the Holy Spirit seems to be necessary for the consistency of Niebuhr's theology as a whole.

Since the heart of Niebuhr's theology lies in the recognition of the depth dimension of sin which is incontrovertible within history, the traditional role of the Holy Spirit as the power of God overcoming sin in the world would be downplayed. Niebuhr did not want to give humankind any grounds for an "easy conscience" or for a progressive view of history. And dealings with the spiritualism of the Social Gospel alerted Niebuhr to the danger of the development of such a progressive view. Consequently, Niebuhr shied away from the idea of a Holy Spirit which was operative in the world.

Yet Niebuhr never fully revealed how the Holy Spirit bequeaths enabling grace to humans. Instead, he seemed to include the traditional understanding of an indwelling Holy Spirit primarily as a means of countering those who would contend that the positive change in a person away from sinfulness was due to the activities of the human spirit rather than to the grace of God through the Spirit.

> The Spirit is not merely...the development of the highest development of the human spirit. He is not identical with the most universal and transcendent levels of the human mind and consciousness.(111)

Talk of the Spirit thus seems like an apologetic appendix to Niebuhr's thought. Nowhere did he explain how the Spirit works in the world. Nor did he adduce any concrete transformation of the world as a result of the activity of the Spirit. His theology, constructed around the insight of the depth dimension of sin, appears to leave little function for the Spirit. In fact, a developed doctrine of the Spirit would only detract from that central insight because it would render sin something which can be overcome in history through the action of God.

Niebuhr's treatment of the Kingdom of God, a concept which traditionally was used relate God and world, does not overcome in any real manner the disjunction of God and world in Niebuhr's theology. For Niebuhr, the Kingdom of God was "not of this world".(112) The relationship between Kingdom and world was basically one of discontinuity, in which the Kingdom is not only not present in the world, but has little concrete effect in the world. A focus on the Kingdom as an immanent force in history is disallowed. Thus, in refuting what he considers to be liberal theological errors, Niebuhr states that a primary error of liberal Christianity is its contention that The Kingdom of God seemed to be an immanent force in history, culminating in a universal society of brotherhood and justice.(113)

When Niebuhr does speak of the continuities between Kingdom and world, he tends to existentialize the kingdom into human conscience or into an ideal which can stand in history, but only as a call to decision for the development of more harmonious relations between people in history.(114) Again, however, Niebuhr's thought on the Kingdom still remains somewhat abstract and existential. He remains silent about any influence of the Kingdom on human history in its concrete development.

The relationship between the Kingdom of God and history, therefore, does not open up the historical process to the activity of God in any real manner. Niebuhr's understanding of the relationship between God and world emphasizes the preserving activity in the world, but not the transformative activity. Rather, Niebuhr seems to have produced an existentialized version of Luther's two-kingdom doctrine.(115)

For both Luther and Niebuhr, reality consisted of two realms, one eternal and divine, the other secular and human. Both Luther and Niebuhr drew a sharp distinction between the two: the eternal is not to be confused with the temporal. Yet Niebuhr maintained contact between the two realms in the human conscience.(116) Conscience, understood as the uneasy feeling of being judged and having demands and decisions forced upon one from outside of oneself, creates a situation in which one is called upon to make a decision. Through one's response to that call to decision, one's consciousness is changed and consequently one's behavior also changes.(117)

When Niebuhr does speak of the relationship between the transcendent God and the world, it is usually in a hermeneutical sense: God is the principle of interpretation for the world, God grants coherence of meaning to history, but God does not *act* in the world in any concrete manner. The eternal always remains separate from the temporal.(118)

The hermeneutical character of Niebuhr's understanding of the relationship of God and world is also seen in his treatment of the Incarnation. For Niebuhr the incarnation seems to be understood primarily in terms of its symbolic function; it provides the world with meaning than a real incarnation of the divinity:

> If men recognize the fragmentariness of all human virtue, Christ becomes to them the *symbol* of an ultimate mercy which overcomes the hiatus between human and divine righteousness.(119)

The importance of this statement turns on the use of the word "symbol". When used by Niebuhr in his discussion of myth, "symbol" refers to a means of representing certain meanings that are not obviously present to human thinking or consciousness. Symbols do not represent *facts* or *realities*, but the *meanings* of certain facts or realities.(120) It seems consistent with the remainder of Niebuhr's thought that "symbol" here is used in the sense of a representative presence of God's mercy in the world, not an actual presence of that mercy. Niebuhr was concerned with showing the disjunction of God and world, of eternal and temporal. Acknowledging the fact that in Christ the eternal actually entered the world would be grounds for identifying the eternal and the temporal. By understanding this presence to be symbolic, there is no means whatsoever for claiming possession of the eternal within the processes and events of history.(121)

What we are thus left with in our discussion of the relationship of God and the world is a contradiction in Niebuhr's thought itself. As D.D. Williams points out, sometimes Niebuhr speaks of the absolute distinction between God and world in such a way that God's being is sharply separated from the world. At other times, he speaks of the relationship of God and world in terms of a drama. This would seem to suggest that God and the world have a mutual effect, cause changes in each other, and thus have a somewhat intimate relationship.(122) Williams leaves the decision on which position is more appropriate to the individual reader of Niebuhr's work. Based on the foregoing, I contend that the primary paradigm in Niebuhr's thought for the relationship of God's relationship to the world is one which emphasizes distinction and separateness. There is not an insurmountable barrier between God and world as R. King has contended. Yet I think that Niebuhr felt the need to fight the dangers of a liberalism which emphasized the continuities of God and world caused him to stress the distinction between God and world.

Similarly, God's transcendence in Niebuhr's perspective is primarily vertical, stressing disjunction between the world and God. This disjunction is such that the grace of God does not penetrate the world in any concrete manner beyond the mere preservation of the world. And the near absence of a doctrine of the Holy Spirit, the traditional means of relationship between God and world, further dissociates God from the world.(123)

While Niebuhr's perspective primarily emphasizes the disjunction of God and world, Moltmann's view tends to emphasize the conjunction of God and world. The strengths of this perspective of God and world in Moltmann's Political Theology lie in its ability to locate the immanence and transcendence of God in the nature of God himself. By adopting a trinitarian perspective of God, Moltmann is able to speak about God's presence in the world in varying degrees. The Father, Son and Spirit are thus not equally related to nor present in the world to the same degree nor in the same manner. The trinitarian perspective allows Moltmann thus to avoid both the dangers of pantheism, which understands the world to be God, and of a deism, which understood the God-world relationship in dualistic terms.

Moltmann's perspective is also more inclusive than Niebuhr's. When Niebuhr speaks of "world", he seems basically to be referring to the humanly-created world; there is little regard given to the non-human, natural world in Niebuhr's thought. Moltmann's thought, on the other hand, includes Nature (as part of God's creation) as an essential element of "world". The human cannot be separated from Nature and Nature cannot be separated from the human.

While Moltmann's perspective has much to commend it, it seems to overemphasize the immanence of God to the detriment of the transcendence of God. As we saw above, God's transcendence is understood by Moltmann in a temporal sense: the presence of God in creation is always incomplete and fragmentary until God becomes all-in-all at the eschaton. While Moltmann does maintain a dialectical understanding of God's relationship to the world, he does not emphasize strongly enough the way in which this future wholeness of God can be understood as judgment against all that is only fragmentary in the present. For Niebuhr, God's transcendence is perceived in the sense of God's judgment against all that exists. Moltmann, however, downplays this idea in favor of a "facilitative" understanding of God's transcendence. In this view, God's transcendence is that which provides the source and content for the anticipation of the future glory of God in the present, but does not seem to emphasize strongly enough the basic over-againstness of God's transcendence in relation to the world. Whereas Niebuhr, in an attempt to counter liberal thought, overemphasizes God's closedness to the world, Moltmann emphasizes too strongly the openness of God to the world in an attempt to stress the liberative aspects of Christian thought. Consequently, Moltmann's theology does not develop to the same extent the critical "over-againstness" of God's transcendence which marked Niebuhr's theology so strongly.

Without a stronger understanding of God's transcendence as judgment, Moltmann's theology seemingly links the grace of God with the movements of human history. If the world contains *vestigia Dei*, and human history participates in the working out of God's promise, if human history is taken into divine history and anticipates the union of the two histories in the present, then the world is given a certain stature of openness to God. Yet theology in general, and Protestant theology in particular, has always emphasized to one degree or another the *closedness* of God to the world. Human history at times runs contrary to God's history. The world is both for God and against God. The human will at times coincides with God's will, yet at other times is in opposition to it. Moltmann's theology does not fully reflect this ambivalence of God and world. Rather than maintain the dialectical tension between God and world in which the world is both for and against God and God is both for and against the world, Moltmann, with his emphasis on the mutual openness of God and world, may underestimate both the intransigence of the world and the wrath of God toward the world. Unlike Barth, who saw the difficulty of understanding the *Ja* of God's mercy behind the *Nein* of God's wrath, Moltmann sees predominantly the *Ja* of God's mercy, while neglecting the *Nein* of God against the world.

The above comparison reveals the different perspectives adopted by both Niebuhr and Moltmann in regard to the God-world relationship. Niebuhr's perspective emphasizes the transcendence of God over and against the world, yet downplays the creative and redemptive activity of God transforming the world. Moltmann's perspective, on the other hand, emphasizes the immanence of God to the world, yet downplays the judgmental transcendence of God over and against the world. As will be examined in the next chapter, a similar pattern can be discerned in their respective understandings of history.

Notes to Chapter 2

1. Cf. K. Barth, *Church Dogmatics*, III/2, (Edinburgh: T&T Clark, 1960): "Even linguistically, the one term 'creation' includes not only the action of the Creator but also its product, the creature....Creator and creation belong together as an integral whole....The creature of God is the totality, the whole cosmos of the reality posited by him and distinct from him....This being the case, it is a serious question whether the theological doctrine of the creature should not be expounded as a doctrine of the totality, of the whole created cosmos..."; Cf. also L. Gilkey, *The Maker of Heaven and Earth*. (NY: University Press, 1959) 4: "...the idea that God is the Creator of all things is the indispensable foundation on which the other beliefs of the Christian faith are based....On this affirmation logically depends all that Christians say about God, about the world that they live in, and about their own history, destiny and hope."

2. SDH, 46ff., 84ff.; NDM, II, 36.

3. LJ, 161-2.

4. FH, 126.

5. NDM,II, 46.

6. See Chapter 1.

7. This can also be understood as the primary emphasis of Neo-orthodoxy in general over against Liberal Theology. Cf. J. M. Robinson, *The Beginnings of Dialectical Theology*, vol. I, (Richmond, Va.: John Knox, 1968.

8. NDM,II, 35, 65-66.

9. *Ibid.*, 71.

10. *Ibid.*, 31. This does not mean, however, that Niebuhr annuls the horizontal totally into the vertical. There is evidence of a "horizontal" perspective in Niebuhr's thought. Cf. BT 253-269; CPP, 35,75; NDM,II, 43-45; FH, 128, 136; LJ, 161-166. It is possible to maintain, however, that the "vertical" model of the God-world relationship is predominant and even formative in Niebuhr's work. Rather than explain how the vertical and horizontal elements of God's activity are dialectically related, Niebuhr leans much more toward the distinction between God and world. As will be discussed below, Niebuhr's understanding of God who is involved in history goes against his formative insight that the references to the confluence of eternal and temporal in history is mythical, not literal as in a "crude supernaturalism" which confused the two. Cf. below, p. 41.

11. NDM,I, 300.

12. NDM,II, 36, 47, 49, 52; FH, 107.

13. The references to this are too numerous to mention individually. The idea presented here forms the basis for NDM, as well as Christian Realism in general.

14. NDM,I, 92, 165-166, 209-212, 213, 240, a.o.

15. NDM,II, 167, 305-306.

16. NDM,I, 129, 137, 140, 141; FH, 113.

17. For a complete discussion of Niebuhr's concept of image of God, see below, Chapter 4.

18. FH, 48, 55, 64, 66.

19. R. Niebuhr, "Truth in Myth", in R. Stone, (ed.), *Faith and Politics* (NY: Brazillier, 1968) p. 17.

20. *Ibid.*, 16.

21. *Ibid.*, 28.

22. Stone, *Faith and Politics*, 105. Cf. also FH, 102, 103, 105.

23. NDM, II, 98-99.

24. *Ibid.*, 99. Cf. also FH, 105, 108.

25. *Ibid.*, 99.

26. *Ibid.*, 99-100.

27. *Ibid.*, 114.

28. *Ibid.*, 58.

29. NDM,I, 127.

30. NDM,I, 136-7. Cf. also FH, 105-108.

31. NDM,I, 139, 132ff.

32. *Ibid.*, 134.

33. TH, 34.

34. FC, 29, TH, 16f.

35. TH, 17, FC, 30.

36. TH, 16.

37. *Ibid.*, 16.

38. *Ibid.*, 21. Cf. also TH, 18, 19, 34, 35, 37, 86; FC, 39, 40.

39. TH, 34.

40. *Ibid.*, 21.

41. *Ibid.*, 37, 41.

42. Cf. T. Fretheim, *The Suffering of God: An Old Testament Perspective*, (Phila.: Fortress, 1984) 35ff.

43. TK, 98; Cf. GC, 13; TK, 99.

44. TK, 3-4, 98.

45. TK, 104.

46. GC, 96-97.

47. TK, 108; GC, 94-98.

48. TK, 104.

49. FC, 81; TH, 202; TK, 90-97.

50. FC, 82.

51. CG, 240.

52. GC, 10, 14-15.

53. TK, 149, 150.

54. *Ibid.*, 172, 173.

55. *Ibid.*, 174.

56. *Ibid.*, 151, 174f.

57. *Ibid.*, 175.

58. *Ibid.*, 4, 19, 64, 93, 94.

59. *Ibid.*, 178.

60. TK, 64, 122; FC, 82; CG, 265.

61. TK, 4, 64, 75; FC, 84, 85.

62. GC, 96-7.

63. CG, 255. Cf. also CG, 266 and GC, 96.

64. CG, 276-277, 321.

65. *Ibid.*, 265, 320-321.

66. FC, 83, 84; TK, 74, 97.

67. FC, 84; TK, 4.

68. FC, 90; TK, 124, 127f., 170.

69. GC, 17. Here Moltmann adopts the idea of the *Schekinah* as a model for the interpenetration of God and world. Cf. CG, 321f.

70. GC, 10. Cf. also GC, 209.

71. GC, 16.

72. *Ibid.*, 96.

73. *Ibid.*, 269.

74. *Ibid.*, 267.

75. TK, 104.

76. CG, 4.

77. GC, 63.

78. CG, 321.

79. *Ibid.*, 320.

80. PS, 205.

81. GC, 308, 309.

82. *Ibid.*, 90, 91.

83. GC, 75, 79-80; TK, 105. Moltmann makes it clear, however, that the resolve to create is not limited to God's will alone. Rather, it is also consistent with God's being. Cf. TK, 106; GC, 81ff.

84. GC, 86,87; TK, 109f.

85. TK, 109, 111.

86. GC, 102.

87. GC, 102-103.

88. FC, 94; GC, 120-122, 124, 280.

89. TK, 198.

90. *Ibid.*, 198.

91. *Ibid.*, 210.

92. *Ibid.*, 210, 211.

93. TK, 210; CG, 265.

94. J. Gustafson, "Theology in the Service of Ethics: An Interpretation of Reinhold Niebuhr's Theological Ethics", in *Reinhold Niebuhr and the Issues of Our Time*, (Grand Rapids, Mich: Eerdmans, 1986) 24-45.

95. Cf. *NDM*, II, 99: "Grace is, on the other hand, the power of God in man; it represents an accession of resources, which man does not have of himself, enabling him to become what he truly ought to be."

96. *Ibid.*, 100.

97. *Ibid.*, 109.

98. FH, 102-103.

99. Cf. CPP, 18. For a similar view, see D. McCann, CRLT, p. 51, note 4.; Chiba, *Transcendence and the Political*, 88; E. Brunner, "Some Remarks on Reinhold Niebuhr's Work as a Christian Thinker", in RN, 85-86.

100. NDM, II, 116.

101. *Ibid.*, 117.

102. *Ibid.*, 98-99.

103. MMIS, 3, 6, 19; IAH, 12; NDM, II, 71.

104. FH, 139.

105. R. Stone, *Faith and Politics*, p. 81. Cf. also, R. Fitch, *RN*, pp. 371-2. Here the distinction to be made is between preserving and enabling

grace. Preserving grace is the activity of God directed toward maintaining creation in existence. Enabling grace, on the other hand, is the activity of God in the world in order to transform the world. Cf. "Grace", in K. Rahner and H. Vorgrimler, *Theological Dictionary*, (NY: Herder and Herder, 1965) 196-197.

106. D. McCann, "Hermeneutics and Ethics: The Example of Reinhold Niebuhr," *Journal of Religious Ethics* 8/1 (1980), pp. 27-53.

107. T. Minemma, "Reinhold Niebuhr's Concept of Power", *Christianity Today*, VI (January 19, 1962), pp. 212-15.

108. E. Brunner, "Some Remarks on Reinhold Niebuhr as a Christian Thinker," RN, pp. 81-8.

109. DCNR, 237 (emphasis mine). P. Lehmann also recognizes the fact that Niebuhr does not understand the cross as operative in the world in any real way except as an idea. P. Lehmann, "The Christology of Reinhold Niebuhr," RN, pp. 327-356.

110. R.H. King, *The Omission of the Holy Spirit from Reinhold Niebuhr's Theology.* (NY: Philosophical Library, 1964). P. Lehmann also contends that Niebuhr's thought tends toward a binitarianism of Father-Son rather than a trinitarianism. Cf. Lehmann, in RN, p. 353.

111. NDM, II, 99. Cf. also, NDM,II, 100: "Yet the Holy Spirit is never a mere extension of man's spirit or identical with its purity and unity in the deepest or highest levels of consciousness. In that sense, all Christian doctrines of 'grace' and 'spirit' contradict mystical and idealistic theories of fulfillment." Niebuhr does not neglect the Holy Spirit altogether. He does speak of an indwelling of the Spirit in human beings (Cf. NDM,II, 110-11) He does not, however, develop this into an effective doctrine of the operation of the Holy Spirit in the world.

112. BT, 273ff.

113. NDM,II, 245.

114. Cf. D. Lange, *Christlicher Glaube und soziale Probleme: Eine Darstellung der Theologie Reinhold Niebuhrs*, (Gutersloh: G. Mohn, 1964) pp. 51f.

115. *Ibid.*, 52.

116. NDM,II, 247.

117. Here again we see the existential aspect of Niebuhr's thought.

118. Cf. McCann, "Hermeneutics and Ethics." Niebuhr's understanding of conscience as the link between the temporal and eternal must be maintained here. Cf. BT, 278-9.

119. "Mystery and Meaning", in *Pious and Secular America.* (NY: Scribners, 1958) 133 (emphasis mine). Cf. NDM,II, 88-9. R. Fitch points out that Niebuhr lacks an understanding of Christ's activity as a power open to human beings rather than as a sign of God's mercy. Where he does speak in terms of power, says Fitch, he qualifies it so many times that it is doubtful whether it can be said to be operative in his thought at all. Cf. R. Fitch, "Reinhold Niebuhr's Philosophy of History," RN, pp. 367-386.

120. Cf. DCNR, 235-237; BT, 4, 7. This seems to be the thrust of Niebuhr's argument that myths are to be taken seriously, but not literally.

121. McCann also understands Niebuhr's Christology to be "cognitive" rather than "real". Cf. CRLT, 51.

122. D. D. Williams, "Niebuhr and Liberalism," RN, 269-290.

123. R. King, *Omission*, 2. This aspect of Niebuhr's thought has been criticized from within the Christian Realist camp, itself. J. Bennett, Niebuhr's friend and colleague, views this tendency in Niebuhr's thought as a weakness which has to be corrected in such a way that it could take into account the openness of the future. Cf. John Bennett, "Christian Realism", *Christianity and Crisis*, XXVIII,(August 5, 1968) 176.

CHAPTER III

THE PERSPECTIVE OF CHRISTIAN REALISM

AND POLITICAL THEOLOGY

ON HISTORY

3.1 *The Place of Theology of History in the Thought of*
Christian Realism and Political Theology:

For both Niebuhr and Moltmann, an essential element of the Christian message is the contention that the human being is historical. This is not a philosophical speculation about what history is, but it means that the human past, present, and future are laden with meaning. And the term "historical" encompasses that meaning.

Niebuhr's view of history is, in effect, the capstone of his theology proper. His understanding of human existence as historical and his understanding of the nature of human history tie together many of the disparate elements in his theology. His anthropological insight that human nature is paradoxical, takes on its broadest meaning in the paradox of historical existence. His understanding of the egoism of groups gets played out in his understanding of the fragmentary character of history. Finally, as we shall see in this chapter, Niebuhr's understanding of the transcendence of God to the world culminates in a view of history which allows for no ultimate meaning to be found in the vicissitudes of the historical process.(1)

Moltmann's understanding of history, on the other hand, while not the capstone of his thought, provides the foundation for the other aspects of his theology. The historical nature of existence (both divine and human) is the starting point for Moltmann's theologizing. Thus, the God-world relationship is an historical one.(2) The primary characteristic of the human being is his or her historicity.(3) Nature, itself, has a history.(4)

3.2: *The Understanding of History in Christian Realism*

Niebuhr's perspective on history begins with anthropological insights: the whole history of humanity is comparable to the individual's life.(5). According to Niebuhr, human existence can not be reduced to mere natural existence nor to mere spiritual existence, but is a combination of both in a variety of ways.(6) This combination of spirit and nature makes human existence historical. Human beings transcend nature and history enough to develop rational structures of meaning for their lives.(7) At the same time, however, the human being is intimately involved in history and therefore can only understand history in a fragmentary way.(8) History, therefore, remains somewhat hidden and enigmatic to the human being.(9)

Given this understanding, Niebuhr's task was to explain how history, in light of fragmentary human existence, can attain overarching, universal coherence and meaning.(10) Without a means of granting coherence to history, history remains a collection of unrelated, meaningless events.

Niebuhr was discouraged by the response that modern culture and religion offered to this problem. Following his usual style of distinguishing between various alternatives of an issue, Niebuhr distinguishes between classical, modern and Christian perspectives on history.

The classical perspective on history, as represented by Platonists and Aristotelians, both ancient and modern, tended to identify the processes of history with the processes of nature.(11) Just as nature undergoes cyclical transformations from season to season, so too does history take on a cyclical character. History becomes an "eternal recurrence" of the past.(12) The result of this view is that the historical process had no ultimate meaning or importance. In fact, the strict bifurcation of body and soul, a conception which lies at the heart of classical anthropology, demands an escape from history into the realm of pure being.(13) When viewed in a classical manner, history offers "no hope for the fulfillment of the unique capacities of human personality" because it reduces human existence to a mere repetition of the past.(14)

The modern perspective toward history, on the other hand, does allow for growth and fulfillment. The modern perception of time is not cyclical, but linear. The future is understood as being qualitatively different from the past and present. Time flows from past through the present into the future in a progressive manner in which subsequent generations reveal development over previous ones.(15)

For Niebuhr, the modern perception of history maintains a basic truth: both nature and historical institutions are subject to development in time. History takes on a dynamism, a variety and a sense of novelty which is absent from the classical view.(16) At the same time, however, modern perceptions of history distort this truth into an illusion: they do not understand the pervasiveness of sin in human existence because they hold that development *within* history fulfils (or will fulfil) the ultimate meaning of life.(17)

According to Niebuhr, neither of these perspectives adequately explains the aspects of freedom and finitude in history. Whereas the classical view of history overly limits human freedom and possibility, the modern view does not take adequate account of the finiteness of history. The classical perspective places the possibilities of attaining any fulfillment outside of the realm of history, and consequently renders history meaningless. The modern perspective considers partial and fragmentary fulfillments in history to be ultimate fulfillments and thus grants history meaning beyond the scope of its possible accomplishments.(18)

Over against these two alternatives, Niebuhr places his understanding of the Christian perspective of history. Niebuhr's Christian perspective attempts to overcome the deficiencies of the Greek and modern perspectives on history by combining the cyclical Greek perspective on history with an Hebraic, dynamic/dramatic perspective developed in the Old Testament.(19)

Although Niebuhr is not in agreement with the dualism presented in the Hellenic view, he does finds two elements to his liking. On the one hand, the dualism of body and soul in Hellenic anthropology emphasizes the ability of the human being to transcend natural processes and to create constellations of meaning for his or her life.(20) At the same time, however, Hellenic philosophy also maintains that ultimate historical meaning transcends both the natural and the historical.(21)

Hellenic philosophy, however, because of an ontologism which emphasizes the orderly structure of being over the "disorderliness" of dynamic becoming, has difficulty in relating the Ultimate to historic temporality.(22) Historical existence consequently takes on a certain orderliness which derives its form apart from the eternal.(23) History, itself, however has to look to the realm of the eternal (external to itself) in order to find its meaning.(24)

The Hebrew view, on the other hand, presents history as a drama between Israel and its God and between individuals, communities and nations as historical actors.(25) As a dramatic encounter between individuals and others and between individuals and God, history takes on central importance as a carrier of meaning. History becomes the framework within which meaning is derived.(26)

For Niebuhr, however, neither of these two perspectives individually does justice to the historical character of human existence:

> The Hellenic is defective in understanding the self and its dramas because it tries to understand both rationally and ontologically. The Hebraic, on the other hand, is defective in analyzing any permanent structure in the flow of events. For the one history is made into another dimension of nature; and for the other nature is subsumed under history.(27)

Niebuhr's interpretation of the Christian perspective of history combines the Hellenic insight that history has a transcendent source of meaning with the Hebraic notion of constellations of meaning within history. Coherence and ultimate meaning of history must be found outside of the historical process. At the same time, however, history is not stripped of all meaning, as was the case in the classical view, because the ultimate meaning of history is apprehended in faith within the historical process itself:

> The meaning of history is not completed within itself. It is only completed from beyond itself as faith apprehends the divine forgiveness which overcomes man's recalcitrance.(28)

It is Niebuhr's understanding of the relationship of the End of history to history itself that provides the theological underpinnings for maintaining the coherence of history without granting history the power to form its own coherence. According to Niebuhr, the End of history must be understood dialectically in the sense of both a *finis* and a *telos*.(29) For Niebuhr, the eschatological symbols of the Bible (when interpreted mythically) point to the ultimate fulfillment of history as the actual end (*finis*) of history. According to Niebuhr, history no longer exists after its end, and consequently any ultimate fulfillment of history can not fall within the bounds of history itself.(30)

With this understanding of a non-teleological "End" of history, Niebuhr effectively undercuts the modern perspective of history as progress. The End of history understood as *finis* leads to the assertion that history, in and of itself, is meaningless. God ends history as a human enterprise and renders any historical accomplishment, striving, and development null and void. What is considered meaningful in life, according to the doctrine of progress, is judged by God as ultimately meaningless because it is without reference to a reality which transcends the end of history.(31)

Understood as *telos*, however, history does take on coherence and meaning.(32) Niebuhr explains the teleological dimension of the End of history with the distinction between those religions in which a christ is expected and those in which a christ is not expected.(33)

Those religions in which a christ is not expected tend either to grant no coherence to history (the Greek perspective) or to locate final and ultimate meaning within the historical process itself (modern religious naturalism).(34)

Those religions in which a christ is expected, on the other hand,

> look forward at first to a point in history and finally toward an *eschaton* (end) which is also the end of history, where the full meaning of life and history will be disclosed and fulfilled.(35)

Christianity, as a religion in which a christ is expected, understands history to have coherence and meaning:

> Christianity enters the world with the stupendous claim that...in the life, death and resurrection of Christ, the expected disclosure of God's sovereignty over history, and the expected establishment of that sovereignty had taken place. In this disclosure of the power and will which governs history, both life

and history had found their previously partly hidden and partly revealed meaning, though it is not denied that God remains, despite this revelation, partly *Deus absconditus*.(36)

It is in the Christian reinterpretation of prophetic messianism that Niebuhr finds the insight that Christianity is a truly historic religion (it makes history a central category). From the perspective of Old Testament prophetism, humans have both the capacity and the inclination to disturb the harmony and order of human life.(37) Human life is thus always in defiance of God's laws and will.(38) The whole of the human enterprise is in contradiction to God.(39) Understood in this manner, the only coherence of history possible would be that all human striving is under the judgment of God.(40) God's judgment is trans-historical and ubiquitous.(41)

Jewish messianism attempted to resolve this dilemma of the ubiquity of God's judgment. Messianic prophetism of the Old Testament anticipated the disclosure and fulfillment of the meaning of history through the revelation of God and through the establishment of God's sovereignty in history.(42) History, therefore, is the stage upon which God is revealed.(43)

For Niebuhr, however, messianic prophetism does not completely resolve the problem of God's judgment. Implicit in the idea of the expectation of a messiah is the belief that history is not self-fulfilling.(44) If history cannot find its meaning except in the disclosure of divine sovereignty from without (in a messiah), history cannot find its full meaning from within itself. Fulfillment, consequently, must enter history from without.

Niebuhr held that the dual nature of history, as the locus of the disclosure and fulfillment of God's sovereignty and as pointing to the need for a solution to the meaning of history from a perspective transcendent to it, implies that meaning in history always remains enigmatic. Evil persists in all that is good. Ultimate meaning in history is always threatened by the attempt to make partial meaning into ultimate meaning.(45) Prophetism, which emphasized the absolute judgment of God, left unresolved the question of the relative good and evil that occurs within any specific historical time period.(46) If all human activity is deemed sinful, and is thus under the judgment of God, then the good in history has no value, and moral striving is hindered.(47)

In Niebuhr's view, the Christian reinterpretation of prophetic messianism in the doctrine of the Atonement, resolves the issue of relative good and evil in history. The doctrine of the Atonement combines God's ubiquitous justice with his all encompassing mercy.(48) According to Niebuhr, the Old Testament understood well the wrath of God, but did not have a complete understanding of the mercy of God. In the Atonement, however, the wrath and mercy of God are both present. God is both the propitiator and the propitiated.(49) The suffering of Christ is both the result of human sin and the response of God's mercy to that sin:

> ...the sufferings of the Son of man are the disclosure of God's suffering. The suffering of God is on the one hand the consequence of sin's rebellion against goodness; and on the other hand the voluntary acceptance by divine love of the consequence of sin.(50)

Through the vicarious suffering of Christ, the meaning of history becomes clear: vicarious love is defeated in history, but will triumph at the end of history with the establishment of God's sovereignty.(51) God is engaged in history, but is engaged not as a victor, but as a sufferer.(52)

The doctrine of the Atonement becomes the key for interpreting history for Niebuhr. Since God's wrath and mercy are paradoxically related in the Atonement, the moral imbalances of history are never completely overcome.(53) The righteous do not triumph over the unrighteous. Consequently, history remains morally ambiguous to the end.(54) It means that the moral ambiguity of history is recognized on every possible level of achievement; yet a power has been disclosed in history which will neither overcome the compound of good and evil in history, nor allow for the belief that the triumph of relative good over relative evil can be raised to ultimate, final level.(55) The persistence of moral ambiguity in history means that the perfect love practiced by Jesus is defeated in history, and thus must become suffering love.(56) Yet this suffering love which reveals the moral ambiguity of history is also the answer to the ambiguity of history. It points to the mercy of God which is beyond the ebb and flow of history.

The atoning power of Christ on the Cross, however, is not derivable from observable facts of history. Neither does it seek a resolution to the ambiguity of history from within history itself. Rather, it points to the resources of the power of the sovereign God who brings history to its fulfillment.(57)

When viewed in this manner, history since Christ must consequently be viewed as an interim period between the disclosure of meaning of history and the fulfillment of that meaning.(58) For Niebuhr, this understanding of history as an interim meant that history remains paradoxical to the end. History partly realizes its true meaning, but also stands in contradiction to that meaning:

> The idea that history is an "interim" between the first and second coming of Christ has a meaning which illumines all the facts of human existence. History, after Christ's first coming, has the quality of partly knowing its true meaning. Insofar as man can never be in complete contradiction to his own true nature, history also reveals significant realizations of that meaning. Nevertheless history continues to stand in real contradiction to its true meaning, so that pure love in history must always be a suffering love. But the contradictions of history can not become man's norms, if history is viewed from the perspective of Christ.(59)

In this perspective, since revelation is needed to bring to light the ultimate meaning of history, coherence in history is thus apprehendable only through faith.(60) The classical view of history denies meaning in history. The modern, progressive view of history ignores the facts of the suffering which belie progress. In the Christian view, revelation provides that through the atoning work of Christ history includes the possibilities of fulfillment, albeit from without. The atoning work of Christ's suffering does not deny the suffering of the world but validates it. Faith understands that despite increased antinomies and contradictions between good and evil the whole drama of history is under the sovereignty of divine love which has been revealed in Christ.(61) History can thus be understood as more than the judgment of God. The promise of history can be fulfilled at the Eschaton, and history gains coherence of meaning.(62)

Revelation also brings to light the nature of the content of history. For Niebuhr, if the End of history were understood merely as *finis*, history would take on a tragic character.(63) History would have no ultimate or even penultimate importance or coherence because all human striving would only be negated by the End. Understanding the End of history as *finis* and *telos*, however, means that history takes on meaning beyond the tragic.(64) As both *finis* and *telos*, history links forward to an end in which history is transfigured, but not annulled.(65)

Niebuhr uses the symbol of the bodily resurrection as a means of supporting the idea that the End of history is the fulfillment, not the annulment of the meaning of history.(66) Over and against the theories of the immortality of the soul, which Niebuhr feels ultimately deny the meaning of history, Niebuhr understands the genius of the Christian symbol of the resurrection to maintain the coherence and meaning of history in spite of its end.(67)

For Niebuhr, the fact that the resurrection is the resurrection of the body symbolizes that not just the transcendent aspects of human existence, but also the finite aspects of that existence, will be lifted up in the end. Thus, in terms of history, all partial fulfillments of historical meaning will not be destroyed, but will be teleologically fulfilled.(68) Consequently, the Christian hope in the fulfillment and coherence of history is based on faith in the biblical symbol of the resurrection of the body.

Understood in this manner, history takes on an *ironic* character; history is not ultimately meaningful, but contains ultimate meaning within it. All things in history move toward fulfillment, but also always contain elements of dissolution within them.(69) The ironic character of history means that good is therefore always intermixed with evil. The human being is at once both one with his or her true self, and in contradiction with it.(70) Human development and evolution are concomitantly tainted with the potentialities for human regression and devolution. So, for Niebuhr, the biblical interpretation of the human situation is ironic rather than tragic or pathetic, because of its unique formulation of the problem of human freedom. The evil in human history is regarded as the consequence of man's wrong use of his unique capacities. The wrong use is always due to some failure to recognize the limits of his capacities of power, wisdom and virtue. Humans are ironic creatures because they forget that they are not simply creators, but also creatures.(71)

Although for Niebuhr good and evil are inextricably intermingled with human freedom in history, the great evils in history are not inherent in human freedom, but are the result of human pretensions. Consequently these pretensions are the source of the ironic contrasts of strength leading to weakness, of wisdom issuing in foolishness. The crown of irony lies in the fact that the most obvious forms of success are involved in failure on the ultimate level.(72)

The ironic interpretation of history is not only drawn from the Christian conception of human freedom, but also from the Christian faith in a source of meaning outside of history which forms the basis for all meaning in history. This divine source of meaning, understood through faith as divine judgment, allows for real human freedom, yet condemns the human pretensions committed in the expression of that freedom.(73)

The implications of Niebuhr's understanding of the ironic nature of history for the modern view of history as progress becomes obvious. The ironies of history, as was the case with Hegel's "cunning of history," effectively eviscerate the progressive understanding of history held by modern society and Liberal Theology. For Niebuhr, history remains self-contradictory, even in its highest expressions. Any progressive view of history is therefore merely human pretension.(74)

Understood in this manner, human existence is always contingent existence until the End arrives. Thus, meaning in history is always partial and fragmentary. Coherence in history cannot be found within history itself, but can only be found outside of history, in its End.(75)

Niebuhr's perspective on the historical nature of the human being is thus the logical culmination of his theological anthropology and social thought. The qualities of freedom and transcendence which make human life truly historical, which make existence truly human, which allow for creative interplay between vitality and form, and which allow a person to find some sense of coherence and importance to life, are the same elements which ultimately cause the fragmentation of human existence, the conflict between individuals and between groups. The human capacity to "make history" is at one and the same time the highest expression of true human nature and also the greatest threat to existence as human.

3.3 The Understanding of History in Political Theology

Moltmann develops his theology of history in contradiction to what he considers the turning of Christianity toward a logos-centered emphasis on "being" over "becoming". According to Moltmann, the early Christian understanding of history was based on a view of God's presence as dynamic, historic and in the process of becoming.(76) God revealed himself in the movement and moments of history.(77) When Christianity moved into the Hellenistic world, however, it adopted a perspective on history which emphasized the eternal being of God.(78) The dynamic aspect of God's becoming was turned into the revelation of God's being.(79) The *logos* character of God (his eternal presence of being) replaced the idea of the dynamic becoming of God's being within history.(80)

For Moltmann, a perspective on history based upon Christian eschatology, rather than a transcendental perspective developed in the so-called epiphany religions, provides a better framework for speaking about history in a modern age of rapid change and development. The perspective of history in the epiphany religions emphasized the eternal presence of God in history. In the modern world, however, the interest in the present is replaced by an interest in the future.(81) More to the point, in Moltmann's perspective, only by understanding the world from the future and God not as eternal being, but as eternal becoming, can both freedom within history and coherence of history be maintained in a world of crisis.

Moltmann's view of history, derived from his eschatology, is also intimately related to his understanding of modernity.(82) For Moltmann, the modern age is a heritage of the Enlightenment's move toward freedom.(83) Historical criticism which developed in the Enlightenment freed humanity from a stultifying dependence on tradition. New sociological insights provided the basis for a critique of institutions. Politically and socially, the Old Regime was overthrown and replaced by republicanism. Advances in science made possible a great deal of freedom from natural determinism.(84) Thus, for Moltmann, the Enlightenment can be viewed as an age of revolution which freed the present and future from absolute dependence on the past. It was an age of novelty and possibility. It was a freedom "in time", that is, a freedom which is revolutionary, which strives for political and social transformation, for the development of new social and political structures and institutions not based on old models. It was a freedom of the future, a freedom which opened new possibilities which had before only been dreamed.(85)

At the same time, however, Moltmann views Enlightenment thought as the source of the historical crisis of the modern age. With the beginning of modernity, the traditions and institutions which have regulated and guided life become uncertain and insecure.(86) Modern people's experience of history is grounded in the experience of the infinitely new and overwhelming possibilities for good and evil.(87) The American, French and Communist revolutions produced epochal changes in the social and political structure of the Western world.(88) Rapid development of technology has created a situation in which the human being is confronted by myriad possibilities for advancement or for decline.(89) The modern age is thus imbued with an impermanence, a transience, a lack of directedness.(90) This rapid social, technological and economic change has created a multifaceted crisis for those living in this age. The flood of newness confronts modern persons with unfamiliar situations which cannot be mastered by the customary methods which had been used so often before.(91)

This rapid change presents a crisis also for historical consciousness. Coherence of history is derived from the understanding that the past, present and future are somehow causally related to each other. The present is somehow continuous with the past and the future will be somehow constructed from the foundation laid in the present and past. In the modern age of rapid change, however, the present and future are disjointed from the past. The death of permanence and the ever-increasing novelty in the world mean that the past cannot be looked to in an attempt to solve present or future difficulties:

> The historical outlook leaves the future without roots because it destroys our illusions and robs things of the atmosphere in which they alone can live and in which they alone can acquire potentialities.(92)

The radically new destroys any continuity and coherence of history, and thus destroys history itself:

> Every crisis throws up the question of the historic future. For when the whole existing situation is in a state of crisis, it becomes evident that the future can no longer arise automatically out of the past, that it can no longer be the natural repetition and continuation of the past, but that something new must be found in it.(93)

Moltmann's theology of history is an attempt to maintain the Enlightenment inheritance of freedom, yet to regain a sense of the coherence of history in the modern world. It attempts to provide a modern answer for a modern age. It neither ignores nor derides the novelty of the modern world. Rather, it attempts to develop a sense of history which can aid a person in finding coherence to history within a situation of novelty.

According to Moltmann, in eschatology, as in Enlightenment thought, the future becomes the primary focus of history. It is the future which illumines all previous history. Moltmann bases his understanding of history on the distinction between the future understood as *futurum* and the future understood as *adventus*.

Understood as *futurum*, the future is that which arises from fundaments already extant in the past and present.(94) Thus, the future is actually extrapolated from the past and present.(95) This understanding emphasizes the continuity of past, present and future. What "will be" presupposes what has already occurred.(96) The form of the future is "new" only in the sense that prior structures are reorganized or are mutated into alternative forms.(97)

The future as *adventus* on the other hand, emphasizes the anticipative aspect of the future. Understood as *adventus*, the future is not extrapolated from the past but exists in itself, and is "coming to" the present and the past. It means the arrival of something "other", something new, which has not been present before.(98) This understanding of the future emphasizes the discontinuity of the future with what has gone before. The future thus maintains the possibility for true novelty, of truly new forms and structures.

Understanding the future as *adventus* means that history takes on an anticipative, proleptic character. What constitutes the future is already extant, in fragmentary form in the past and present:

> An anticipation is not yet a fulfillment. But it is already the presence of the future in the conditions of history. It is a fragment of the coming whole. It is a payment made in advance

of complete fulfillment and a part possession of what is to come.(99)

Moltmann contends that Christian eschatology emphasizes the future as *adventus* more than *futurum*:

> [Past events] were not the background of the now existing present, but were themselves the present and the frontline towards the future. It is the open future that gives us a common front with earlier ages and a certain contemporaneity which makes it possible to enter into discussion with them, to criticize and accept them.(100)

The essence of Christian eschatology, for Moltmann, is that the End of history thus becomes determinative for interpreting all that has occurred previously:

> What unites our age with past ages in history is...not a common core of similarity nor a general historic character attaching to human existence as such, but the problem of the future. The meaning of each several present becomes clear only in the light of the hopes for the future. Hence a 'historic' relationship to history will not seek merely to illumine the factual sequence of events and their laws, but will search the reality of the past for the possibilities which lie within it.(101)

By maintaining the openness of the future and the possibilities for future novelty, Moltmann has sought to maintain what is valuable in the Enlightenment idea of freedom. Old structures need not remain in force into the future. Change and transformation are possible because the future is open. The emphasis on the discontinuity of the future from the past, however, does not help resolve the crisis of historical consciousness which was derived from just that disjuncture of past, present and future. In order to resolve this problem, Moltmann turns to the idea of Promise.

The fundament of Moltmann's eschatological interpretation of history is the Promise of God implicit in the creation of the world and explicit in the Covenant with Moses and in the resurrection of Christ.(102) For Moltmann, history is not merely defined by promise, but it is the promise which gives the modern world its historical sense:

> Beneath the star of the promise of God it becomes possible to experience reality as history. The stage which can be experienced, remembered and expected as 'history' is set and filled, revealed and fashioned, by promise.(103)

Over and against the Hellenistic idea of history as an eternal recurrence, understanding history in terms of promise provides history with a linear quality. For Moltmann, a promise is a declaration which announces the coming of a reality which does not yet exist. Promise thus sets a person's sights on a future history in which fulfillment of the promise is expected. The history which is initiated by promise thus gives historical process a determined, irreversible directedness toward the future.(104) The promise of God provides and discloses the horizon of history which can only be fulfilled in the future.(105)

Within the horizon of remembered and expected promises, history is understood as a dynamic and creative interim between the uttering of the promise and the fulfillment of the promise:

> Under the guiding star of promise...reality is not experienced as
> a divinely stabilized cosmos, but as history in terms of moving
> on, leaving things behind and striking out towards new horizons
> as yet unseen.(106)

Understood eschatologically in this manner, history therefore has not only an accidental, individual and relative character, but also an unfinished, provisional character which constantly points forward to as yet unrealized, open future.(107)

With the idea of Promise, Moltmann has found a means of maintaining the freedom inherent in the modern age, and also of granting modern history a continuity and a coherence. Whereas for Niebuhr, faith revealed history as an interim between the disclosure and fulfillment of history's meaning, for Moltmann, history understood from the perspective of promise is the interim between the uttering of the promise and the redeeming of the promise.(108) History, therefore, becomes a realm of freedom to obey or disobey, to accept the promise and its responsibilities, or to reject it, to be hopeful, or to be resigned.(109) Thus, for Christian theology,

> ...'history' cannot mean that it has again to proclaim the truth of
> God in combination with old experience of fate and chance, but
> that it has to give this world a place for the process that begins
> with the promise and is kept going by hope.(110)

Since the Promise is a promise of God, the expected future does not of necessity have to develop out of the possibilities inherent in the present, but rather is determined only by that which is possible for the God of the promise.(111) Consequently, since the horizons of human history are limited only by the possibilities which reside in the promise of God, human history takes on a totally open character within which human freedom is limited only by God's freedom. In this sense, the reality associated with history (*Wirklichkeit der Geschichte*) becomes the working out of the promise of God (*Wirkungsgeschichte der Verheissung Gottes*).(112)

Understood in this manner, history contains tendencies and impulses which are not bound by causal necessity inherent in the historical process itself. Rather, the tendencies and impulses of God are sometimes at odds with human tendencies and impulses. At other times, however, God's tendencies give shape and direction to the human aspirations and tendencies within the historical process.(113) History, therefore, is an anticipation of the promised fulfillment: the horizon of expectation within which a Christian operates is the horizon of the expectation of the kingdom of God, of the coming of God's righteousness.(114) History is not yet the fulfillment of the promise. There is no sense of a progressive growth of fulfillment in history, nor is there a sudden perfection of history. Rather, history as the anticipation of the Kingdom of God is a preliminary taking possession of what is to come in the future.(115)

At the same time, however, the Promise provides history with a certain coherence:

> The whole history of Israel shows again and again that the promises to which Israel owes its existence prove amid all the upheavals of history to be a *continuum* in which Israel was able to recognize the faithfulness of its God.(116)

History in light of the Promise forms a continuum because God pledged to follow through on the promise, regardless of human disloyalty. Thus the guarantee of the promises' congruity with reality lies in the credibility and faithfulness of him who gives it.(117) Because the God who made the Promise is the self-same God who brings the promise's redemption, history understood in light of promise is given coherence due to the fidelity of God to the promise.

The coherence of history does not, however, diminish the aspects of freedom inherent in history. If the promised fulfillment is entrusted to the

God who is true to his word in the Promise, the fulfillments can contain elements of novelty because the promise as it was received can never be exhausted or destroyed within history.(118) The promise never becomes totally congruent with reality because promise as the horizon of history "moves" as the horizon of history moves. As history progresses or declines, as partial fulfillments of the promise are attained, the promise expands to include an ever wider fulfillment:

> ...The facts of history can never be regarded as processes complete in themselves...the events that are 'historically' remembered in this way do not yet have their ultimate truth in themselves, but receive it only from the goal that has been promised by God..The events that are thus experienced as 'historic' events give a foretaste of the promised future.(119)

While Moltmann does speak of promise in general terms, he finds the concretization of the promise in the history of Jesus. The future of Jesus becomes the anticipation of our own future. For Moltmann, the Easter proclamation took up and expanded what had previously been promised. Thus,

> The proclamation and the history of Christ which opens up faith is not a past history in the historical sense, but in the eschatological sense it is an event of the past which opens up the divine future...(120)

Moltmann thus gives history a christological focus. For Moltmann, the crucifixion/resurrection of Christ is the concretization of the promise. Since the God of the promise to Israel is the selfsame God who crucifies and resurrects Jesus, this event becomes the *continuity* and *validation* of the promise which was made to the Israelites in the Old Testament.(121) The resurrection, therefore, is the "stamp of approval" of the promise. It is the manifestation of the continued existence of the promise into the time of Jesus.

At the same time, the future of Christ is not only the validation of the promise, but also the *extension* of the promise into the future. Because the Gospel finds the promise validated in the event of Christ, Christ's future becomes both indicative and determinative for the future of history itself. As an indicative, the future of the resurrected Christ as the extension of the promise points to an analogous situation for the future of humankind:

> The path leads from the *concretum* to the *concretum universale*...It is not that a general truth becomes present in Jesus, but the concrete, unique, historic event of the crucifying and raising of Jesus by Yahweh...becomes general through the universal eschatological horizon it anticipates.(122)

Thus to recognize the resurrection is to recognize the future of God for the world and the future which the human being finds in God and his acts.(123) It means that the future of Jesus is analogous with what is to come for human history itself.(124)

As a determinative factor of history, the resurrection of Christ not only points to what is to come, but in some sense brings what is to come to the present. Christ's future is a goal to be maintained and a promise to be fulfilled, yet at the same time it is a reality that can be grasped, in anticipatory form, in the present:

> If the event thus contains the validation of the promise, then this means no less than that through the truthfulness and truth of God the promise is made true in Christ....Hence the promise now determines the existence of the recipient and all he does...(125)

Given this understanding of the efficacy of the resurrection to determine existence, history as an interim between the uttering of the promise and the fulfillment of that promise is not a mere time period devoid of content. Rather, history, for Moltmann, is under the reign and lordship of Christ.(126) Understood eschatologically, the lordship of Christ is not a mere ontological statement, explaining the nature of Christ. Rather, the lordship of Christ is understood by Moltmann to have an active side. Christ's lordship is Christ acting as lord to bring history toward the fulfillment and consummation which was promised to Abraham, Moses, and others.(127) Christ's lordship over history is thus provisional and incomplete. It is not until the Eschaton that the promised fulfillment reaches completion.(128) At the same time, however, history does not become the working out of the kingdom of God, as understood in Liberal Theology. Rather, world history is subjected to an eschatological process in which Christ as Lord calls, sends, justifies and sanctifies humanity.(129) With the cross and resurrection of Christ, the promised future of righteousness, life and freedom becomes manifest in the lordship of Christ and has begun to move towards humans from the future.(130)

While it is true for Moltmann that Christ's lordship brings the promised future into the present, Moltmann understands the lordship of Christ not only as the lordship of him who was Victor over death, but also as the one who was put to death. For Moltmann, the lordship of Christ is always the lordship of the Crucified One.(131)

The identifying of the Exalted One with the Crucified One means that history will always be an arena of suffering.(132) Since the Crucified One is also the Resurrected Lord, suffering takes on historical importance in two senses. On the one hand, the lordship of Christ is in actuality a *passio activa*.(133) Through his death, the risen Christ brings the future kingdom of God into the present through his suffering. Thus, those who suffer in history also have a share in the kingdom of God which is announced to them by Christ and is brought to them, in anticipatory form, by Christ.(134) By sharing in the fellowship of Christ's suffering, they gain a share in Christ's resurrection.(135) In effect, by linking the cross with the resurrection, Moltmann makes it possible to understand the kingdom of God as a real force in history. The fact that it is the Crucified One who is resurrected means that the kingdom has *actually entered history in the history of Jesus*. The kingdom is not totally trans-historical and utterly future. Rather, it is incarnated in history, and thus has effect within history, because the Resurrected One (who is supra-historical) is also the Crucified One (who is intra-historical).(136)

The second sense in which the suffering of Christ takes on historical importance is that it points to the fact that the lordship of Christ within history is not yet complete or consummated.(137) Consequently, the overcoming of suffering and death in the world has not yet reached fruition, but lies within the realm of the future. History, therefore, must always contain suffering until Christ's lordship is completed, and history in turn, is consummated and turned over to the Father.(138)

In conclusion, Moltmann's eschatological view of history, as delineated above, means that, in light of the resurrection, we have a means of granting coherence and meaning to history. Theology, in effect, creates its own concept of history based on the resurrection. For Moltmann, history in light of the resurrection is characterized by openness and possibility. It is human history understood within the confines of God's history. It is a history which is experienced forward, from past through the present into the future, but is understood backward, from the future into the present and into the past. The End has already been written, and needs only to become manifest in the present.

3.4 *Evaluation*

The central issue between Niebuhr and Moltmann in regard to history lies in the content and meaning of the interim period we know as history. For both Niebuhr and Moltmann, the ultimate disclosure of the meaning of history is in the life, death and resurrection of Christ.(139) In Christ, the revelation of the character of God and the meaning of history completes what is fragmentary in the human understanding of history, clarifies obscurities in comprehending meaning, and corrects falsifications and distortions of meaning introduced by human egoism and self-interest.(140)

For Niebuhr, however, the clarifications of the meaning of history always include an obfuscation of the meaning of history.(141) It is only with and through the end of history that the meaning of history becomes ultimately clear.(142) Yet the ultimate fulfillment of history does not enter into the historical process. Rather, the fulfillment of history is also the end of history.

One of the strengths of this perspective on history is that it does justice to the paradoxical Biblical understanding of the relationship between the first and second coming of Christ. A central biblical theme is that somehow history has ended with Christ, yet the ultimate fulfillment of that end is yet to come. It is a tension between the "already, but not yet" of the Biblical proclamation of the Atonement.(143) In his understanding of the persistence of the antinomies of history until the End of history, yet also maintaining that the meaning of history has been fully revealed in Christ, Niebuhr maintains the paradoxical tension of human history between the disclosure of history's meaning and its fulfillment.

This perspective also protects both individuals and nations from undue pretensions which could lead from self-aggrandizement to a moral imperialism which causes friction between the self and others. By understanding history as an ironic mixture of good and evil which cannot be overcome by history itself, Niebuhr calls on us to guard against self-righteousness and to be wary of our own one-sided self-interest and egoism. The problem of history is thus the Promethean urge to strive for more than is our due. It is the desire of Icarus, to reach for the sun without realizing that wax wings will melt and we will fall to earth again. At the same time, however, it is precisely this absolute distinction between the disclosure and fulfillment of the meaning of history that leads one to question whether history, for Niebuhr, ever transcends the tragic.

For Niebuhr, the tragic character takes on two forms. In the first instance, the tragic person is one who suffers because he is strong, not because he is weak. He is one who suffers because of virtues, not because of vices. It is a person whose strength demands action which causes suffering.(144) Thus a tragic person does not succumb to suffering, but freely takes on suffering for the sake of a higher good.(145) Prometheus becomes the paradigm of the tragic hero, for here is revealed the perennial self-destruction of humans who attempt to overreach the divinely instituted limitations.(146) In the second instance, the tragic person is one who succumbs to base desires inherent in his or her own constitution. The person allows passions to overcome logic. Rather than being a failure derived from strength, the tragic character is derived from weakness.(147)

Niebuhr recognized certain parallels between the tragic Greek and Christian views of history. Both Christianity and Greek tragedy agree that guilt and creativity are interwoven in history. Both agree that sin (transgression) is possible only in freedom.(148) However, for Niebuhr Christianity transcends the tragic because it points beyond the tragic elements of history to an end of history which will fulfill and redeem history. History is not viewed as the eternal recurrence of the past, but is ever open to novelty, and therefore, is open to new complexes of meaning and fulfillment. The Kingdom of God, although "not of this world", impinges upon the world and is the ultimate fulfillment of the world.(149)

Yet, Niebuhr never really develops the manner in which the world is fulfilled. Rather, the emphasis in Niebuhr's thought is on the fact that history has a structure of meaning which is never fulfilled in the vicissitudes of history itself.(150) By identifying the *telos* of history with the God-initiated *finis* of history, Niebuhr in effect "brackets off" the flow of history from any real significance. Meaning is disclosed *to* history, but is never realized *in* history because the fulfillment of history results in the overcoming of the process of history. While Niebuhr does contend that the End of history will complete the partial fulfillments of meaning in history, from a perspective within history itself, history and its meaning are always under the threat of destruction until the End. Human existence remains tragic in a Sisyphean sense: the greater the heights one tries to attain, the steeper the incline. The steeper the incline, the more resistance to achievement, until the incline becomes so great that all achievement comes crashing down. Similarly, for Niebuhr, the more one attempts to attain fulfillment within history, the more forces of egoism come into play, until all attempts at fulfillment come crashing down under the weight of self-aggrandizement.(151) Only through the End of history is history fulfilled.

In this perspective, history is not understood as the realm of freedom and creativity which Niebuhr often says it is. Rather, Niebuhr's interpretation emphasizes inertia and cautiousness. It is a realm in which one would feel loathe to extend oneself, for fear of over-extending oneself. It is a realm in which one does not place an emphasis on hope, but on soberness and watchfulness.(152) Although one must attempt to right injustice in history, one must also be modest about that which one expects to attain.(153)

The persistence of the tragic character of history in Niebuhr's interpretation, seems to render history hopeless: the aspirations toward which humans strive are doomed to failure within history itself; it is only with the destruction of history, not its transformation, that those failures become victories. For those still within history, however, life remains essentially tragic.

Niebuhr's use of the symbol of the resurrection as a means of maintaining the fulfillment of history must also be questioned. The difficulty is two-fold. The first difficulty concerns the amount of conceptual weight that the symbol of the resurrection is supposed to carry. In Niebuhr's thought the symbol of the resurrection does not play a central conceptual role. It is not used as a primary hermeneutical category. And it does not play a formative role in his thought in general. In his understanding of the coherence of history, in particular, it is overshadowed by the symbol of the kingdom of God. To entrust the task of maintaining the coherence of history's meaning to a secondary conceptual symbol seems to be asking it to do too much. If a symbol is called on to carry the weight which Niebuhr expects of it, it should be incorporated into his thought in such a way that it relates to other central themes.

Along the same lines, Niebuhr's understanding of the resurrection must be questioned in regard to the manner in which he validates its symbolic character. While it can be argued that the Christian hope in the fulfillment and coherence of history rests with the resurrection, the resurrection symbol, in order to be avoid being nothing more than a consoling illusion, needs to be grounded and validated in Christ's resurrection. The resurrection as the symbol of the fulfillment of history in the End is only valid if Christ's resurrection was its "first fruits". Nowhere, however, does Niebuhr ground his symbolic use of the resurrection in the actual event, in history of the resurrection of Christ. Rather, he speaks about resurrection, whether of Christ or of others in purely symbolic terms, as a carrier of meaning, but not as an actuality in history. As we saw in the previous chapter, Niebuhr does not allow God to operate in the world in a causal manner. Consequently, the resurrection of Christ remains an impossibility within the world.

Moltmann adopts a somewhat different perspective on history. History, since it is constituted by the impulses and tendencies of the resurrection, takes on an open character. It is capable of transformation because with the resurrection the end of history is not only disclosed, but is also made manifest as a power within history.(154)

This perspective also has much to commend it. From a theological viewpoint, this perspective does justice to the understanding of history as developed in the Old and New Testament. From the perspective of Old Testament theology, as Gerhard von Rad and others point out, the covenant promise was what formed the identity of Israel, and was the hermeneutical principle of its interpretation of history.(155) Moltmann's use of the promise as a category of interpretation is consistent with this perspective. From a New Testament viewpoint, Moltmann's futurist eschatology is consistent with the

New Testament writers' understanding of the End of history being determinative for developing their own theologies of history.(156)

Moltmann's theology of history also presents us with a means of grasping the freedom inherent in the modern world, without falling into a progressive view of history which hearkens back to a return to Liberal Theology. Moltmann is careful to maintain that the future of humanity is directed to its end not through human activity, but through an act of God. In this way the Kingdom of God and its initiation in history remains *God's* kingdom, and is not to be confused with any human attempts at bringing about the kingdom through human power.(157)

The weakness in Moltmann's presentation of his theology of history, however, lies in his underdevelopment of precisely how human and divine history mutually condition each other. Moltmann makes much of understanding history as the "tendencies and impulses" of the resurrection.(158) He also contends that the "tendencies of the world" are often in conflict with the "tendencies of God". If this is the case, how are these tendencies overcome (if they are at all)? Does the final act of God in the Eschaton destroy these "tendencies of the world"? Or, are the "tendencies of the resurrection" made manifest in history through the overcoming of the "tendencies of the world" through anticipation of the End? If the former were the case, then human aspiration is rendered meaningless, for then it is the sole action of God which gives history its meaning. If the latter were the case, would this not be a form of cooperation between God and human in bringing history to its end? Is this consequently a slip back into the perspective of Liberal Theology which he attempts to avoid by insisting on the future first and foremost as God's future?

This ambiguity also produces a moral dilemma. If (as Niebuhr pointed out) the End of the world is brought about by God's action, then it removes from the human any sense of moral responsibility for his or her actions. If, on the other hand, humans somehow cooperated in bringing about the kingdom, as Moltmann's idea of history as the anticipation of the Eschaton seems to be inferring, how can a view of progressive morality be avoided? Moltmann seems to insist on the possibility of an increased rationality appearing in the world, yet is not totally clear about how this is possible within the world.

The above comparison of Niebuhr and Moltmann on history thus reveals the difference of emphasis which constitutes each perspective. Niebuhr's emphasis on history as an interim within which irony of meaning dominates, brings to light the ambiguous nature of historical progress. At the same time, however, it also can lead to the downplaying of the varied aspects of fulfillment and possibility within the historical process itself.

Moltmann's understanding of history as an interim which is stamped by the promise of God and marked by God's activity, causes him to understand the fulfillment and possibilities of history in a broader sense than does Niebuhr. This selfsame perspective, however, causes him to neglect those elements of history which militate against fulfillment and possibility. A similar pattern can be discerned in the anthropologies of each, the topic of the next chapter.

Notes to Chapter 3

1. For Niebuhr's view of God's transcendence see above, Chapter 2; For his view of anthropology, see below, Chapter 4.

2. TK, 24-5; GC, 118-124; FC, 80-96.

3. TH, 106-112; GC< 215-275.

4. This is the general perspective of Moltmann's book, *God in Creation*, See below, Chapter 4.

5. FH, 233.

6. For a detailed discussion of Niebuhr's anthropology see below, Chapter 4.

7. NDM,I 3, 15, 17, 156, 164-6; FH, 231.

8. FH,17, 36-37, 214; SDH, 41; NDM,I, 3, 170, 178-9.

9. FH, 126ff., 135ff.; SDH, 46-47, 49.

10. CRPP, 175-203.

11. SDH, 76, 77; NDM,II, 11, 58.

12. FH, 16, 38, 40, 64; SDH, 50; NDM,II, 9.

13. According to Niebuhr, because the classical view of history was cyclical, it underestimated the importance of history, the conception of pure, ahistorical "being" took predominance in Greek thought as a means of explaining the essence of human existence. Even those strands of classical thought which did, to some degree, affirm history (for example the thought of the Roman Stoics) were not enough to offset the ahistorical aspects of classical thought in general. Cf. FH, 58.

14. FH, 58.

15. *Ibid.*, 66.

16. *Ibid.*, 41.

17. *Ibid.*, 69.

18. Cf. FH, 14-34.

19. For Niebuhr, this combination forms the heart of the New Testament view of history. The New Testament did not simply adopt a precursive

Hebrew view of history, but alloyed it with a Hellenistic perspective of eternal being to create a new understanding of history. Cf. SDH, 74-78; NDM,II, 37. It must be noted, however, that Niebuhr believed that the Christian perspective adopted more of its historical outlook from the Hebraic perspective than from the Hellenistic one. Cf. SDH, 77-78.

20. NDM,II, 37.

21. *Ibid.*, 37; FH, 58-9.

22. NDM,II, 58-60; FH, 58.

23. NDM,II, 60; SDH, 76.

24. Following the Platonic idea of forms, the realm of the historical and the realm of the eternal coexisted, but eternity never took on being within history. In this perspective, truth rested in the eternal, not in the historical. History, therefore, remains without ultimate meaning. Cf. Plato, *Republic*, vi, 515a-517a.

25. SDH, 46ff., 84ff.

26. *Ibid.*, 85.

27. *Ibid.*, 77.

28. FH, 144.

29. FH, 235-236; NDM,II, 287ff.

30. FH, 235; NDM,II,287.

31. NDM,II, 287.

32. FH.

33. NDM,I, 4-34.

34. *Ibid.*, 6-15.

35. *Ibid.*, 4.

36. NDM,II, 35.

37. FH, 124, 133.

38. FH, 125.

39. FH, 125.

40. *Ibid.*,127.

41. This idea is derived by Niebuhr from his interpretation of the condemnation by Yahweh directed to all nations (including Israel) in the prophetic writings of Isaiah and Amos in particular. Cf. NDM,II, 23-34.

42. NDM,II, 36.

43. This idea is inherent in Niebuhr's understanding of history as "drama" in SDH. Cf. also NDM,II, 36.

44. NDM,II, 36.

45. NDM,II, 19-23, 43; FH, 239.

46. NDM,II, 31.

47. See Niebuhr's explication of the difficulties of Barth's theology in NDM,I, 220, 269, 289; NDM,II, 66-67, 116, 117.

48. NDM,II, 55, 56, 59.

49. NDM,II, 56.

50. *Ibid.*, 55-56.

51. *Ibid.*, 45-46.

52. NDM,II, 46.

53. NDM,II, 213.

54. FH, 135; NDM,II, 211, 212.

55. R. Niebuhr, "Revelation and the Meaning of History," Dudlean Lecture, Harvard University, April 14, 1942.

56. FH, 135; NDM,II, 47.

57. FH, 125, 133, 137.

58. NDM,II, 213.

59. *Ibid.*, 48 Cf. also NDM,II, 51: The idea of an interim between the incarnation and parousia is not new with Niebuhr. A. Schweitzer developed this idea nearly a half century before in *The Quest of the Historical Jesus.* (NY: Macmillan, 1968).

60. FH, 20-33.

61. FH, 236.

62. NDM,I, 27.

63. BT; NDM,II, 287; FH, 236-7.

64. This is the thrust of Niebuhr's book, *Beyond Tragedy*. Cf. also, IAH, and NDM,II.

65. FH, 137.

66. NDM, II, 294.

67. *Ibid.*, 296.

68. *Ibid.*, 297.

69. NDM,II, 287.

70. NDM,I, 1, 2, 13-15.

71. IAH, 155.

72. *Ibid.*,157.

73. *Ibid.*, 169.

74. BT, 18.

75. FH, 28-9, 48, 57, 237.

76. TH, 41, 76-91.

77. *Ibid.*, 97.

78. *Ibid.*, 40-41.

79. Moltmann includes Kant and Hegel and most of the Neo-Orthodox theologians in the category of a logos-based historical perspective. Cf., TH, Chapters 1 and 2. Moltmann understands those religions which emphasize being over becoming to be epiphany religions, focusing on the appearance of the eternal in the temporal in the present. He opposes his idea of the future presence of God against this appearance in the present.

80. TH, 40-41. This is a reversal of E. Jüngel's perception of Barth's Theology in his book *The Doctrine of the Trinity: God's Being is Becoming*. (Edinburgh: Scottish Academic Press, 1976).

81. A survey of literature, both secular and theological alike, show the interest of modernity in the future. Cf., A Toffler, *Future Shock* (London: Pan, 1970); C. Braaten, *The Future of God* (NY: Harper and

Row, 1969); R. Jenson and C. Braaten, *The Furturist Option* (NY: Newman, 1970).

82. Here "modernity" or the "modern age" has the same sense as the German word *Neuzeit*. Used throughout this work, it means the change of consciousness concerning the social world, politics, history, and the individual, which began with the Enlightenment.

83. J. Moltmann, "Toward a Political Hermeneutic of the Gospel", *Union Seminary Quarterly Review*, 4, (Summer, 1968) 303-323. (Hereafter, "Toward...").

84. *Ibid.*, 304-305.

85. RRF, xii; "Toward...", 303.

86. "Toward...", 303.

87. TH, 230.

88. *Ibid.*, 231.

89. TH, 230; Man, 22-23.

90. TH, 232; Man, 25.

91. TH, 230 A foremost example of this is the development of nuclear weapons. The advent of these weapons demanded a new way of thinking about modern warfare which had little relationship to methods of conventional warfare. Niebuhr maintained that there was a necessity of keeping these weapons despite the threat of world annihilation. Here the limits of his balance of power thinking did not allow him to understand any alternative. Cf. IAH, 1. Moltmann, on the other hand attempts to find ways beyond this impasse through a new, "participatory" manner of understanding human relations. Cf. GC, 2-4.

92. TH, 237. Cf. also, "Toward...", 304.

93. TH, 233. This view of modernity can be understood to be consistent with the view of the Critical Theory of the Frankfurt School. Cf. M. Horkheimer and T. Adorno, *Dialectic of Enlightenment*, (NY: Seabury, 1972) and R. Bernstein, (ed.) *Habermas and Modernity* (Cambridge, MA: MIT, 1985).

94. FC, 29.

95. *Ibid.*, 41-45.

96. *Ibid.*, 30.

97. FC, 30, 42-43; TH, 102, 107.

98. FC, 29; TH, 104.

99. PS, 193.

100. TH, 269. Cf. also FC, 18-45.

101. TH, 189.

102. *Ibid.*, Chapter 2.

103. *Ibid.*, 106.

104. *Ibid.*, 103.

105. *Ibid.*, 106.

106. *Ibid.*, 102.

107. *Ibid.*, 107.

108. *Ibid.*, 104.

109. *Ibid.*, 104.

110. *Ibid.*, 93.

111. *Ibid.*, 103.

112. *Ibid.*, 108.

113. *Ibid.*, 142, 162-3, 194.

114. *Ibid.*, 334.

115. PS, 195.

116. TH, 109.

117. *Ibid.*, 117, 119. This understanding of the fidelity of God to his promise is consistent with the understanding of God's HESED witnessed to in the Old Testament. Despite the bretrayal of the covenant by humans, God's HESED (loving-kindness, steadfastness) maintains and nourishes the covenant. Cf. W. Zimmerli, *Man and His Hope in the Old Testament* (London: SCM, 1971) and Fretheim, *The Suffering of God: An Old Testament Perspective* (Phila.: Fortress, 1984).

118. TH, 104.

119. *Ibid.*, 107. This coincides with the understanding of "horizon" set forth by H-G. Gadamer in *Truth and Method* (NY: Crossroad, 1982) 217.

120. PS, 121. Cf., also, TH, 191.

121. TH, 152.

122. *Ibid.*, 141-2.

123. *Ibid.*, 194. Cf., also, CG, 171-172.

124. TH, 180, 195; TK, 85, 91.

125. TH, 147.

126. TH, 139, 325; TK, 87, 89, 93.

127. TH, 92.

128. TK, 92.

129. TH, 179, 325.

130. TH, 139; CG, 180.

131. TH, 197ff.; CG, 160ff., 183ff.

132. TH, 197, 199ff.; CG, 178ff.

133. TK, 81.

134. CG, 184.

135. *Ibid.*, 185.

136. *Ibid.*, 187.

137. TK, 83-88; CG, 187-200.

138. TK, 94; CG, 263, 265; GC, 7-9.

139. NDM,II, 35; FH, 139.

140. NDM,II, 81. Niebuhr, however, draws a sharp distinction between the disclosure of the meaning of history and the fulfillment of that menaing, while Moltmann maintains a more flexible boundary between the two.

141. FH, 233.

142. NDM,II, Chapter 10; FH, Chapters 13 and 14.

143. Cf. N. Perrin, *The New Testament: An Introduction.* (NY: Harcourt, Brace, Jovanovich, 1974) pp. 40-41.

144. BT, 156.

145. *Ibid.*, 160.

146. *Ibid.*, 161.

147. *Ibid.*, 163.

148. BT, 166; NDM,I, 178, 182-3, 189.

149. BT, 277.

150. IAH, 6; NDM,II, 4. Cf. R.E. Fitch, "Reinhold Niebuhr's Philosophy of History", in RN, 367-386. Fitch contends that Niebuhr posits a moral law, but never inserts it into the historical process.

151. This is also the thrust of Niebuhr's argument that Christ's kingdom is not of this world. Cf. BT, Chapter 14.

152. "Christ the Hope of the World", *Religion in Life*, (xxiii/3, 1954).

153. "Walter Rauschenbusch in Historical Perspective", *Religion in Life*, (Fall, 1958), pp. 527-36. P. Riemer reaches a similar conclusion about Niebuhr: "His 'realism' leads, I believe, to a failure to press even more vigorously on behalf of the least free...So it is that the Niebuhrians fail to explore more creatively and courageously the possibilities of a more prophetic politics. Fundamentally, I suppose, they fail to explore the possibility of creative breakthroughs in politics because they indescriminately associate such bold efforts with modernity's betrayal of our prescriptive constitution." Cf. P. Riemer, "Beyond Marx and Niebuhr" *The Drew Gateway* 48,(1978) pp. 14-27.

154. TH, 243, 268-9; TK, 84-90; GC, 228f., 278f.

155. For a discussion of this understanding of promise, Cf., Fretheim, *The Suffering of God*, pp. 36f. Cf. A. Schweitzer, *The Quest of the Historical Jesus* (NY: Macmillan, 1968) 330-397; E. Käsemann, *New Testament Questions of Today* (Phila.: Fortress, 1982) 169-195; W. Kümmel, *The Theology of the New Testament* (Nashville: Abingdon, 1973) 40-43, 48-58, 325-335.

156. TH, 103: "It is not evolution, progress and an advance...but the word of promise cuts into events and divides reality into one which is passing and can be left behind, and another which must be expected and sought."

157. *Ibid.*, 162-163, 179, 180, 194, 195.

CHAPTER IV

THE ANTHROPOLOGY OF CHRISTIAN REALISM
AND POLITICAL THEOLOGY

As was stated in the Introduction, the different political stances adopted by Christian Realism and Political Theology are grounded in their respective theological perspectives. These perspectives include the God-world relationship, history and its end, and anthropology. This chapter examines the last of these three perspectives, anthropology. The chapter begins with an explication of the role of anthropology in the thought of Christian Realism and Political Theology, moves through a description of the anthropological thought of each and then concludes with an evaluation of each.

4.1: *The Place of Anthropology in Christian Realism and Political Theology*:

The role of anthropology in Niebuhr's thought is central, while for Moltmann, anthropology, for the most part, remains implicit. The basic distinction in the role that anthropology plays in the theologies of each lies in the fact that Niebuhr's theology moves logically from human nature to human destiny, while the eschatological nature of Moltmann's understanding of what it means to be human begins with a discussion of God's nature, moves into a discussion of human destiny and then moves into a discussion of human nature.

The place that anthropology occupies in Reinhold Niebuhr's Christian Realism has been highly disputed in recent literature. Some interpret Niebuhr's theology as essentially anthropology writ large.(1) Others contend that Niebuhr's thought betrays an implicit Christological core which would relegate anthropology to a secondary position.(2) The truth of the matter is that the place of anthropology in Niebuhr's thought probably falls between the two extremes.

Anthropology is most certainly a central category for Niebuhr. Unlike Karl Barth and Emil Brunner, two theologians with whom Niebuhr is often compared, Niebuhr does not begin theologizing from a certain understanding of God and then move on to a discussion of creation and the world. Niebuhr instead begins with human nature, and then moves on to discuss creation and ultimately God. The format adopted by Niebuhr in his *magnum opus*, *The Nature and Destiny of Man*, delivered as the Gifford Lectures in 1939, betrays the centrality of anthropology in his thought. In those lectures, Niebuhr begins with an analysis of human nature, and then moves on to an analysis of history and human destiny.

Furthermore, as John Bennett has frequently remarked, Christian Realism is based on a specific understanding of human nature, which in turn informs its subsequent political perspective.(3) Niebuhr, himself, has stated that the Christian understanding of human nature could solve many of the crucial issues of our day,(4) and that one of the greatest resources that Christianity has to offer politics is the understanding of human sinfulness.(5)

In a manner similar to Paul Tillich, Niebuhr understands the human being to be at the intersection of the divine and the world. The human being's questions about his or her own existence lead to the consideration of the meaning of history and finally to a consideration of those things which concern the human being ultimately.(6) The question of human existence does not determine the nature of God, but rather forms a logical means of connection for understanding God and the world and for understanding history. It provides Niebuhr with a "middle-concept" which in its very nature allows him to deal with God, world and history simultaneously. Thus, for Niebuhr, anthropology is inextricably tied in with other aspects of his thought such as his analysis of historical existence, social existence and the existence of the world with God. While it can be rightfully argued that Niebuhr's understanding of the social world does lean heavily on his understanding of individual human nature, the same can not be said for his theory of history. In fact, Niebuhr places the Christian view of anthropology and of history on equal conceptual footing in regard to their social relevance.(7)

Understood in such a way, anthropology functions as a principle of organization for Niebuhr. It is not totally determinative for the content of his subsequent thought, but allows him to use one category to relate diverse theological elements.

Moltmann, on the other hand, does not begin with anthropology, per se, but places anthropology firmly within a theocentric framework. Consequently, for Moltmann, in order to arrive at an anthropo-logy, one must first begin with theo-logy.(8)

When understood in this way, theology and anthropology have a reciprocal relationship for Moltmann. Human nature develops only "in relation to the Godhead of his God...The divine is the situation in which man experiences, develops and shapes himself."(9) Consequently "God-talk" must logically precede "human-talk"; yet to talk of the human is also to talk of the God who is the milieu within which the human being is created and formed.(10)

4.2: *The Anthropology of Christian Realism*

Within the limits of the discussion above, it can be stated that Niebuhr's theology begins with anthropology. It must also be stated, however, that Niebuhr's anthropology is most definitely a theological anthropology: it is the content of Christian myths (primarily those of the Creation and Fall) which forms the foundation for Niebuhr's anthropology.

Niebuhr places the problem of human *identity* at the center of his anthropology. He begins his discussion of human nature by describing several different ways in which human nature can be perceived.(11)

According to Niebuhr, the Classical view of man, derived from the thought of Plato and Aristotle, is primarily a rationalistic one: the human being is understood from the standpoint of his or her unique rational abilities. This rationalism results in an unfortunate dualism in which human rationality (spirit) comes to be considered as good while human body (nature) comes to be considered as evil.(12) Because spirit is considered good while body was considered evil, body is understood as the "tomb of the spirit". As such, body is understood as that which is passible, while the spirit (*Nous*) was that which is impassible and eternal. Consequently, spirit is capable of living through ever-renewing cycles of nature. History is understood as cycles of endless recurrences. When understood in cyclical terms, history loses its sense of meaning. The new is much like the old, which is simply coming around again.

The Modern view of the human being, according to Niebuhr, suffers from a "confusion of rationalist and naturalist elements."(13) The Modern perspective begins with the Renaissance rationalist attempt to distinguish rationality from faith. Later, in the nineteenth and early twentieth centuries, a very strong naturalist perspective gained the upper hand. Instead of identifying the human being in relation to possessed rational faculties as did the rationalists, the naturalists identified the human being in relation to the natural elements of the human constitution.(14)

The naturalist rebellion against rationalism was not the last word in the modern attempt to define human nature. A modified rationalism again gained favor in the form of Marxism. Although Marxism has certain affinities with the naturalist distrust of the omnipotence of human reason, (it understands reason to be "deceptive") at the same time it looks forward (after the revolution) to the creation of a society founded upon the pillars of rationality.(15) For Niebuhr this confusion of rationalism and naturalism in modern thought becomes the dilemma of modern humanity:

> [He] cannot determine whether he shall understand himself primarily from the standpoint of the uniqueness of his reason or from the standpoint of his affinity with nature...Thus some certainties of modern man are in contradiction with one another; and it may be questioned whether the conflict can be resolved within the terms of the presuppositions with which modern culture approaches the issues.(16)

The resolution of this dilemma of human identity obviously lies in the Christian perspective for Niebuhr. Rationalism relates man to the presence of his rational powers, to the detriment of his natural ones. Naturalism relates man to his natural affinities to the detriment of his rational ones. Thus, the question "Who is the human being?" still lingers. Only in the Christian perspective, where the human being's primary relationship to God becomes the principle of identifying human nature, can both elements of nature and rationality be kept in dialectic tension to the detriment of neither. In such a view:

> ...[the human being] is understood primarily from the standpoint of God, rather than the uniqueness of his rational faculties or his relation to nature. He is made in the "image of God," It has been the mistake of many Christian rationalists to assume that this term is no more than a religious-pictorial expression of what philosophy intends when it defines man as a rational animal.(17)

Unlike the rationalist and naturalist perspectives, the Christian perspective, as Niebuhr understands it, does not identify transcendence with good and finitude with evil or vice versa. Instead, it understood both transcendence and finitude to have impulses to good and to evil. Because the human being is to be understood from the perspective of God rather than from the uniqueness of his rational faculties or his relation to nature, ultimate human meaning is thus found outside of the world, not in it, and the human being can therefore not completely understand himself or herself from the world alone:

> The only principle for the comprehension of the whole (the whole which includes both himself and his world) is therefore inevitably beyond his comprehension. Man is thus in the position of being unable to comprehend himself in his full stature of freedom without a principle of comprehension which is beyond his comprehension.(18)

For Niebuhr, the Christian perspective, rather than Classical or Modern theories, best illumines human nature and the situation of the human being in the world. These religious perspectives embodied in the Christian narratives first and foremost revealed to Niebuhr the depth dimension of human life, and the paradoxical nature of human existence:

> The distinctive contribution of religion to morality lies in its comprehension of the dimension of depth in life.(19)

In Niebuhr's perspective, it is in the depths of life that God is found. However, it is in the depths of life that sin is also found. This paradoxical understanding of human existence is what Niebuhr gleans from his interpretation of the creation and fall narratives.

Niebuhr interprets the creation and fall narratives in strictly mythical terms. They are not literal accounts of an actual fall from a state of innocence, as the orthodox theologians tend to interpret them.(20) Neither are they merely stories which attempt to present us with a moral message, as the liberal theologians interpret them.(21) Instead, they are to be interpreted as stories which reveal the depth dimension of human nature.(22) The creation account thus make clear the essential nature of human being, while the fall narrative reveals the nature of the human being as he or she exists in the world.

According to Niebuhr, the human being is created in the image of God, and thus is essentially good. Being in the image of God means that the human being is transcendent to history and can view it from a trans-historical perspective. It emphasizes the vertical aspects of human nature. Since the human being is the image of God, he or she is limited only by the nature of God. Human transcendence is possible to the point where it encounters its limit in God.

At the same time, however, the human being constantly and unavoidably (but not necessarily) sins. It is this tension between created good, yet unavoidably sinful that drives Niebuhr's anthropology. Being understood as a *human* being, however, means that the human being is inexorably within the ebb and flow of both history and nature. Niebuhr summarizes the biblical account of human nature:

> It emphasizes the height of self-transcendence in man's spiritual stature in its doctrine of "image of God".... It insists on man's weakness dependence and finiteness, on his involvement in the necessities and contingencies of the natural world, without, however, regarding this finiteness as, of itself, a source of evil in man.(23)

The myth of the fall reveals to Niebuhr the degree to which the human being refuses to live within the limitations of being in the image of God.

It affirms that the evil in man is a consequence of his inevitable though not necessary unwillingness to acknowledge his dependence.(24) Human beings in the world, as God's images, thus overlook their dependence on God. They tend to view themselves as the center of their own existence, thus denying their contingency on God.

In Niebuhr's perspective, then, the creation and fall myths more realistically express the depth and breadth of human existence because they present life as a paradoxical existence in which human freedom and human finitude are maintained in a dialectical tension. For Niebuhr, freedom and finitude refer to human capacities and limitations. Freedom refers primarily to the human capacity for transcendence. Human beings, as the image of God, have the capacity to survey their own situations from a vantage point above history.(25) Consequently, they also have the capacity for imagining ever new possibilities for history and can thus find coherence in history which is not readily apparent.(26)

Finitude, on the other hand, represents those aspects of human existence which cause human beings to have a partial perspective of meaning in regard to their own lives, to history and ultimately to the socio-political realm.(27) Being finite means being limited by the historical situation and by human nature itself. Thus one has incomplete powers of creating coherence for one's own world. Because human beings are historical, they are subject to a certain degree of historical determination. The historical era and socio-political situation within which people live do not allow the fulfillment of all possibilities capable of being imagined.(28) Consequently, finitude is understood by Niebuhr primarily as an element of the human constitution which limits human freedom.(29)

Since, in Niebuhr's view, the elements of freedom and finitude constitute what it means to be human, human existence is defined according to the relationship of these two elements. Rationalistic theories tend to neglect the finite aspects of human existence. Naturalistic theories tend to neglect human freedom in their estimation of human nature. Only Christian mythos maintains both.

For Niebuhr, it is only in this dialectic of freedom and finitude that human existence becomes truly *historical*. The Classical perspective denies the historicity of human existence because human existence comes to be understood as cycles of endless recurrences, and loses its sense of ultimate meaning. The new is much like the old, which will return again in new forms. Human creativity in history is thus severely curtailed. The modern view of anthropology in its naturalist perspective also strips human existence of its true historicity. By understanding human existence exclusively from the perspective of nature, the naturalist perspective denies the spirit's ability to transcend natural forms and historical conditions.(30)   Naturalism thus denies the human capacity to *create* history.

Understanding the human being as a compound of freedom and finitude makes the historicity of human existence apparent. Human freedom makes history possible, makes it known as history and makes it infinitely creative by allowing humans to look beyond the extant situation and to imagine new possibilities:

> The freedom of the human spirit over the natural process makes history possible. The transcendent perspective of the individual over the historical process makes history perpetually creative and capable of creating new forms; but it also means that the individual finally has some vantage point over history itself. Man is able to ask some questions about the meaning of life, for which the course of history cannot supply adequate answers; and to seek after fulfillments of meaning for which there are no satisfactions in the moral ambiguities of history.(31)

Finitude, on the other hand, means that the human being is fully immersed in the historical process and thus is to a degree determined by the contingencies of history:

> The individual is conceived of as a creature of infinite possibilities which cannot be fulfilled within terms of temporal existence....It [Christianity] knows of the finiteness of the self and of its involvement in all of the relativities and contingencies of nature and history.(32)

Consequently, any attempt at imagining any new coherence of history are doomed to be always partial and unfulfillable within history itself.

It is thus the freedom and finitude of the human constitution which makes life truly human. Human life is life "at the juncture", and thus is paradoxical life. This paradox, however, presents the greatest challenge to human existence, because along with its benefits, it also leads to sin.

The genius of Christian thought, for Niebuhr, is that it reveals how human nature is historical and thus creative, yet still within the vicissitudes of nature. Accordingly, human nature is ambiguous existence at the nexus of finitude and freedom. Human freedom allows for creativity and historical existence. Finitude, however, places limits on that freedom. It is this paradoxical existence of finite yet free which for Niebuhr becomes the source of the *primum datum* of human existence: anxiety leading to sin.(33)

The source of anxiety, according to Niebuhr, results from, but does not lie within the human constitution itself. Anxiety, rather than being the *result* of the human constitution, is understood by Niebuhr as the *response* of the human being to his or her paradoxical constitution. In order to flesh out this insight, and to show its relatedness to human experience, Niebuhr turns to a discussion of "vitalities" and "forms" within the human being.

Since the human being is created both free and finite by God, each person has elements of vitality and form respectively. Vitalities are human impulses and drives (both biological and spiritual) while forms consist of those elements (natural, racial, historical, geographic, etc.) which provide limits on the vitalities.(34)

Neither vitality nor form, in itself, is considered by Niebuhr to be evil. Instead, the vitalities and forms of nature and of spirit have a role in both human creativity and human destructiveness. The sex impulse (a natural vitality) can function creatively to ensure the continuation of the species. It is, however, also a primary source for many of the sexual aberrations which plague society. Spiritual vitality, such as intellectual desire, is what allows science and culture to flourish. At the same time, the intellectual impulse can result in a Faustian desire for knowledge without regard for the consequences.

Likewise, forms also have negative and positive consequences. Racial distinction (a "form" of nature) for example, lends cohesion to racial groups. When it is understood in an exclusionary manner, however, it can be the source for discrimination and bigotry. Similarly, a spiritual "form" such as inculcated patterns of thought and behavior lend a society cultural cohesion, but can also become the source of a militant nationalism or a cultural arrogance.(35)

The difference between Niebuhr's Christian view, and that of naturalism or rationalism should be clear. Naturalism locates the truly human in natural vitalities, tending to understand the source of evil to be the loss of the harmony of natural existence.(36) Rationalism locates human transcendence in human rational powers, and thus tends to understand the source of evil to be the lower, natural impulses.(37) Niebuhr's perspective allows for no determination of absolute evil (or absolute good!) in either nature or in rational faculties. Similarly, Niebuhr does not identify either freedom or finitude as the source of human sinfulness. The self, even in its freedom, is still the finite self. Human finitude, even though it is fragmentary existence, is also considered good because it is created by God. The goodness of creation again rests on the absolute transcendence of God. In the Biblical perspective taken by Niebuhr, God the Creator's transcendence is absolute over his creatures. This does not mean, however, that creaturely existence is evil because of its fragmentary character. As a consequence of God's absolute transcendence, fragmentary human existence is given a coherence because it is considered an integral part of God's will as Creator.(38) Finitude, then, takes on a certain moral stature of its own.

From this understanding of vitality and form, it becomes obvious that human existence at the juncture of nature and spirit is precarious. Human beings are forced to live in a world of which they are part, but also one which they transcend in very real ways. On the positive side, being forced to live in this paradoxical situation is what makes human existence creative. It allows human transcendence and human finitude to interact in such a myriad of ways that human life is always novel and pregnant with possibility. Anxiety, understood positively, provides the impetus for all human achievements. It allows no complacency:

> Man is anxious not only because his life is limited and dependent....He is also anxious because he does not know the limits of his possibilities. He can do nothing and regard it perfectly done, because higher possibilities are revealed in each achievement....There is therefore no limit of achievement

in any sphere of activity in which human history can rest with equanimity.(39)

On the negative side, however, paradoxical human existence is always an existence of anxiety. And anxiety is both "the source of creativity and a temptation to sin."(40) Life at the juncture of freedom and finitude is wrought with tension between the vitalities of nature and spirit and the forms of nature and spirit. Because the contradictory elements of freedom and finitude are constituent parts of human existence, the human being can not identify himself or herself fully with God or fully with nature. In a sense, human beings are "gods with anuses," both transcendent to the world yet also inextricably part of it.(41) Consequently, people are "homeless" in the world and can find no place to rest in which they are completely at ease.(42) This "homelessness" results in anxiety which could provide the impetus for a fall into temptation and sin:

> Obviously the basic source of temptation is, therefore, not the inertia of "matter" or "nature" against the larger and more inclusive ends which reason envisages. It resides in the inclination of man, either to deny the contingent character of his existence...or to escape from his freedom...(43)

Sin, for Niebuhr, then, is an act of the human will which attempts to overcome the paradoxical nature of human existence. It is the attempt of the human being to deny the "homelessness" of existence and to find a home exclusively in his or her own freedom or finitude. It is, in a sense, the human "will-to-security," the attempt to reduce the insecurity of paradoxical existence by retreating to one or the other poles of the paradox. It is the attempt of the human being to secure his or her selfhood. The ironic aspect of this attempt is that in the very act of attempting to find oneself, one loses oneself. In Niebuhr's words:

> Anxiety tempts the self to sin; the sin increases the insecurity which it was intended to alleviate until some escape from the whole tension of life is sought.(44)

Because sin is related to the paradox of the human constitution, its resolution is not an easy task. The task is made even more difficult by the fact of original sin.

Niebuhr's understanding of original sin is derived from the paradoxical presentation of sin in the Bible interpreted through the

Reformation doctrine of *simul justus et peccator*. According to Niebuhr, the Bible consistently maintains that sin is not an *essential* part of the human constitution, but is located in the human *will*.(45) Due to a defect in the human will (the desire to "overestimate one's stature") even the most generous acts of human beings are tainted with sinful proclivities.(46)

Central to Niebuhr's understanding of original sin is his mythic interpretation of the Fall narrative. The Fall for Niebuhr is not the literal fall from one state of existence (paradise) to another (fallenness). Instead, it is an expression of a defective will in the human being which is the prerequisite for sin.(47) Niebuhr explains this in psychological terms. While the human being may consciously desire to do good, unconsciously, he or she desires things contrary to the good. This unconscious desire becomes a "directedness", a general attitude which determines subsequent behavior.

This general attitude, given human existence at the juncture of freedom and finitude, takes the form of an overstatement of human stature which ultimately leads to the temptation to sin and actual sin itself.(48) Thus, human freedom, as a constituent part of the human person, makes possible a variety of responses to any historical situation. The human will, understood by Niebuhr as defective due to original sin, falls into anxiety about paradoxical human existence. The response to this anxiety can either cause one to adopt the perspective of faith or tempts the human being to sin in an attempt to relieve the tension created by paradoxical existence. Sin, therefore, is not rational error, nor is it finitude in general; it is a response to anxiety which results in a false interpretation of human stature in which one is tempted to consider oneself more or less than one really is.(49) Accordingly, Niebuhr distinguishes between two types of sin: the sin of sensuality and the sin of pride.

The sin of sensuality is the result of dealing with anxiety by retreating into the self and into bodily existence. It is a denial of transcendence. Niebuhr considers the sin of sensuality to be the consequence of excessive self love which is expressed in sexual aberration, gluttony, drunkenness and the succumbing to various other forms of physical desire. At its heart, however, it is the turning of the self away from infinite possibilities of spirit, and turning toward the mundane tediousness of human existence and its limited values.(50)

The sin of pride, on the other hand, is grounded in the human capacity for transcendence. Because the human being is capable of self-transcendence and world-transcendence and is capable of viewing the world and history as a whole from a vantage point above it, there is great temptation for a person to envision himself or herself as the whole, to envision his or her perspective as an all-inclusive, omniscient one.

But what is the situation which is the occasion of temptation? Is it not the fact that man is a finite spirit, lacking identity with the whole, but yet a spirit capable in some sense of envisioning the whole, so that he easily commits the error of imagining himself the whole which he envisages?(51)

The sin of pride, then, is the attempt of the human will "to obscure...blindness by overestimating the degree of...sight...."(52) It is the attempt of the human being to transcend natural limits by denying those limits which are inherent in his or her constitution.

Niebuhr believed that the sin of pride took three forms: pride of knowledge, pride of virtue and pride of power. Of the three, pride of power is considered by Niebuhr to be the most basic. Pride of power is either the lust for power of those who deem themselves superior to others, or the attempt of an insecure ego to find security through the attainment of power over others. Pride quickly transmutes the will-to-security into the will-to-power.(53) It is this transmutation, according to Niebuhr, which gives form and content to the relationship between the individual and the social world.

For Niebuhr, the individual is never an individual-in-isolation, but is dependent on others for fulfillment.(54) Niebuhr's anthropology, therefore, also includes an inherent relationship between the individual and society. Niebuhr understands the human being to be an "incomplete" creature. Consequently, human fulfillment finds its source and its end only in others. The human being can not exist only in isolation, but must "seek the realization of his true nature; and to his true nature belongs his fulfillment in the lives of others."(55) The transcendence of the human being thus not only makes individual existence possible, but also forms the bond of cohesion for ever-larger social groups:

> The individual cannot be a true self in isolation. Nor can he live within the confines of the community which "nature" establishes in the minimal cohesion of family and herd. His freedom transcends these limits of nature, and therefore makes larger and larger social units both possible and necessary. It is precisely because of the essential freedom of man that he requires a contrived order in his community.(56)

Niebuhr begins his treatment of the social world with a discussion of the divinely ordained sociality of human beings. As God's creature, the human being is part of the animal kingdom in that both share common attributes of nature. Animals and humans have common impulses and drives which, in varying degrees, determine their behavior. There is thus an organic relation between animals and humans. Family and racial organization, for example, is primarily dependent on "natural" cohesion.

> The natural impulse of sex is, for instance, an indispensable condition of all higher forms of family organization....In the same way the natural cohesion of tribe and race is the foundation of higher political creations.(57)

The individual, however, is also part of the human kingdom in that he or she shares transcendent, spiritual characteristics with other humans. Merely existing bodily is not sufficient for humans. They have a "will-to-live-truly" which demands that their existence must be fully human, that is, both bodily and transcendent.(58) Niebuhr locates the difference between the animal kingdom and social groups of humans in the human faculty for spiritual life:

> ...The most significant distinction between the human and the animal world is that the impulses of the former are "spiritualized" in the human world...(59)

Human life, since it includes the possibilities of transcendence, never includes impulses in their pure biological essence, as is the case in the animal world. In humans, biological impulses are always interconnected with psychological and spiritual elements, resulting in a complex mix of nature and spirit. Niebuhr speaks about the primary drive in both animals and humans, the life drive:

There is, of course, always a natural survival impulse at the core of all human ambition. But this survival impulse can not be neatly disentangled from two forms of its spiritualization. The one form is the desire to fulfill the potentialities of life and not merely to maintain its existence. Man is the kind of animal who cannot merely live. If he lives at all he is bound to seek the realization of his true nature...the will-to-live is thus transmuted into the will-to-self-realization...On the other hand, the will to live is also spiritually transmuted into the will-to-power or into the desire for "power and glory". Man, being more than a natural creature, is not interested merely in physical survival, but in prestige and social approval.(60)

In humans the will-to-live thus no longer remains in its pure, biological state, but becomes the "will-to-live-truly," the will to attain the full realization of human capabilities.

Niebuhr connects the will-to-live, the will-to-security and the will-to-power in his understanding of the human situation. The human being in society finds himself or herself in a situation of scarcity. There is an ever-increasing desire to realize one's capabilities to the fullest. These needs can not be met merely biologically, but demand spiritual satisfaction as well. In human culture, however, these demands cannot be easily met. Prestige and glory are not easily forthcoming. Desires must be sublimated and repressed:

However much human ingenuity may increase the treasures which nature provides for the satisfaction of human needs, they can never be sufficient to satisfy all human wants; for man, unlike other creatures, is gifted and cursed with an imagination which extends his appetites beyond the requirements of subsistence.(61)

Under such conditions, the "will-to-live-truly" becomes quickly transmuted from a biological impulse into the "will-to-power" or the "will-to-glory."(62) The person seeks unfair advantage over another and seeks to expand his or her will to its fullest extent in an attempt to either maintain the security of one's position in society, or to improve it. The human response to scarcity is thus self-interest and egoism.(63)

Niebuhr believes that on the level of limited relationships between individuals, this egoism could be overcome or at least restricted. A person could disregard his or her self-interest and develop a loving, altruistic relationship with others. In a sense, the will-to-live-truly does not transmute into its negative forms as the will-to-power and the will-to-glory. Instead, it remains as a force of cohesion and unity between the self and others. Niebuhr, however, considers this altruism to be impossible in larger groups, and especially not possible between nations:

> While it is possible for intelligence to increase the range of benevolent impulse, and thus prompt a human being to consider the needs and rights of other than those to whom he is bound by organic and physical relationship, there are definite limits in the capacity of ordinary mortals which makes it impossible for them to grant to others what they claim for themselves.(64)

This situation is in part the result of the increased complexity of larger groups. As individuals band together in ever-larger groups, conflicts in self-interest grow geometrically. Even when it is possible for a larger group to claim a common purpose, that purpose is always a partial one. The single purpose which binds a group together never satisfies all of the interests of the individuals in the group. In many cases, it may even bring interests into greater conflict because a group is never merely the sum of its constituent vitalities and interests. The group itself has vitalities and develops interests which are in conflict with many of those held not only by the individuals who constitute the group, but also those held by other groups.

Niebuhr draws another distinction between the activity of individuals and that of groups: group pride is of a different order from that of individuals. In individuals, the desires of the will can be militated against by opposing desires of altruism. The group, however, has an "inchoate 'mind' and its organs of self-transcendence and self-criticism are very unstable and ephemeral compared to its organs of will."(65) Thus, for Niebuhr the internal dynamics of the individual and of the group are qualitatively different.

For Niebuhr, then, human existence is marked by a paradoxical combination of innately human characteristics and social influences. The attempt to reduce the tension of existence at the juncture of freedom and finitude, God and world, leads one to sin. The necessity of a social existence for human fulfillment, combined with an antagonism toward surrendering one's own interests leads to injustice. The tension is, and should be unresolvable. If it is resolved, then life loses its human essence.

4.3: *The Anthropology of Political Theology*

A reading of Moltmann's works reveals that although he finds many of the issues dealt with by Niebuhr as central to his own interest, he approaches human nature from a different perspective than does Niebuhr. Whereas Niebuhr operates from a dialectic focused primarily on the *phenomenon* of human being as a dialectic of freedom and finitude based on an eschatological understanding of human existence, Moltmann uses a temporal dialectic which emphasizes the past and present situation of human existence in dialectical tension with the possibilities of the human future.(66) This means that the human being cannot be examined according to what he or she is, but rather by what he or she is in light of what he or she will be. Consequently, for Moltmann, a phenomenological approach to human nature of the sort that Niebuhr offers provides only a partial answer to the question of human identity.

In a way that parallels Niebuhr in some respects, Moltmann understands the basic problem of anthropology to be the problem of *identity*.(67) Human existence is an existence of questionableness. The question "Who am I?" becomes "man's greatest puzzle"(68) Moltmann, however, understands the source of this questionableness of human nature to be different from what Niebuhr contends. For Niebuhr, the questionableness of human existence is produced by the ambiguous relations of freedom and finitude in the human constitution.(69) For Moltmann it is the openness of human nature and the concrete alienation of the human being in the modern world which create human questionableness.

Moltmann views human nature to be open in regard to three primary relationships which the human being has: biology (one's relation with Nature), sociology and politics (one's relation with others), and theology (one's relation with God).

The relationship of the human being with Nature reveals that the human being is both an incomplete creature and a transcending creature. The human being is an incomplete creature because, unlike animals, the human being has no set nature. The instinctive knowledge of one's environment, so prevalent in animals, is lacking in the human being. In effect, the human being is not born with a fixed nature, but is charged with finding his or her true nature.(70)

At the same time, this lack of distinct human nature is also the human being's greatest asset because it allows for human creativity and adaptability.(71) Since humans are not totally bound to their environment, and indeed create their own environment, human beings have an innate ability to create and change themselves. This in itself makes the human being superior to and transcendent to the animals.

The openness of human existence also arises through the comparison of human beings with each other. From this perspective, human *individuality* and *sociality* are stressed. In relation to others, the human being is at one and the same time a discrete person with specific characteristics (a member of a certain race, gender, nationality, etc.) yet also a common member of human culture.(72) The human being is thus unique, yet social. It is the social nature of the human being which provides human nature with its openness. Because human nature is social, there are no human characteristics apart from the strictly biological which delimit a person's nature. Race, for example, may tempt a person to identify himself or herself with a specific group to the exclusion of others. Other social arrangements (nationality, for example) demand that the boundaries between races be destroyed in order for one to perceive oneself as a member of a national group. The factors through which one identifies oneself, are thus perceived to be fluid.

The openness of human nature can also be seen through comparison of human and divine. Comparison with the divine in the first place reveals to the human being the finitude, transitoriness and fallibility of human existence.(73) At the same time, however, this relationship to the divine deepens the mystery that the human being is. It calls human nature into ever deeper questionableness by demanding a transvaluation of all values which only serves to deepen human ambiguity. The question "Who am I?" can no longer be answered by looking at the individual's constitution or qualities, but must be viewed in light of "Who am I, my God, before you?"(74)

For Moltmann, then, human identity rightfully remains a question mark when viewed in light of these three sets of relationships, since the human being is always open to change and transformation. Human nature is not bound to specific instinctive patterns of behavior or to specific forms of culture. In fact, when the quest for human identity reaches a comparison of human and divine, the human identity question becomes even more ambiguous. The openness of the future creates a situation in which the human being becomes the *homo absconditus*. The true reality of human nature will only be revealed in the attainment of those prospects which the open human future holds.(75)

The ambiguity of human identity is further compounded by the fact of alienation. For Niebuhr, the human being is alienated primarily due to the dialectic of freedom and finitude which is part and parcel of the human constitution. While Moltmann does recognize this problem,(76) he nevertheless emphasizes much more the concrete alienation the human being experiences in the relationships within which the human being lives in modern, technological society. Following the above discussion, these relationships correspond to one's relationship with Nature, others and God.

For Moltmann, the human being's relationship with Nature is alienated to the degree that the human being dominates and exploits Nature.(77) Pollution, population increases, waste of resources, and the paving of huge chunks of the industrial world all point to the skewed relationship between humanity and Nature.

The human being's relationship with others also takes on an alienated form. Modern society is marked by the fragmentation of human relationships.(78) Racism, nationalism and other factors tend to drive wedges between people. People no longer view their destinies to be linked with those of others'. In effect, modern society divides and isolates people.

The relationship of humans to God also takes on an alienated character. In the domination of Nature and of others, human beings deny their contingent relationship to God. They remove themselves from the ranks of creation and attempt to take on the role of creator, a role reserved for God. In an attempt to find themselves, they really lose themselves.(79)

Given this understanding of the questionableness of human existence, comparison with animals, with other humans or even with God does not, for Moltmann, reveal the true basis for the identity question which humans face. Rather, the human question, "Who am I?" can only be answered in light of the divine mission and call which points the human being ahead to the future.(80)

In light of the divine call, the human being does not come to a knowledge of himself or herself as he or she is in the present, but comes to self-knowledge through being charged with something impossible by the demand of God.(81) God's call points out to the human being both the limits and possibilities of human life. In the call human beings recognize their own shortfalls; they recognize what they should be, but cannot attain of their own volition. In the discrepancy between what a person is and what he should be, the human being attains knowledge of self, of others, of sin, and of guilt.(82) Thus, for Moltmann, the human being is not constituted by a dialectic of freedom and finitude as with Niebuhr. Rather, the human being's identity is formed by a dialectic of being called from a certain past and present into an open future.

This does not mean that the human being is in fact a person without attributes, a *tabula rasa*. If the human being is constituted through God's call, then he or she is given certain qualities in light of the relationship he or she has with God. Since God is true to the covenant and shows himself to be the same God throughout history, the "essence" of the human being, understood as the person's identity and continuity is determined by the continuity of the relationship which God has with the person.(83) The continuity of human existence is thus maintained through the constancy of the God who calls the human being.

At the same time, the call opens up new possibilities for the human being. The divine call does not merely reveal to the human being his or her essential character. Rather, new possibilities are revealed and opened up for the human being, and he can become what he is not yet.(84) It is the divine call which, for Moltmann, also points to the historical nature of human existence. The real mystery of human nature is discovered in the missionary history, initiated by the divine call, which discloses to the human being his or her future. Since human beings attain selfhood only in relation to the future which is opened up to them, history not only becomes the stage upon which humans act, but also constitutes the essential nature of human existence. Because humans only become who they are through their determination to the future, human existence is given a historic character.(85)

In this perspective, therefore, human beings can not be identified by extracting permanent, unalterable characteristics which remain constant through history. Since human existence develops in and through history, life is an *experiment*.(86) It suffers no presumptive closure. It is a constant testing and risk, attaining and losing of identity.(87) Since God is true to the covenant and maintains his identity as covenant partner, then human life becomes a *project* to be lived out. Consequently, human existence has a directedness and a goal: the subsequent working out of the covenant demands within the future which is open to the human being. Moltmann points to three different aspects of the covenant toward which the human being is called to attain:

1. *Imago mundi*
2. *Imago Dei*
3. *Imago Christi.*

Each of these foci will now be examined in turn.

The concept of the human being as *imago mundi* emphasizes the involvement of the human being in the created order. Moltmann uses the concept, *imago mundi*, in an attempt to counter a prevailing theological notion, borrowed from Greek thought, that the essence of the human being lies in the intellect or soul.(88) This Greek view was theologically developed most strongly in the thought of Augustine and Aquinas, who considered the similitude between God and human to lie in the intellect.(89)

For Moltmann, this conception not only fails to do justice to the true stature of the human being as transcendent to Nature, yet part of Nature, but is also one of the primary causes for human domination of Nature.(90)

Moltmann counterposes the idea of the *naturalization of human being* as being a more adequate means of understanding the human being.(91)

By the naturalization of human being, Moltmann does not suggest a return to Nature in the Romantic sense of a pan-naturalism which absorbs human being. Instead, he considers Nature to provide the framework for understanding the human being.(92) Understood in this way, Nature is the subject which brings forth the human being. Thus, the human being is in actuality a product of Nature.(93)

The human being is not merely one product of Nature among others, but due to its unique place as the most developed form of Nature also exists as the microcosm of Nature as a whole.(94) This can be understood in two senses. On one hand, from an evolutionary perspective, the human being is the recapitulation of Nature as a whole (ontogenesis recapitulates phylogenesis). On the other hand, the human being as the microcosm of Nature also has a priestly function of representing the whole of creation to God.(95) The human being lives, speaks and acts on its behalf.

If he stopped here, Moltmann would indeed fall into the Romantic error of understanding the human being to be totally absorbed in Nature. Moltmann, however, understands the human being to be in an ec-centric relationship to Nature.(96) In this perspective, even though the human being is a product of Nature, and thus *is* Nature, the human being also stands over and against Nature due to the fact that he or she is transcendent to Nature.(97) Moltmann interprets this transcendence of Nature in terms of the human being as the *Imago Dei*.

Moltmann's hermeneutical treatment of the theological concept *imago Dei* differs greatly from Niebuhr's treatment of the same concept. For Niebuhr, the concept *imago Dei* is a means of talking about the freedom and transcendence inherent in the inner constitution of the human being. In this sense Niebuhr uses the concept in a strictly anthropological manner, i.e., to refer to factors in the human being. Moltmann, however, understands the concept *imago Dei* to be primarily a theological term, relating first to God and only secondarily to humans.(98) Understood in this manner, the term *imago Dei* becomes a relational term dealing first and foremost with God's creation of and relationship with his *imago* and only then with the relationship of the *imago* to God. Moltmann thus views as invalid the attempt (as in Niebuhr and the Christian tradition in general) to use the concept of *imago Dei* as a means of developing a "phenomenological" understanding of the human being from his or her personal characteristics and qualities.(99)

Understood in relational terms, the human being as God's image is God's representative on earth.(100) As such the human being is the "emblem of God's sovereignty" on earth, the one who rules over earthly creatures as God rules over all of creation.(101) Moltmann is quick to point out, however, that the sovereignty role of the human being as God's representative is always a role of stewardship of creation. Understood in this way, the responsibility of the human being toward nature is one of nurturing, preserving and renewing creation for the glory of God.(102)

Acting as God's representative also means that the human being is a reflection of God on earth. As God's reflection, the human being is a mode of God's appearance in the world. Since only the human being is the image of God, through the human being God is present in the world in a manner different from the way in which he is present in creation in general.(103) Humanity therefore has a special role to play in the working out of God's creative activity.

In effect, for Moltmann the *imago Dei* is the obverse side of the *imago mundi*. In both cases the human being plays a priestly role. Whereas the human being, as the *imago mundi*, represents the world to God, as the *imago Dei*, the human being represents God to the world. Consequently the human being has elements of both immanence to the world, but also transcends the world. The human being is both part of the world, yet also in some ways "above" it.

Moltmann uses the idea of the human being as *imago Christi* to provide him with a means of conceptually linking his understanding of *imago mundi* and *imago Dei*. Moltmann understands the *imago Christi* as the messianic calling of the human being to bring to fulfillment his or her true nature as *imago mundi* and as *imago Dei*.(104) This has two different implications for Moltmann. On the one hand, the human being as the *imago Christi* is a constant reminder of the reality of sin and suffering in the world.

In Christ we know both God and our own wretchedness.(105) We are called by the Crucified God to take part in the pathos of God; we are called to suffer actively, as did Christ.

On the other hand, the fellowship of believers with Jesus brings about the restoration of the likeness of God which had been lost.(106) By conforming oneself to Christ, one moves on the way to becoming the likeness of God through the reordering of one's relationship with God.

In fellowship with Jesus, the human being also takes part in the promise given to Creation at the beginning: the *dominium terrae*. For Moltmann the sovereignty of the crucified messiah is the only true *dominium terrae*. Yet, to the degree that we conform ourselves to Christ, we too can take part in that *dominium* here on earth. Thus, conformity with Jesus brings us into the eschatological history of the New Creation.(107)

These three paradigms of the future toward which the human being is called have implications not only for understanding the relatedness of God with the human, but also for understanding how Moltmann views sin.

Moltmann bases his understanding of sin on what he considers to be the foundation of the Christian life: hope. For Moltmann, "Hope is the inseparable companion to faith," without which faith loses all content.(108) Consequently, the Church is called to answer for its hope, and in doing so reveals its true character.(109)

If hope is the true character of the Christian faith, then sin is not only the absence of hope, it is also that which militates against hope. For Moltmann, temptation is not in the "titanic desire to be like God, but in weakness, timidity, weariness, not wanting to be what God requires of us."(110) In Moltmann's perspective, God has created us with an open future and therefore demands that we live up to it by filling that openness with content. It means responding to God's call to become the *imago Dei* by reflecting the divine will on earth. It also means accepting the appellation *imago mundi*, by fulfilling the representative function of the world to God. Finally, it means also fulfilling the call to become the *imago Christi* by entering into the suffering of God through active suffering in the world and through solidarity with those who suffer.

From this perspective, sin is not so much an act of commission, but an act of omission which plunges the human being into disaster.(111) It is an attempt to disregard God's call by avoiding necessary suffering.(112) In doing so, we deny the openness of our own future.

This inadequate response to human openness can take two forms: presumption and despair. Presumption is the self-willed, premature anticipation of what we hope for from God. It is not so much the prideful desire for acquisition, but more the impatience for fulfillment of what will come in the future.(113) The greatest sin for Moltmann, however, is the sin of despair. Despair is the anticipation of the non-fulfillment of what is hoped for. It is *acedia, tristesse*. It can take the form of acquiescence to fate, the denial of meaning, purpose and future. It is the gravest of all sins because it is also the denial of faith and the denial of God's promise and call.

4.4: *Evaluation*

From the foregoing, it becomes evident that Niebuhr and Moltmann present us with two diverse perspectives in anthropology. Each of these perspectives has its own strengths and weaknesses.

Niebuhr often speaks of the "essential nature" of the human being as opposed to the nature of the human being in the world.(114) Inherent in this perspective is Niebuhr's distinction between Nature and history.

For Niebuhr, Nature and history are mutually independent aspects of human existence. A "clear biblical insight into the nature of history, the freedom of man and the corruption of sin in that freedom" makes clear to Niebuhr that "history cannot be equated with nature."(115) This distinction means that the historical judgments we make cannot be equated with the judgments which are made by a scientist in regard to the natural world:

> It is because historical causation is endlessly complex...that history is not subject to the generalizations of either the scientists or the philosophers who insist on trying to comprehend its multifarious themes in terms of either natural or ontological necessity.(116)

The strength of this perspective is that it brings to light the depth dimension of human motivation in the political sphere. The qualities of freedom and finitude which constitute the human being are not peripheral elements of human nature, but make up the very core of what it means to be human. As such, they prove to be primary motivators of human actions and thus must be taken into account when one makes ethical decisions. The depth dimension of such qualities, as we have seen above, thus provides Niebuhr with a means of grounding his ethical thought in certain "constants" of human nature. It gives him a foundation for a critical perspective on the social world and politics. The freedom inherent in the constitution of the human being, for example, demands for Niebuhr that the social world reflect that freedom in its structures.(117)

By adopting such a perspective, Niebuhr avoids the "easy conscience" of the idealists who believe that one can alter human political behavior by merely changing the historical conditions which they assume form such behavior.(118) In Niebuhr's view, since the primary motivator of human action lies in the human constitution as such, the idealist perspective of political behavior, which believes political change possible through the manipulation of historical structures, does not understand the true, deep forces which guide political decisions.

At the same time, however, Niebuhr's anthropological perspective presents some difficulties. Because of his dependence on unchangeable essential qualities, Niebuhr's anthropology remains somewhat abstract, which in turn has the surprising result that his analysis is often individualistic. For Niebuhr the essential nature of the human being is beyond the reach of historic change and conditioning: "Nothing can change the essential nature and structure..." Because of this bifurcation in human nature, Niebuhr does not seem to have a feel for the ways in which socio-political and historical forces impact on the human being in such a way that human nature is formed or re-formed. Is it true that vitalities and forms are the same for everyone? May not one person have different vitalities than others? May there not be different degrees of vitalities and forms?

The neglect of this perspective is not merely an oversight on Niebuhr's part. He utilizes the idea of an ahistorical, unchangeable core as a means of countering the claims of utopians who base the possibilities of historical transformation on the malleability of human nature. According to Niebuhr, the utopians feel that:

> ...pessimistic reservations upon utopian dreams are predicated upon the assumption that human nature does not change, while it is their belief that human nature is surprisingly malleable and is to a large degree the product of its environment. The question is whether they have not confused human nature with human behavior. Human behavior is constantly changing under the influence of various stimuli...But a certain common human nature underlies all this varied behavior.(119)

In adopting such a view, Niebuhr draws too sharp a distinction between nature and history.(120) If Niebuhr would allow for more interplay between nature and history, his critique of society would become even more effective. When he deals with alienation, for example, Niebuhr speaks almost exclusively of the internal alienation of freedom and finitude. Seldom does he refer to the alienation inherent in the social structures surrounding the human being. If he did take this latter form of alienation more seriously (by, for example, including some idea of the reification of history into human nature) he would be able to bolster his case that what seems like human progress is really just a new form of human alienation.(121)

The fact that he does not link history and nature adequately also points to an inconsistency of logic in Niebuhr's thought. Niebuhr contends that the genius of Christianity is that it takes history seriously. He also wants to maintain the historical character of human nature. It seems incongruous, therefore, that he refrains from allowing history to penetrate to the depths of human nature.

This bifurcation between nature and history also confuses the manner in which Niebuhr deals with his primary concept of freedom. Niebuhr speaks of freedom in at least two senses. On the one hand, freedom is a capacity located in the essential nature of the human being. In this perspective, the human constitution has the *capacity* for self-creativity.

From such a vantage point, freedom means that there are

> ...no limits to the possibilities of refining a culture or expanding the treasures of art and science....[the human being] has, therefore, the ability to imagine a more perfect goal or a more consistent application of a technique or a more satisfying fulfillment of a desire.(122)

Niebuhr sometimes talks of freedom and possibility in terms of a realistic *ability* of the human being in the world to determine himself or herself and to express that creativity which allows for self-determination. Freedom in the political realm, for example, refers to the ability to reach one's desired ends without being subject to coercion. In maintaining that the possibilities for the refinement of culture are unlimited, Niebuhr seems to be contradicting the major emphases of his own realist perspective that history reveals equal progress toward cosmos as chaos.(123) According to Niebuhr, because all political relations involve coercion, the material means of fulfilling possibilities are always limited. While it can be stated that possibilities are indeterminate, this does not mean unlimited. As we have shown, Niebuhr understood all political relations to be coercive and therefore subject to powers which hinder the expression of freedom in the world. It would seem that when Niebuhr speaks about "no limits to the possibilities of refining a culture," he is talking in an abstract sense: because we are capable of transcendence and therefore of imagining ever greater refinements of culture, they are possible for us to attain. In making this statement, however, he downplays the fact that possibilities also have a material side which limits their realization. In the concrete, socio- political, historical world, the ability to express that creative freedom is definitely curtailed.(124)

It must be remembered that, for Niebuhr,

> ...no matter how wide the perspectives which the human mind may reach...there is no level of human moral or social achievement in which there is not some corruption of inordinate self-love.(125)

What Niebuhr does not do, however, is draw out the necessary connections between freedom as a capacity in human nature and freedom as an ability in the social world. To say that a person has unlimited possibilities of creating new forms of social arrangements belies the fact that the material conditions for attaining those possibilities may not exist in any real way in the world.

Niebuhr's presentation of sin, which forms the heart of his anthropology, also has inherent weaknesses. As has been presented above, Niebuhr understands the human being to be a paradox of transcendence and finitude. The interplay of both of these factors creates a situation which produces anxiety and ultimately the temptation to the sin. Niebuhr includes both pride and sensuality in his discussion of sin. However, the sin of pride takes priority over sensuality in his thought.(126) *Hubris* is the human being's greatest sin.

While this view has much to commend it, the consequence of sin still remains ambiguous in Niebuhr's thought. One of the statements central to Niebuhr's thought on sin is that the human being sins inevitably, but not necessarily.(127) As has been often pointed out by others, Niebuhr nowhere gives a precise definition of what this means, and he uses it in such an ambiguous way that it is rendered ineffective as a guiding principle of his thought.(128)

A second weakness of Niebuhr's anthropology is that it speaks primarily to those who are powerful, not to those who are powerless. Pride is a problem for those who have attained some sense of identity, some sense of subjecthood. As J. B. Metz points out, however, a major problem of modernity is the problem of gaining subjecthood.(129) Whole groups of society (in American-U.S. culture, especially women and Blacks) have not gained their own independent identity. Women are still often looked at as appendages of their husbands and blacks are still looked at as second-class citizens. The questions which must be asked: What does an interpretation of sin as pride have to say to these people? Does Niebuhr's call for self-sacrifice aid these people in attaining their identity and their subjecthood? Or does Niebuhr's view of sin really hinder the growth of people into subjecthood? Does not Niebuhr's view of sin really represent one of the obstacles which women and other groups have to overcome in order to attain full subjecthood?(130)

Moltmann's relational anthropology, on the other hand conceives of the relationship between nature and history in a much more fluid way. For Moltmann, history penetrates nature and nature penetrates history.(131) Creation, itself, has a history.(132) The human being as the *imago mundi* participates in the history of creation.(133) There is no set human nature because the human being is constantly creating and re-creating himself or herself within history.(134)   For Moltmann, then, human nature, is, in its entirety, historically conditioned.

This perspective has many positive aspects.   The recognition of the historical element of human nature allows Moltmann to speak in concrete terms about the human being.   The human being is not partially constituted of an admixture of freedom and finitude or vitality and form.   Instead, the concrete particularities of history penetrate to the core of human nature.

Moltmann's perspective also takes into account the creative elements in human nature more completely than does Niebuhr's.   The interpenetration of nature and history provides an openness to the human constitution.   For Moltmann, the forms of nature are open because they too are constituted historically.(135)

This interpretation of anthropology provides a means for understanding the interrelatedness of the human being with all other members of creation.   Whereas Niebuhr spoke of an unchanging, ahistorical human essence, as we saw above, Moltmann considers the essence of human nature to be relational.   Human nature thus has an inherent "sociality."

Moltmann's approach to anthropology also maintains a concrete perspective.   Moltmann speaks of the human being as he or she is found in the world.   For Moltmann, human nature is not a mixture of diverse, abstract elements, freedom/finitude, vitality/form, but in its essence is historically conditioned human nature engaged in the world, in the concrete living out of life.(136)

There is an inherent weakness to Moltmann's anthropology, however.   In attempting to maintain the fluid relationship between history and nature, Moltmann has, in effect, slipped into some of the idealist weaknesses against which Niebuhr warns.(137)   From Moltmann's recalcitrance to define human nature in any but a relational manner, it follows that one can not speak of what one *is*, but only of what one *is becoming*;(138) it becomes questionable whether Moltmann grants to human nature any inherent content which exists over time at all.   One gets the impression that historical experience and relationship exclusively give human being its character.(139)

Elsewhere, Moltmann states that "The recognition that man does not have nature, but history means an overcoming of all naturalistic or quasi-naturalistic ways of thinking".(140) Several questions become evident at this point. Are there no constants of human nature which limit the possibilities of human activity? Does human nature also have an "ontological" aspect, not merely an historical aspect? If the human being is purely historically-conditioned, is it possible to produce an anthropology at all? Can one evaluate human behavior if that is the case? According to what standards? Moltmann does speak of certain aspects of human nature that are obviously unalterable (race, for example). But he glosses over the limiting effect which these qualities have in an attempt to show how they are historically perceived.(141)

From an ethical perspective, this one-sidedness toward history seems to argue that unjust social arrangements can be overcome by reshuffling historical structures and institutions. This is most obvious in Moltmann's understanding of sin. A result of the historicizing of the human being in Moltmann's thought is that sin then becomes "externalized", that is, the source of sin is located not in human beings themselves, but in the social and political world.(142) In presenting sin in this manner, Moltmann loses any sense of original sin. Moltmann seemingly lacks a sense of the deep motivators of human action which Niebuhr brings to light in his anthropology.

What is curious about Moltmann's seeming idealism is that there is, in his latest work, *God in Creation*, a basis for understanding nature and history as somewhat distinct and independent realms. In this work, Moltmann makes a case for the subjecthood of nature over and against humanly created history. Moltmann contends that theology must free its belief in Creation from an overemphasis on history.(143) Furthermore, Nature has a certain subjectivity to the systems of life and matter.(144) History is not the framework for nature; nature is the framework for history which sets limits on the historicization of the world.(145)

However, even though Moltmann states that we need to rediscover Nature within the human being,(146) nowhere does he define what that Nature is within the human, or how it limits or opens human possibilities. Instead, he speaks again in relational terms which return to the human being's historical nature.(147)

Moltmann's treatment of the relationship between theology and psychoanalysis in *The Crucified God* also falls prey to the historicizing of the human being. In his comparison of theology and psychoanalysis, Moltmann, following Neo-Freudian interpreters, disregards the depth dimension of the psychological aspects of human existence. He speaks of "cycles of ritualized behavior" and "neurotic pattern formations", but nowhere ties them in with inherent human qualities as did Freud. Instead, he speaks of them as illusory symbolizations which can be overcome by a new symbolization process based on recognizing the pathos of God.(148) In effect, Moltmann places the "cycles of ritualized behavior" on the same level as the "cycles of domination" which he sees evident in the historical world. In doing so, he loses the deep motivators of human behavior which Freud (and Niebuhr) understand to be inherent in the human constitution itself.

Moltmann's neglect of a substantial link between historical events and human nature itself weakens the effectiveness of his political program. It betrays a utopian (in the strict sense of the word) emphasis which does not take into account the intransigence of human nature, the understanding of sin as an inherently human proclivity (whether located in the will or somewhere else). Consequently, what Moltmann sees as realistic possibilities, may only be imaginative constructs of human wishes.

The different anthropological emphases evident in the theologies of Niebuhr and Moltmann only partially explain the different ethical perspectives adopted by each theologian. In the next chapter, the three strands of the theologies of Political Theology and Christian Realism examined heretofore will be tied together by an examination of the ethical thought of each theological perspective.

Notes to Chapter 4

1. Cf. Shin Chiba, *Transcendence and the Political*. Ph.D. Dissertation, Princeton Theological Seminary, 1983, for an overview of the discussion.

2. Cf. Paul Lehmann, "The Christology of Reinhold Niebuhr", in Kegley, *RN*, 328-356. Focusing on Niebuhr's understanding of the incarnation and atonement, Lehmann contends that christology is the *leitmotiv* of Niebuhr's anthropology. For what follows, however, I am in agreement with Dietrich Bonhoeffer's conclusion that Niebuhr is on the right path in making Christ the midpoint and end of human history, but falls short because he lacks a doctrine of the person and redemptive work of Christ. Cf. D. Bonhoeffer, *No Rusty Swords*. (London: Collins, 1958) p. 112.

3. Cf. J. Bennett, "Reinhold Niebuhr's Social Ethics", in Kegley, *RN*, pp. 99-141 and J. Bennett, "Realism and Hope after Niebuhr", *Worldview*, (May, 1972) 4-14.

4. R. Niebuhr, "Ten Years That Shook My World", *Christian Century* (April 26, 1939) 542-546.

5. Cf. NDM,I, Chap. 5; ICE, 107-8.

6. Cf. Niebuhr, "Reply to Interpretation and Criticism", in *RN*, 508f.

7. NDM,I, vii-viii.

8. CG, 267; *Man*, x.

9. CG, 267.

10. *Man*, 107.

11. NDM,I, 181. In the present work, the focus will be on Niebuhr's mature thought, particularly his Gifford Lectures. This choice has been made because it is in his later works that Niebuhr presents the most systematic and complete development of his Christian Realist perspective. Other sources will be used as noted.

12. *Ibid.*, 7.

13. *Ibid.*, 188f.

14. Niebuhr understood Freud's biological instinctivism to be a primary example of this type of thinking. Cf. NDM,I, 43.

140

15. Cf. Marx's conspectus on Bakunin's book, *Statecraft and Anarchy*, in R. Tucker, *The Marx-Engels Reader* (NY: Norton, 1978) 542-548.

16. NDM,I, 21.

17. *Ibid.*, 13.

18. *Ibid.*, 125.

19. *ICE*, 5.

20. *Ibid.*, 14.

21. *Ibid.*, 16.

22. *Ibid.*, 46-7.

23. NDM,I, 150.

24. *Ibid.*, 150.

25. *Ibid.*, 3,16,17,57,164-5.

26. CRPP, 175-203; NDM,I,164; DCNR, 36; GU, 135.

27. CRPP, 178; NDM,I, 165f.

28. Cf. Niebuhr's reply to his critics in *RN*, 510.

29. It is important to note here that Niebuhr does not equate finitude with sin. See the discussion of sin below.

30. NDM,I, 27.

31. CLCD, 42.

32. NDM,I, 170.

33. Niebuhr arrived at this insight both through investigation of the creation and fall myths and through an examination of the works of Karen Horney and Alfred Adler. Cf. NDM,I, 44 and D. McCann, *Christian Realism*, 55.

34. NDM,I, 48.

35. Cf. EAC, 313; CRPP, 28-29, 35; CPP, 65; ICE, 106,106.

36. Cf. H. Bloom's quote of Wordsworth: as a poet, he desires to "arouse the sensual from their sleep of death...by words which speak nothing more than we are. *The Visionary Company* (Ithica: Cornell, 1971) 3.

37.   This is the main thrust of the Platonic worldview. Cf. NDM,I, 4-12.

38.   *Ibid.*, 168.

39.   *Ibid.*

40.   *Ibid.*

41.   E. Becker, *The Denial of Death* (NY: Free Press, 1973) 51.

42.   NDM,I, 14.

43.   *Ibid.*, 185.

44.   *Ibid.*, 235.

45.   *Ibid.*, 241ff.

46.   *Ibid.*, 150.

47.   *Ibid.*, 142.

48.   *Ibid.*, 241-261.

49.   *Ibid.*, 183.

50.   *Ibid.*, 185.

51.   *Ibid.*, 181.

52.   *Ibid.*, 181.

53.   *Ibid.*, 188ff.

54.   SDH, 32; CLCD, 5, 48.

55.   CLCD, 19.

56.   *Ibid.*, 5.

57.   NDM,I, 27

58.   CLCD, 20.

59.   *Ibid.*, 8-9.

60.   *Ibid.*, 18.

61.   MMIS, 1.

62.   CLCD, 20.

63. *Ibid.*, 20.

64. MMIS, 3.

65. NDM,I, 21. Cf. IAH, 169; MMIS, 15.

66. Cf. TH, 21,25,42ff.,195,261; FC, Chapters 1 and 2; UZ, 119-123, 148-167. At this point this thesis will only be stated. It will be dealt with in detail only later on in this work.

67. Man, 2; TH, 285.

68. *Man*, 2.

69. See above, pp. 11-17.

70. *Man*, 5; HP, 105.

71. *Man*, 6.

72. *Ibid.*, 7ff.

73. *Ibid.*, 13.

74. *Ibid.*, 14.

75. TH, 286.

76. *Man*, 54.

77. GC, 23.

78. Man, 24.

79. Matthew 10:39.

80. TH, 285, 287; *Man*, 16; HP, 105.

81. *Man*, 16.

82. TH, 285.

83. HP, 106.

84. TH, 286, 288.

85. *Ibid.*, 286.

86. EH, 107,188; TH, 265-270.

87. HP, 24, 107; EH, 188.

88. EH, 160.

89. Augustine, *de Trinitatis*, xii,5,6; Aquinas, *Summa Theologica*, I,93:5.

90. GC, 256.

91. *Ibid.*, 49.

92. *Ibid.*, 50

93. *Ibid.*, 187.

94. *Ibid.*, 186.

95. *Ibid.*, 190.

96. GC, 38; TH,64; *Man*, 1-4.

97. GC, 52.

98. *Ibid.*, 220.

99. *Ibid.*, 221.

100. *Ibid.*, 220.

101. *Ibid.*, 219.

102. *Ibid.*, 224.

103. *Ibid.*, 188,208,218.

104. *Ibid.*, 225.

105. *Man*, 18.

106. GC, 226.

107. *Ibid.*, 228.

108. TH, 20.

109. *Ibid.*, 22.

110. *Ibid.*, 22.

111. *Ibid.*, 32.

112. CG, 16, 47, 63.

113. TH, 22.

114. NDM,I, 16,242,267-268,275f.

115. TPTW, 257; Cf. also NDM,I, 99,126.

116. SDH, 45.

117. CLCD, 3.

118. NDM,I, 93-96.

119. CPP, 154-155; Cf. also NDM,I, 269.

120. Cf. D. Brown, "Hope for the Human Future: Niebuhr, Whitehead and Utopian Expectation", *Iliff Review*, 32/3 (Fall, 1975) 3-18. For an opposing view, see D. Griffin,"Whitehead and Niebuhr on God, Man and the World", *Journal of Religion*, 53/2 (April, 1973) 149-175.

121. Dietrich Bonhoeffer raises a similar objection. Cf. *Ethics* (NY: Macmillan, 1955) 195f.

122. SDH, 21.

123. ICE, 97-98.

124. In point of fact, Niebuhr reveals many limitations to the possibilities of the refinement of culture: He doubts that it is possible to form a world community ("Can We Organize the World?", *Christianity and Crisis*, XIII/1 (February 2, 1953) 1-2.) He doubts that nuclear disarmament will be possible ("Coexistence under the a Nuclear Stalemate", *Christianity and Crisis*, XIX/5 (September 21, 1959) 121-122. He doubts that perpetual peace and brotherhood will ever be developed (MMIS, 21-22).

125. CLCD, 16-17.

126. NDM,I, 186.

127. *Ibid.*, 242.

128. Cf. R. Wolf, "Niebuhr's Doctrine of Man", in RN, 315.

129. J.B. Metz, *Faith in History and Society* (NY: Seabury, 1980) Chapters 3 and 4. Hereafter, FHS.

130. This question is raised with the greatest poignancy by feminist theologians, especially in J. Plaskow, *Sex, Sin and Grace: Women's Experience and the Theologies of Reinhold Niebuhr and Paul Tillich* (NY: University Press, 1980) and Daphne Hamson, "Reinhold Niebuhr on Sin", in R. Harris (ed.), *Reinhold Niebuhr and the Issues of Our Times* (Grand Rapids: Eerdmans, 1986) 44-60. Cf. also Wolf's article in RN, p. 317.

131. GC, 16-17.

132. *Ibid.*, 42-45; FC, 129.

133. GC, 187.

134. *Man*, 2.; EH, 187.

135. GC, 5.

136. This is the emphasis of Moltmann's interest in atheistic philosophers. In Moltmann's perspective, the horizon of theology is not heaven, but the concrete existence of humans in the world in light of the Eschaton. Cf. UZ, 15-22; TH, 25,265.

137. His is also a criticism of Moltmann by J.B. Metz, in FHS, p. 55.

138. GC, 265.

139. Cf. TH, 287: "Man has no subsistence in himself, but is always on the way towards something and realizes himself in the light of some expected future."

140. HP, 122-123.

141. Nowhere, for example, does he speak of Nature as a limit. Rather, he always refers to the openness of nature. Cf. FC, 115-127; GC, 33-64.

142. Consequently, Moltmann's thought would, for Niebuhr, fall squarely under the idealist heading.

143. GC, 32.

144. *Ibid.*, 50.

145. *Ibid.*, 56.

146. *Ibid.*, 47.

147. For an opposing view, see W. French, "Moltmann's Eschatology Naturalized", *Journal of Religion*, 68/1, (January, 1988).

148. CG, 314-315. For a general introduction to the history of neglecting the depth dimension of Freud's psychological theories, see R. Jacoby, *Social Amnesia* (Boston: Beacon, 1975).

CHAPTER V

THE ETHICAL IMPLICATIONS

OF CHRISTIAN REALISM

AND

POLITICAL THEOLOGY

5.1 *Introduction*:

For purposes of analysis, the foregoing chapters have lifted up elements of each theology for comparison and of necessity neglected what makes each a whole. This chapter attempts to rejoin what has been rent asunder. It will focus on the ethical implications of both Christian Realism and Political Theology in such a way that the disparate strands of each will again be woven into whole fabric.

The divergencies in the ethical thought of Christian Realism and Political Theology revolve around two issues. The first is the nature and function of utopia. Niebuhr's primary ethical opponents (secular liberalism, Christian liberalism, Marxism) according to Niebuhr, all betray a basic flaw: a utopian outlook which taints their political outlook.(1) Niebuhr's theological response to these perspectives is thus strongly based on an anti-utopianism. Moltmann, on the other hand, attempts to utilize utopian thought as a means of understanding the emancipative elements inherent in Christian theology.

The second issue concerns the relationship of theology to the necessity of order in society. This issue reflects the need in theological discourse of maintaining both an *anarchic* moment which is critical of the existing social order and attempts to transform it and also an *archic* moment which recognizes the necessity of speaking about ethics within a framework of an established social order.(2) It will be shown that Niebuhr's realistic thought tends to emphasize the archic function of religion, while Moltmann's emancipative thought tends to emphasize the anarchic.

5.2: *The Nature and Function of Utopia*

Ruurd Veldhuis, in his comparison of the work of Niebuhr and Moltmann, understands the conflict between the thought of each to center on the issue of realism (Niebuhr) versus utopianism (Moltmann).(3) Moltmann would consider this distinction as false, however, because he considers his utopian outlook to be more realistic than that of Christian Realism.(4) Understood in this manner, the issue between the two theological perspectives does not revolve around realism versus utopianism, but around the nature and function of utopia in the thought of each.

When Niebuhr refers to utopianism in his writings, it is predominantly in a deprecatory sense.(5) Niebuhr distinguishes between two types of utopian thought: soft-utopianism and hard utopianism.(6) Soft-utopianism is represented in Niebuhr's thought by secular and Christian liberalism. He understands liberalism both as a creed and as a political program. On its credal side, liberalism is marked by an assumption of a progressive view of history which professes an optimism in regard to human nature and human possibility.(7) From Niebuhr's perspective, this optimistic anthropology developed from the Enlightenment's trust in reason as a force for resolving human conflict.(8) In basic form, this belief entails understanding reason as the basic motivator of human behavior. As rationality is increased, conflicts between people will diminish.(9)

This perspective is maintained in liberalism's view of history as a process of evolutionary progress. In this view, history itself is seen as redemptive in that it translated man from impotence to power, from ignorance to intelligence, from being the victim to being the master of historical destiny.(10)

On its political side, liberalism is the concretization of these credal statements into political stances and action. If the Enlightenment trust in reason were true, then the task of any political program would be to rationalize the world. The aim of politics thus would overcome the differences between people through rational argumentation and appeals to common good. Niebuhr finds this progressive perspective evident in the trust in technology and science as a panacea for social ills that characterize American optimism.(11)

The Christianity of the early years of this century accepted, to one degree or another, this liberal utopianism. The fundamental religious idea behind Christian utopianism is that through the working out of the kingdom of God in history:

> ...the chaos of the world will be overcome and life will be a complete harmony and a fulfilled meaning. They [Christian Liberals] save optimism not by faith, but by hope. Life is not regarded as meaningful as it exists, with all its sad disappointments; but significance is imparted to it by what it will be.(12)

Incarnated in the Social Gospel Movement, this utopianism emphasizes the perfectibility of human relations through the expansion of love in human relationships. As love increases, so too would brotherhood and sisterhood. The political program of the Social Gospel is thus directed toward making manifest within socio-political reality the love demanded by Christ's love command.(13)

Christian liberalism, with its conception of a realm of peace and harmony as the result of the working out of the kingdom of God and the love command in history, carries on a pretense which obscures the coercion which is at the foundation of all societies:

> The religious vision of a final realm of perfect love in which life is related to life without coercion is changed into the pretension that a community, governed by prudence, using covert rather than overt forms of power, and attaining a certain harmony of balanced competitive forces, has achieved a final harmony. A society in which the power factors are obscured is assumed to be a 'rational' society.(14)

For Niebuhr, then, Christian liberalism is really furthering the bourgeois ideology that society is being rationalized. In doing so, Christian liberalism distorts and even hides the true sources of injustice. In this sense, Christian liberalism really hinders the search for justice.(15)

Niebuhr recognizes that this optimistic faith, along with its political program, comes crashing down with social catastrophe. History itself refutes this faith.(16) In Niebuhr's perspective, a utopian progressive view of history obscures the reality of the horrors of injustice and actually supports the moral complacency of society rather than challenges it.(17) Thus, for Niebuhr, utopianism is a source of confusion in political decision making because it looks toward a time when the antinomies of history will be overcome.(18)

Niebuhr's attack on the soft-utopianism of liberalism, in both its secular and Christian garb, began with that element of the modern worldview which supported this perspective: liberal anthropology. In Niebuhr's view, "The real basis for all the errors of liberalism is its erroneous estimate of human nature."(19) Over and against the liberal view of the rational capabilities of the human being to overcome political differences, Niebuhr emphasizes those elements of human existence which work against any easy harmony of peoples. In religious terms, this counterforce to consensus is sin.(20)

The central insight of Niebuhr's thought in regard to sin is that human powers of transcendence, precisely those powers which the Enlightenment contended would allow the human being to overcome conflict, actually increase conflict.(21) The ability of human beings to transcend themselves causes humans to forget that they are also finite beings enmeshed in nature and finitude. They tend to force their own interests onto others. They succumb to a self-centered egoism which does not allow them to recognize, much less concur with, the viewpoints of others. In Niebuhr's view, modern culture (and Christianity to the degree that it corresponds with modern culture) has lost the sense of the *demonic* in life.(22)

For Niebuhr, the difficulty with the political program of liberal culture is that it does not take full account of the elements of dissolution in society.(23) The Enlightenment understanding of progress is guaranteed by increasing intelligence because human sin is attributed to human ignorance which will be removed by proper pedagogy.(24)

It does not understand the power relations inherent in all relations between people or groups.(25) And perhaps worst of all, it leads to disillusionment and ultimately political inertia because it provides a false sense of possibility for social change.(26)

The Christian Liberal ethic of applying the love command of Jesus directly to contemporary life is also problematic for Niebuhr. For him, the weaknesses of this ethic are manifold. On the one hand, Jesus' ethic of absolute love (at least in the form it was being promulgated by Christian liberalism) does not take into full account the complexities of the power relationships which are included in the socio-political dynamics of every society. The foremost element of power is the need for coercion in any social group.

From his understanding of the intransigence of sin in the form of egoism and self-interest as the *primum datum* of personal and socio-political existence, the consequences of this self-interest are most exaggerated in the social realm. Since self-interest and egoism are the hallmarks of human relations, all groups must operate to one degree or another through coercion:

> All social co-operation on a scale larger than the most intimate social group requires a measure of coercion. While no state can maintain its unity purely by coercion neither can it preserve itself without coercion.(27)

Coercion therefore is necessary for the construction of a social world which not only limits people's expression of their individuality, but also provides them with the possibilities of "living truly". This is the tragic situation of humans:

> they need society to realize themselves fully, yet in the process of realizing themselves in society, become the victims of coercion and domination.

Since coercion is part of all interpersonal relations of individuals and groups, "society is in a perpetual state of war" in which "...all human society seems but a tentative peace and uneasy armistice between conflicting interests and passions."(28) The social world is thus a world of power versus power. Those who are fortunate enough to have momentarily gained power have to use coercion to gain it and need it also to keep their power. Those who lack power need coercion to gain it.

The problem is more highly exacerbated on the international level. Relationships between nations are even more complex than between members of the same nation. "National interest" is more difficult to define and satisfy than individual and group interests. The possible permutations of international relations make the sublimation of the interests of specific nations almost impossible.(29)

Beyond the problem of the necessity of coercion, a second problem of this love ethic is its absoluteness. Because Jesus' ethic demands absolute obedience, it of necessity cuts across all human endeavor and judges it invalid. Any situation in which the love command is not being fulfilled is deemed evil. While Niebuhr does make a case for this perspective, he points out that in the real world moral decisions are never made between absolute and contingent moral options, but between choices of "less and more" justice.(30)

Hard-utopianism, in Niebuhr's perspective, was represented by the utopianism inherent in Marxism. Although the earlier Niebuhr found in Marxism a possible cure for many of the ills in society, the later Niebuhr finds it "an absurd religio-political creed"(31) and "an organized evil which spreads terror and cruelty throughout the world and confronts us everywhere with faceless men who are immune to every form of moral and political suasion..."(32) Thus for Niebuhr Marxism turns out "worse than the disease it was supposed to cure."(33)

What Niebuhr finds at the center of Marxism, and indeed of liberalism in general, is a utopian attitude based on the perfectibility of humans, on the rational basis of society and on the possibilities of the progressive perfectibility of history.(34) As opposed to the soft-utopianism of liberalism that maintains faith in the evolution of historical progress toward a more rational world, the hard-utopianism of Marxism adopts a revolutionary view of progress in which a specific class (the proletariat), through its own actions of overthrowing the class structure of society, will create a society in which coercion is not necessary and in which all social ills will be abolished.(35) As opposed to the followers of liberalism the Marxist utopia,

> In place of confidence in a simple harmony of all social
> forces proclaimed confidence in a new harmony of society
> through a revolutionary destruction of property, thus making a
> social institution the root of all evil in man and promising
> redemption through its destruction.(36)

From both his reading of historical events, and from his theological insight that the antinomies of history are ever-present as long as human nature is what it is, Niebuhr feels that one of the great flaws of Marxist theory is its reduction of the power conflicts in society to one cause: class struggle.(37) According to Niebuhr, this is far too simplistic because the intransigence of sin in the world cannot be reduced to class conflict alone. In Niebuhr's reading of Marx, once the class struggle is overcome through a socialist revolution, the need for coercion and thus power against power will also be overcome. But for Niebuhr, the persistence of sin (in the form of egoism and self-interest) means that once the underclasses have gained power, they will not be satisfied with equality and will in turn fall prey to egoism and self-interest themselves.(38) Thus, in Niebuhr's view, the acquisition of power carries along with it the temptation to utilize power in a way that dominates others. For Niebuhr, Marxism's failure is that it believes in the "innocency and virtue of a nation which stands on the other side of the revolution."(39) It does not recognize the persistence of the interests specific to the proletariat after the revolution, but instead contends that the proletariat is primarily a disinterested group which will rule in a disinterested manner after the revolution.(40) This miscalculation produces, for Niebuhr, a situation which is ripe for injustice. The proletariat, newly in power, considers itself to be ultimately righteous and therefore understands its use of power as ultimately right. It has lost any self-critical perspective it once had as an underclass.

A second way in which the Marxist theory is too simplistic is that it does not understand the different ways in which power is wielded by groups in society. From Niebuhr's perspective class conflict (based on economic differences) is only one conflict among many power conflicts in the dynamics of any and every society.(41)

Niebuhr's response to soft-and hard-utopianism is based, again, on his understanding of sin. In Niebuhr's perspective, since sin and coercion are parts of all relationships, maintaining justice in the political realm takes on a priority. The stronger will always use the coercive power open to them in order to dominate those who have less power. While Christian liberalism concerns itself with justice, in Niebuhr's view, its response to injustice (simplistically applying the command to love to the problems of injustice) is ineffective. What is needed, and what Niebuhr supplies, is a means of applying the love command to socio-political reality in such a way that it does not obscure, but rather takes into account, the complexities of the social world caused by human self-interest and egoism. Christian liberalism obscures the sources and manifestations of injustice in the world. Niebuhr wants to lay them bare and find a means of producing justice within the possibilities inherent in any political situation.

Central to Niebuhr's ethical thought is his understanding of justice and its possibilities. For Niebuhr, the social manifestation of human sin is injustice. It is the assertion of the self over and against others.(42) Solving the problem of injustice becomes most difficult in the political realm. While sacrifice of one's own interests for the sake of justice may be an effective way of ending injustice, political leaders who may be interested in the attainment of the most perfect of forms of justice must be wary of relinquishing any political stance which is not in their countries' best interest. Self-sacrifice by political leaders becomes the sacrifice and betrayal of others.(43)

Niebuhr's solution to maintaining a realistic picture of the possibilities of the search for and attainment of justice in the world lay, as in Liberal Christianity, in the application of the love command to socio-political reality. While Liberal Christianity identifies the possibilities of attaining justice with the possibilities of achieving true, selfless love, Niebuhr understands the love command as an *ideal* unable to be fully manifested in history rather than as a possibility inherent in history. Consequently, justice may be attainable within history, while love certainly is not.(44)

As we saw above, beginning with Jesus' ethic of love, Niebuhr contends that the demand of this ethic is so absolute, it does not provide us with an adequate ethic if applied to society in simple form (as a call to love everyone, to put others before self, to look to others' interests before one's own).(45) Rather, the ethic of Jesus must act as an ideal which lures us on to realizing love within society, but does not provoke the pretensions of actually reaching the goal of absolute love within society itself.(46)

In order to understand this insight, we must return again to Niebuhr's theology. As discussed above, the paradoxical aspect of human nature as a mixture of freedom and finitude does not allow us to overcome social conflict by expecting love (or rationality) to conquer all. Human egoism and self-interest are rooted in the human constitution itself, and therefore political conflicts will never be resolved fully because their source is within human nature itself. Selflessness is not a simple possibility in history because selflessness always is counteracted by sin.(47)

It is, however, Niebuhr's understanding of history which best supports his contention that love is related to ethical action as an ideal. Past history revealed to Niebuhr that progress within the social realm is ambiguous and perhaps even questionable. Any attempt to deny this either through a secularized view of the resolution of the antinomies of history through the overcoming of political strife (e.g., Marxism) or the religious perspective of the kingdom of God in history (e.g., Social Gospel) is contrary to the facts of history themselves. Consequently, Niebuhr's understanding of the Kingdom of God as *finis* of history is his means of maintaining historical antinomies and disallowing a progressive interpretation. History is fulfilled, but only through its end as history.

Niebuhr's understanding of the permanence of coercion directs him toward understanding politics as a realm of power conflict and its mitigation. From Niebuhr's perspective, politics is basically the use and distribution of power.(48) The complexity of society as a multi-layered, multi-faceted association of people with varying degrees of power leads Niebuhr to question any theories of politics which does not take into account this diversity.

Again Niebuhr's theological insights aid him in reaching a decision as to what form his political ethics is to take. Basic human sinfulness means that power struggles are necessarily part of any social order. His view of history maintains the existence of those power struggles, for the kingdom of God is beyond history. His (perhaps unconscious) conviction that God does not relate to or operate in the world in any way which is effective in ameliorating social conflict means that we must look to human ingenuity alone for solutions to the problems which plague society. In other words, we must take a "realistic" approach which does not allow for the resolution of social problems from any source except the human.(49)

Basic to this realistic approach is the contention that:

> The Christian faith in its profoundest versions has never believed that the cross would so change the very nature of historical existence that a more and more universal achievement of sacrificial love would finally transmute sacrificial love into successful mutual love, perfectly validated and by historical social consequences.(50)

Given this understanding, Niebuhr feels that politics is the search for "proximate solutions", not absolute ones.(51) Solutions to the problem of justice are never really solutions, but merely changes in degree of injustice. Justice, understood by Niebuhr as total brotherhood with no conflicts of interest,(52) could not be attained; only more just social arrangements could be reached.(53)

Niebuhr concentrates less on how to overcome power conflicts and more on how to use inherent power struggles to create a tolerable harmony of powers which would approximate justice.(54) Niebuhr bases this perspective on his understanding of the vital nature of social relations. For Niebuhr, both individual and social existence are constituted by certain vitalities which can be endlessly and creatively elaborated.(55) At the same time, however, the expansiveness of the vitalities either causes vitalities to come into conflict with one another or one may suppress another. This suppression of one vitality by another is manifested in the political realm by the utilization of one power over another. Consequently, for Niebuhr, all political relations are power relations. Each party in social relations utilizes coercion to achieve the expansion of its own interests and the limitation of the interests of others.(56)

Given this understanding of the political situation, Niebuhr contends that the only way to dislodge power is to raise a countervailing power against it.(57) Yet not all actors in a political drama wield the same amounts of power. In such relationships a disproportion of power, and hence injustice, always occurs.

Niebuhr's answer to the problem of injustice is to call for an equilibrium or balance of power between political actors, for only in this way can proximate justice be attained:

> For even the most perfectly organized society must seek for a decent equilibrium of the vitalities and forces under its organizations. If this were not done, strong disproportions of powers develop; and wherever power is inordinate, injustice results.(58)

Niebuhr then applies this basic idea to all areas of society in which injustice appears. He feels that workers who are being exploited by owners should organize into unions to increase the political power and clout.(59) Only by increasing their power can they wrest power from others. Race relations can only be improved through the empowerment of racial minorities, not through discussions between oppressed and oppressor.(60)

In domestic affairs, according to Niebuhr, the responsibility falls to the government to strive for and maintain this equilibrium of forces. In Niebuhr's perspective, the government is the only force in society which has the power and the ability to organize means of maintaining relative justice in society. Consequently, the role of the government is to guide, direct, deflect and rechannel conflicting forces in a community in the interests of a higher order. It must provide instruments for the expression of the individual sense of obligation to the community as well as weapons against the individual's anti-social lusts and ambitions.(61)

For Niebuhr, only democracy is capable of maintaining both the openness to allow individual expression and yet the power to squelch anti-social behavior. Dictatorships, monarchies and oligarchies only increase the possibilities for injustice because both economic and political power is centered in the hands of the few. In a democracy, however, power is disseminated among the many. Only in this way is the citizen protected from the expansive power of his or her own government:

> Man's capacity for justice makes democracy possible; but man's inclination to injustice makes democracy necessary.(62)

To the extent that a government fulfills its duties in this regard, we are to appreciate it as divinely ordained and established.(63) At the same time however, we are to be aware that governments, because of this power, also tend to create injustice by attempting to usurp divine majesty and claim it for their own.(64)

While many of Niebuhr's writings are directed toward domestic issues, it is in the field of international relations that he develops his theory most completely. For Niebuhr, one of the great problems of international relations is how to maintain relative justice in a world in which some nations hold considerably more power than others. In specific, Niebuhr approaches the issue of how the United States, the most powerful country, relates itself to a weak and impoverished world.(65)

The liberal answer to the problem of power relations between countries is to attempt to form a world government based on constitutional lines. This constitution will limit the powers of some countries and bolster the powers of others.(66) The World Federalist Movement and other groups attempted this form of resolution. Niebuhr, however, felt that an approach of this sort is doomed to failure because it, of necessity, is based on mutual trust. And trusts have been and will continue to be broken.(67)

In Niebuhr's mind, the only feasible answer to the question of world peace is the meeting of the power of an aggressor by the countervailing force of an opposing power. Consequently, constitutionally limiting the powers of the strong nations whose powers can be used to create justice (in Niebuhr's eyes, primarily the United States) allows the unbridled expansion of those powers who created injustice (primarily the Soviet Union).(68)

Niebuhr's Christian Realism is thus an "Ethics of the Interim" between the disclosure of the meaning of history and justice by Christ and the fulfillment of that disclosure at the end of history. What Niebuhr does not allow is the confusion of the disclosure of justice with its fulfillment. When this confusion occurred, in Niebuhr's eyes it always created more injustice than it prevented.

Whereas for Niebuhr the ethical enemy to be fought is a liberalism with utopian tendencies, for Moltmann, the ethical opponent is a realism which is not utopian enough in that it functions ideologically to emphasize the maintenance of existing social structures over and against the transformation of those structures.(69) Where theology adopts this realist perspective in one form or another, in Moltmann's eyes it too tends to maintain those structures.

According to Moltmann, the realist perspective, bases its understanding of reality on what it considers to be things "as they really are". The method for understanding things "as they really are" is to look to the past, to find out how they really *were* and then to extrapolate and trace the effects of the past into the present and ultimately into the future.(70) When reality is understood in this manner, present socio-political structures are understood to be basically intractable because they are to some degree predetermined by previous social and political structures. The ethical task, therefore, is to develop the best forms of justice within already existing social structures.(71)

Moltmann's ethics attempts to counteract this realist perspective by developing a utopian ethic based on an eschatological perspective which acts both as a critique of the existing order and as a catalyst for the transformation of society. The utopian aspect of Moltmann's ethics begins with a disavowal of the correspondence between the Christian message and a utopia in the sense that Niebuhr uses the term. For Moltmann, the Christian faith is not a utopia which begins from the world processes and then looks forward to some presupposed future based on that possibility. Rather, Christian eschatology begins from a perspective of God's history which surpasses and discloses the relative character of such utopian thought.(72) Following both Ernst Bloch and Karl Mannheim, Moltmann contends that Christian thought is utopian in that its understanding of the kingdom of God introduces an element of transcendence into the world which, when put into practice in the world, acts both as an iconoclastic impulse, shattering present reality, and as a source of freedom which encourages change in the socio-political sphere.(73)

This Christian utopia begins with the understanding of God as open to the world. As we saw above, God for Moltmann is triune in nature. The Triune God is open to the world, and acts within the world to transform it. Through Christ and the Spirit, the world participates in God and God in the world.

The mutual participation of God and world consequently brings together human history and God's history. For Moltmann, in the Promise of God an element of transcendence enters human history. It is not an "epiphany" of God's presence, but rather, since God's being is primarily future, is the transcendence of the future of God which intersects with, confronts and carries along the human future. In this sense, the Promise announces the coming of a reality which does not yet exist.(74) It stands in contradiction to reality as now experienced.(75)

The event of Christ's resurrection, understood by Moltmann as the continuation and fulfillment of the Promise, discloses the congruence of the horizons of human and divine history in that Christ's future is understood as the "first fruits" of what is to come for human history.(76) If history grounds itself in the resurrection of Christ, then its horizon is enlarged to include the future of Christ, the overthrowing of sin and death by the lordship of God in the Kingdom of God.(77)

Understood in this manner, the horizon of the human historical future and the future of God are placed under a universal horizon of the Kingdom of God toward which both are directed and toward which both strive.(78) The horizons of the political world and of God not only correspond to each other or mutually condition each other, but the destinies of each are interrelated and interdependent. History takes on an open character derived not from the extrapolation of past events as for the realist, but in light of the future of God which encapsulates human history. This eschatological perspective means that history has a new future, a future which originates from God. There is not a mere renewal of what is old, but the entrance of something totally unexpected into history.(79)

From this perspective, the eschatological understanding of history shatters all views of history which base their understanding of what is possible in the future from an understanding of what has been in the past. One is not to look for Jesus among the dead, nor is one to try to refill old wine skins. The Christian message of freedom shatters and overcomes the old for the sake of the new. What stands between possibilities and reality is tendency, trend and specific leanings toward something which can become real in certain historical constellations which, while not currently extant, can become extant in the future.(80)

The possibility of the future as a *novum ex nihilo* means that traditional socio-political relationships are not cast in stone. Eschatological awareness brings with it a crisis of order. The traditions which have guided behavior and have formed the basis for social structure are no longer equal to the new possibilities of history which the eschatological perspective opens up.(81) Consequently, the eschatological message is a message of freedom because it announces the qualitatively new which will overcome and transform the present. Such ideas, when acted upon concretely in history thus have an "explosive effect" which shatters old structures and opens them for the possibilities of the new.(82)

The possibility of the *Novum* in society means that all order is brought into crisis. In light of the fulfillment inherent in the kingdom of God, any existing social order is relativized. It has validity only to the degree that it anticipates and fosters the fulfillment which is to come.

This eschatological perspective also demands that theology reflect this "explosive character" in its proclamation. Moltmann calls theology to forsake dwelling on the maintenance of the old in order to emphasize the freedom of the new. This understanding of the Christian kerygma primarily as an explosive message of freedom gives Moltmann a perspective from which to criticize theological formulations which present the kerygma in a way which might support socio-political structures already in place. Moltmann understands theology to have often functioned to politically support the status quo in two senses. On the one hand, theology acts as an *ideology* which operates as a framework for determining and supporting specific structures of society. On the other hand, theology becomes concretized in the *institutions* of society, and therefore forms the basis for specific political actions which keep present structures in existence. Moltmann contends that theology, in order to become sufficiently critical, must develop both an ideology-critique and an institution-critique.

In order for theology and its utopian message to be truly effective in the world, it must have political actors who affect the political sphere through their actions. Toward this end, Moltmann understands the operation of theological discourse in the world to be concretized in the Church as an institution in society. The Church, for Moltmann, has a paradoxical identity. It is 'at the same time' the object of faith and the object of empiricism. It is 'at the same time' an eschatological and an historical power.(83)

This paradoxical identity of the Church thus makes it the locus of the convergence of the future of God and the future of humans. Thus for the Church, eschatology and history come together at the point when the "eschatological instant" is grasped in faith.(84) In its present tensions between faith and experience, hope and reality, the Church will have to understand itself as part of the history of the creative Spirit.(85) When in the Church the future of God is at hand, people are converted to it and move towards it within its power.(86)

The ethical significance of the paradoxical nature of the Church as an institution is that it can never be neatly absorbed or fitted into any existing social structure.(87) As of this world and not of this world, the Church acts as a source of "eschatological unrest" which calls into question the existing socio-political realm. As a community which cannot become assimilated, the Church holds the social process open through its existence and its witness.(88)

There is also a personal side to the manifestation of the utopian message of Christianity. Individuals within the church, to the degree that they grasp hold of the eschatological message of the kerygma are called to make the utopian elements of that message a reality in the world.

As the reflection of God on earth, the human being as the *imago Dei* is called to become the reflection of the divine sociality represented in the trinity. Thus the human being does not only reflect the outward relationship of God to the world, but also reflects the inward relationship of the three persons of the trinity.(89) In this view, the unity and diversity which constitutes the triune God is reflected in the innate sociality of human beings in community.(90)

According to Moltmann, the isolated individual and the solitary subject are deficient modes of being human because they fall short of likeness to God. The socially open companionship between people is thus the form of life which best corresponds to God. Understood in this manner, the *imago Dei* is, in actuality, the *imago Trinitatis*.

Being the *imago Trinitatis*, above all, places human beings into a relationship of freedom. Moltmann distinguishes two types of freedom: freedom of rule (no external compunction) and freedom of community (the creation of new possibilities).(91) The person who understands freedom as rule in reality becomes individualistic and isolationist. He or she does not really consider others as true persons; the "other" is nothing more than a limitation on one's own self-determination.(92)

The understanding of freedom as community, reflecting the divine triunity, emphasizes that one can attain true freedom only by opening oneself up to others. In such a view, the other person is not a limitation to one's freedom, but an expansion of it.(93) Through relationship to others, new possibilities are opened up which would normally be closed to the isolated individual.

Moltmann considers this type of freedom to correspond to the relationship of the persons of the trinity. Just as each of the persons of the trinity is perichoretically related to one another, so too are humans called to reflect that perichoretic relationship in the world.(94) This demands a solidarity among all people in the world, a solidarity which looks to the as yet unrealized possibilities of the other and allows him or her a future based on those possibilities.(95)

Moltmann's eschatological perspective thus betrays both elements of a concrete utopian ethic. It is iconoclastic in that it shatters existing socio-political ideas and structures. Yet it also contains an imperative character: the divine call includes a sense of mission to attempt to realize the future which God has opened for humanity.

The distinction in perspective between Christian Realism and Political Theology in regard to utopianism can be traced to the different theological perspective of Christian Realism and Political Theology.

As we saw above, the starting point for Niebuhr's theology is Christian anthropology. Consequently, Niebuhr's view on utopianism also adopts anthropology as its starting point. Moltmann, however, develops a much more strictly theological perspective based on an eschatological understanding of history and of the mutual penetration of God and world. This distinction thus forms the basis for the different understandings of utopia of the two perspectives under examination in this work.

From Niebuhr's perspective, the possibilities of human existence are grounded in fundaments located in human nature itself. Niebuhr began from a relatively immutable human essence consisting of freedom and finitude, vitalities and form. The possibilities of human history for Niebuhr are then derived from the interplay of these different elements. History is open to change and ever new structures because these elements can be rearranged in ever novel manners. Consequently, the possibilities for increased brotherhood are boundless because the combinations of freedom and finitude, vitality and form are endless.(96)

In regard to Niebuhr's view of utopianism, a theoretical or political perspective is utopian to the degree that it does not correspond to the possibilities already inherent in human nature itself.(97) The possibilities of history are determined in relation to the development of elements already in place in human nature and thus are modified according to historical exigencies within which they are found. Consequently, for Niebuhr any attempt to locate absolutes (e.g., absolute peace, absolute brotherhood) within history is utopian because human nature will not allow the destruction of the antinomies and conflicts inherent in history.

Niebuhr's understanding of the God-world relationship also affects his perspective on utopianism. As was explained above, for Niebuhr God does not act in the world in any way which would help shape or alter the vitalities and forms inherent in human existence. By removing God from the calculus of the possibilities of human existence, Niebuhr has returned those possibilities to what is feasible from the perspective of human nature itself. From the perspective of human nature, antinomy and ambiguity predominate over any progress and betterment.

In contrast to Niebuhr's anthropological approach, Moltmann approaches the problem of utopianism from a strictly theological perspective. Similar to Niebuhr, Moltmann holds that from the perspective of exclusively anthropological possibility, certain claims (of complete brotherhood, for example) are utopian in nature in that they are beyond the possibilities inherent in humanly formed and altered history.(98) Moltmann, however, believes that this perspective is too restricted and wrong-headed. Rather than view the possibilities of history from the viewpoint of the human being or human nature, Moltmann understands the possibilities of history to be dependent on the possibilities inherent in the nature of God. This does not mean simplistically that "All is possible for God". Rather, for Moltmann, this means that the openness of God to the world and the openness of the world to God creates new possibilities for the world which cannot be derived directly from intra-worldly elements. The world does not develop on its own, but God's history creates new possibilities within human history.

It is here that the distinction between Moltmann's thought and that of the Social Gospel can be brought to light. In his *Theology of the Social Gospel*, Rauschenbusch attempts to make clear the role which we, as Christians, have to play in the work of God's salvation. Through the increasing manifestation of Jesus' love commandment in the world, the kingdom of God becomes present in the world. Consequently, like other Liberal Christians, Rauschenbusch adopts a developmental understanding of the kingdom of God in which humans either already participate in the kingdom or are responsible for bringing it about. Consequently, history itself is looked upon as redemptive.

Moltmann, however, adopts a more apocalyptic understanding of the kingdom in which the kingdom breaks in on the world; it does not develop out of it. Understood in this way, the kingdom of God is not something which *we* create through our own actions, even by our actions aided by God. Rather, it is God imposing his will and creating what *He* desires. We do not progress in the realization of the kingdom of God. Rather, we are only offered the possibility of anticipating that kingdom in our actions.

Moltmann's understanding of God and his kingdom as a future which can be realized for human history thus reverses the perspective from which we are to understand the possibilities of history. Where Niebuhr's theology distinguishes God and world, and consequently views the possibilities of history from the side of anthropology somewhat cautiously, Moltmann's theology speaks of the mutual penetration of God and world and thus understands the possibilities of history to be the possibilities inherent in the kingdom of God. The utopian future is not an extrapolation of conditions in the present, but is the anticipation of the kingdom which is promised by God.

For Moltmann, consequently, utopia must be understood in concrete terms. The future is brimming with promise and fulfillment because God promised such a future for humans. The future which is promised, in the words of Karl Mannheim, thus takes on an explosive character because it not only relativizes the present (as was the case in Niebuhr's thought), but also presents the future promised by God as a real possibility, not attainable solely through the work of humans, but by the work of God which humans anticipate in their own relationships. Thus, Moltmann's theological understanding of utopia discerns unlimited possibilities for the human future because it takes into account the future promised by God.

5.3: *Evaluation of the Perspectives on Utopia*

The foregoing has presented us with somewhat diametrically opposed views of utopianism. The most general criticism of Political Theology toward Christian Realism concerns Christian Realism's interpretation of social reality. As we saw above, in determining what is real and what is unreal socially, Niebuhr moves in a rather consistent direction from anthropological insights about the individual (self-interest and egoism linked to imagination) to social insights (the complexity of social relations aggravating these anthropological elements). He is relatively uni-directional in this regard. The social world is to a large degree a continuation and extension of the conflict which is inherent in the human individual. In making this claim, Niebuhr is granting a relatively unchangeable ontology to the social world: the conflicts which are ontologically human are insurmountable; so too are the "ontologically" social elements, because they are derived from ontologically human elements.(99)

This insight is derived not only from historical experience, but also from Niebuhr's theological interpretation. As we saw above, Niebuhr maintains a basically ahistorical human essence rooted in the conflict of freedom and finitude. Niebuhr's perspective on God and the world and on history does not allow for the transformation of this ahistorical essence.

Moltmann, on the other hand emphasizes the historical core of human nature. In such a perspective, human nature and the social world dialectically condition each other. In other words, the social world is not merely objective in regard to human nature, but also subjective. Niebuhr's perspective, from the vantage point of Political Theology, is limited in its perception of reality because it does not allow for sufficient mutability or transformation of human nature by the social world and vice versa.

Social reality as conceived by Christian Realism also conditions the manner in which politics, itself, is conceived. If social reality is understood as a realm of conflict, then politics concerns itself with the resolution of or at least the controlling of conflict.(100) From the perspective of Political Theology, Niebuhr's balance of power ethic based on self-interest increases conflict rather than ameliorates it. As was delineated above, for Niebuhr anxiety is the root cause of social conflict. In his ethics, Niebuhr demands that power needs to be met with countervailing power in order to approximate justice. Such a process only increases anxiety and distrust, but does nothing to overcome it. Niebuhr's balance of power ethic, therefore, worsens the situation that it is trying to ameliorate.(101)

Political Theology, with its ethic of liberation, attempts to create a situation in which trust may grow and conflict may decline. It is not utopian in the sense that it expects perfect trust and peace. Rather, it works to undermine the impediments which hinder any kind of mutuality. Niebuhr's perspective tends to aggravate them.

Political Theology also criticizes Christian Realism for its abstractness. While Niebuhr does present a viable political ethic, Niebuhr's political thought is fundamentally grounded in paradoxical human nature. Central to Niebuhr's thought is that human nature, at its core, is identical for everyone, everywhere. Such an ethic is doomed to abstractness because different situations present different ethical needs. One cannot base a large part of one's ethics on generalities which apply to everyone in all places and at all times without becoming abstract.(102)

A third critique of Christian Realism concerns the audience toward which it is directed. Without its theological elements, the ethic that Niebuhr produces may be adequate for those who are involved in the exercise of political power already: presidents, members of congress, statesmen and stateswomen. In Niebuhr's case, however, theological insights (particularly the insight about sin) form the heart of his ethic. Can politicians in a pluralistic society be expected to adopt an idea of sin which is particularly Christian in orientation?

This difficulty could be overcome if Niebuhr directed his ethics toward those who held similar views of human nature: other Christians. Niebuhr's theology, however, lacks a cogent doctrine of the Church, within which the theological insights which inform Christian Realism make sense and can be made politically relevant. Without this ecclesiastical framework, Christian Realism remains in the realm of abstract political theory without a means of being manifested in the political realm.

Political Theology, on the other hand, contains the focus on political actors which Christian Realism neglects. It is first and foremost directed to the Christian Church. For Moltmann, the church as an institution among others, of necessity, performs a political function within society. It can become a locus of freedom in society.(103) It exerts both a moral and political influence through its concrete actions (a prime example here is the role of political or civil religion in the development of specific political societies.) Its theological statements, to the degree that they are influential in forming political ideas, affect the political relations of the society within which they are offered. In this sense they act as a means of moral suasion.(104)

Christian Realism's critique of Political Theology is developed out of Niebuhr's anti-utopian perspective. As we recall, utopianism for Niebuhr is a dangerous element in Christian ethics because it neglects the power relations inherent in politics and because it does not provide a strong enough counterforce to human egoism. The broadest critique of Political Theology begins with a criticism of the extent of its ethics in general.

From Niebuhr's perspective, any ethic must be practical in the sense that it provides directives for concrete political action. While Moltmann's theology does present a general ethical perspective, he seldom concretizes that perspective into ethical ideas which direct people's decisions while they are involved in the process of deciding between just and unjust alternatives in history.(105)   Moltmann's eschatological perspective, stressing the anticipation of the future rather than the extrapolation from the past, while suggestive of new possibilities of the transformation of society, gives little direction in critical ethical discernment *among those possibilities which the current socio-political situation offers*.(106) Moltmann's perspective offers few norms for guiding concrete decision-making of those in the process of attaining justice. He does provide a general vision of liberation, but does not provide us with the answers to the question of precisely how we are to organize ourselves in the process of attaining that vision.(107)

Christian Realism, on the other hand, provides us with precise directives for acting concretely in the world. Most of Niebuhr's occasional writings were directed toward such issues as the use and misuse of nuclear weapons, strategies for labor unions for the development of more power and the quest of Blacks for equality.

A second critique of Moltmann's concrete utopianism concerns his neglect of the tendencies of history which militate against the formation of justice in society. Foremost among these is the necessity of coercion in all social arrangements. Although the future promised by God will certainly come to fruition precisely because it is promised by God, it must be anticipated in the realm of present socio-political relations. As Niebuhr has rightly pointed out, these relations always contain coercive elements which will never be overcome within history itself. Consequently, the anticipation of the kingdom of God in history is never quite as easy as Moltmann seems to imply.

5.4: *Archy and Anarchy*

The second overarching ethical issue in the debate between Christian Realism and Political Theology concerns the function of theology in regard to the socio-political order. Two extremes present themselves in this relation: an *archic* understanding of theology which supports the prevailing socio-political structures and an *anarchic* perspective which emphasizes the dissolution of order in society.(108) Neither Niebuhr nor Moltmann adopts these extreme perspectives. Rather each supports a position which lies somewhere in the middle.

For Niebuhr, the political life of all societies must steer between the Scylla of tyranny and the Charybdis of anarchy. Because no sure way has been found to establish an adequate organizing center for any specific society or an international judiciary with the power to make binding decisions, all political orders degenerate into a degree of anarchy. In turn, in an attempt to maintain their own existence in the face of this entropic degeneration, those in power tend to become tyrannical.(109) Niebuhr's ethics attempts to develop a perspective in which these tendencies can be averted.

Niebuhr adopts a "dialectical" approach to the question of social order. On the one hand, government and the order it produces are ordained by God and reflect his majesty. On the other hand, they are subject to the judgment of God because they tend to defy divine majesty.(110) Each side of this dialectic will now be examined in detail.

Niebuhr's understanding of the divine ordination of government rests on his understanding of the necessity of government for the maintenance of justice. From Niebuhr's perspective, government would not be necessary if it were possible to eliminate the need for coercion in political relations. Given that coercion is unavoidable, however, injustice results from the inequalities of power inherent in all societies.

The limitations of the human mind and imagination, the inability of human beings to transcend their interests sufficiently to envisage the interests of others as clearly as they do their own makes force an inevitable part of the process of social cohesion. But the same force which guarantees peace also makes for injustice.(111)

Niebuhr's strategy for overcoming this inequality is in the attempt to balance socio-political powers in conjunction with bringing this balance under the judgment of the necessity of love.(112) The balance of powers, however, presumes an orderly society within which this balance can occur. The movement toward justice can only take place within the framework of an ordered society. Consequently, for Niebuhr "order precedes justice" in the strategy of government; but only an order which implicates justice can achieve a stable peace.(113)

Inherent in this idea is the insight that without some form of order, injustice is totally unavoidable. In a state of anarchy, the strong rule the weak and the weak have no means of redress of grievances. Consequently, Niebuhr attempts to develop what he understands to be "tolerable forms of justice". For Niebuhr, absolute justice within society is a chimera; because of sin, the best we can hope for is an approximation of justice which is the best possible political relations *within the confines of a pre-established social order.* If given the choice, Niebuhr would prefer order to fanaticism because justice is predicated upon order.(114)

Niebuhr's distrust of revolutionary transformations of society is based on the primacy of order over justice. Revolutionary schemes, particularly those of the communist variety, neglect the necessity of defining the possibilities for justice within the new socio-political structures which are to be created. In Niebuhr's words,

> [If] one is not so certain what lies on the other side of the social breakdown, whether in terms of ideal possibilities or actual historical alternatives, one does not lightly hope for the breakdown of any social system in which there is a degree of freedom and the possibilities of achieving better social and economic achievements.(115)

Niebuhr also contends, however, that no socio-political order escapes the judgment of God. Divinely-ordained does not mean divinely legitimated:

> The final majesty of God is centered not so much in his power within the structures as in the power of his freedom over the structures...of reality.(116)

For Niebuhr, the standard by which all orders are to be judged is the standard of justice. Where a government becomes unjust or tyrannical, it may become necessary to resist that government:

> It may become necessary to resist a ruling of class, nation or race, if it violates the standards of relative justice which have been set up for it.(117)

It is precisely in this regard that Niebuhr understands democracy's strength. Unlike other forms of government, democracy allows for the criticism and replacement of those structures of political order which do not meet standards of justice:

...one perennial justification for democracy is that it arms the individual with political constitutional power to resist the inordinate ambition of rulers, and to check the tendency of the community to achieve order at the price of liberty.(118)

Also inherent in this idea, however, is the elevation of the value of order over that of change. If order precedes justice, then dramatic or wholesale change of social structure is a threat to justice. This seems to be the intent of Niebuhr's statement that:

...the first task of a community is to subdue chaos and create order; Order is needed to ensure justice.(119)

Yet the continuation of the statement is equally important:

That task is to prevent the power, by which initial unity is achieved, from becoming tyrannical. Justice is introduced into a field of order if the organizing power is placed under both moral and constitutional checks.(120)

Moltmann's perspective on the role of government and order is not quite so dialectical as is Niebuhr's. The thrust of Moltmann's theology is against the threat of the too close identification of theology and political order either in the form of a political religion or a civil religion. Consequently, his thought tends to emphasize the imperatives of countering social order rather than the correspondences of the two. Moltmann's theology reflects this interest.

From his eschatological understanding of the world and its history, the structures of the future are primarily discontinuous with the structures of the present and past. The present and past contain anticipations of the promised future, but are not structurally formed from them. Consequently, all socio-political structures and political programs are brought under the eschatological reservation. No political program or structure is considered to contain the kingdom of God.(121) Thus, the revolution of the present must not mold itself after the strategies of the world.(122)

In light of this insight, Christianity's message is to be understood in revolutionary, not evolutionary terms. Moltmann understands "revolution" to mean the transformation in the foundations of a system--whether of economics, of politics, of morality, or of religion. All other changes amount to evolution or reform. But transformation in the foundations of a system becomes a genuine possibility only when previously unsuspected possibilities or powers are at hand.(123)

While Christianity is not revolutionary in the sense that Christ was considered among the zealots, its revolutionary potential lies in its prophetic hope of the coming of God's kingdom. This hope is in the possibility of the manifestation of the NEW: the new person, the new covenant, the new people of God, the new creation of heaven and earth.(124)

From the above, it becomes clear that Moltmann understands the *new* to be dependent on the availability to the individual and to society of heretofore unknown powers. Thus, for Moltmann the eschatological interpenetration of the history of Christ and the history of the world, coupled with the indwelling of the Spirit in the world, provide that power.(125)

In relation to the question of political order, Moltmann's anticipatory eschatology leans heavily toward the side of anarchy, or at least toward a state of permanent revolution until the kingdom of God arrives. It would seem that different degrees and forms of order are necessary way-stations along the path to the attainment of justice.

This understanding reverses the perspective of the relationship of order to justice which was held by Niebuhr. For Niebuhr, from the perspective of human history the kingdom of God is an ideal toward which to strive, but never to be attained within history itself. This then allows Niebuhr to maintain the relative intransigence of historical and political forces to change. As we saw above, Niebuhr contends that absolute justice was impossible to maintain within history, and therefore the best that one could hope for is "relative" justice achieved through a balancing of powers. Necessary for the establishment of this relative justice is the overcoming of social chaos and the establishment of a certain degree of order. Order thus becomes the context and milieu within which justice can be achieved, and order involves coercion.

Moltmann's eschatological perspective reverses that relationship. For Moltmann, the kingdom of God is not an ideal, but is a future reality which has import and influence on the present. From this perspective, an eschatological understanding of justice, insofar as justice is an element of the kingdom of God, becomes the context within which order must develop.(126)

For Moltmann, since the horizon of the future kingdom of God is within the horizon of human history, the justice which is inherent in that kingdom becomes a possibility within history.(127)   In this way, the partial manifestations of justice in the world point forward to the achievement of total justice in the kingdom.

At the same time, however, the absolute justice of the kingdom stands over and against all partial forms of justice as an "eschatological reservation."(128) Absolute, eschatological justice can never be contained within any socio-political structure.   Consequently, all political orders inherently limit the degree and form that justice can attain. Peremptorily considering a certain ordering of society to be conducive for producing justice therefore limits the possibilities for the attainment of even greater or newer forms of justice. By emphasizing the mutable elements of politics, the reordering of society along the lines of increased justice would then make the social order produced more just and equitable. If justice grants a social order legitimation, then social orders which are unjust or only approximate justice must be overthrown until absolute justice is achieved.(129)

5.5: *Evaluation of the Perspectives on Archy and Anarchy*

When this perspective of Christian Realism is brought under the ideology critique of Political Theology, the logic of its theological constructs is revealed to be grounded in the assumption that political decisions should be based on the way things are, not on the way they could be or should be.(130) Niebuhr's strong critique of utopianism as the expectation of a perfect realm in the future means that he must concentrate on the present as the stage of time which gives political reality its meaning. In other words, *the form of the present determines the limits of its possibilities.*(131) In the social realm, this means that existing social structures define both the possibilities of any sort of socio-political change and also define the manner in which we are to understand socio-political reality. The definition of the "real" for Christian Realism is thus limited by the way in which things are perceived under current conditions.(132)

Niebuhr's theological perspective regarding the distinction of God and world seems to form the basis of this idea. Because God is not involved in the world in any real way for Niebuhr, the possibilities which are inherent in the political world are primarily derived from past experience.(133) In maintaining this, however, Niebuhr misses the Biblical insight that God has acted in the world and will continue to in one way or another. This claim, which is either folly or a stumbling block to Niebuhr, allows for the discernment of new possibilities in the world which Niebuhr's perspective does not allow. When it functions in this manner, it provides humans striving for justice with an historical vision and motivator for continuing the quest.

When understood in terms of knowledge-guiding interests, Niebuhr's ethic has as its primary interest the attainment of MORALITY, where morality is understood as the attainment of the most just political arrangements within existing social arrangements. All social orders have social norms inherent in them. By demanding order prior to justice, Niebuhr prematurely limits ethical behavior to those pre-established norms.

This emphasis on order over change in Niebuhr's theology also affects the search for justice by oppressed groups in society. While Niebuhr's perspective does emphasize the means to attain justice, increasing one's power, his theology contains few elements which motivate those in search of justice for themselves. Niebuhr's theology offers little of the "encouraging" hope which acts as a motivator for entering the struggle for justice in the first place. It does not provide the future vision necessary for maintaining the struggle for justice in the face of opposition.(134)

From the viewpoint of Political Theology, this ethic is an ethic of compromise, based on a theology of compromise. For Political Theology, the search for justice should be practiced by oppressor and oppressed alike, but for the oppressed the search for justice is more than an attempt to maintain adherence to certain norms; it is an attempt to protect one's own existence in the face of those forces which are attempting to destroy it. Niebuhr's ethic says to those oppressed who are in the trenches of the quest for justice not to expect perfect brotherhood or the end of oppression. Rather, one should accept the fact that because of sin one must compromise on one's expectations of what is attainable within society.(135)   One should look for the relatively good and the relatively evil.(136)

Niebuhr's theological interpretation also reflects this interest in compromise.   From the perspective of Political Theology, Niebuhr's Christian Realism falls into the category of theologies which "flatten out" the eschatological impetus of the Christian message.(137)   Niebuhr's interpretation of the three different theological elements examined in this work, the God-world relationship, his view of history and his anthropology, all support this contention. The lack of contact between God and the world in all but a "psychological" sense, coupled with the "bracketing" of history from the influence of the kingdom of God, means that political reality consists of what is present as potentiality in the social world. What presently exists to a large degree determines, shapes and creates the possibilities and potentialities of the future. Ideals provide new understandings of the goals of history, but the possibilities of attaining those goals are dependent on the potentialities already present in the world. Niebuhr's tendency to understand society as a reflection of anthropology means that the present state of society is dependent to a large degree on what has occurred in the past. Consequently, any changes which occur tend to be "functional" in nature; that is, there is no creation of a *new* structure of reality (in the sense that Moltmann uses the term,) only a reshuffling of elements within the same general structure.

In adopting this perspective, Niebuhr's theology downplays the understanding of the Christian message as one of freedom, and consequently, his thought tends to emphasize the problems inherent in the maintenance of order in society.(138) His theology urges caution rather than calling for the transformation of society.(139)

From Moltmann's perspective, the compromise inherent in Niebuhr's theological ethics resembles too closely that of the modernized two-kingdom ethic of Martin Luther. While the practical intent of Niebuhr's theology does not allow him absolutely to divorce the two realms, Niebuhr adopts a form of the two-kingdom doctrine in his insistence on the distinction between personal and public ethics. A central claim of Niebuhr's is that the love ethic propounded by Jesus, while sufficient for a personal ethic, was untenable when applied to the political world.(140)   The demand of complete adherence to the love command is too absolute to be applied directly to the worldly decisions of politics.   Consequently, Niebuhr's ethics creates a bifurcation between private and public spheres in which each sphere has its own attendant ethical requirements and solutions.   Luther's distinction between sacred and profane is transformed by Niebuhr into the distinction between private and public morality. In order to do this, however, Niebuhr has to compromise the love ethic of Jesus by turning it from a command into an ideal.

In contrast, Moltmann's emphasis on the revolutionary, anarchic function of Christian theology neglects the fact that all anticipations of the future kingdom must take place within the structure of one form of political order or another. A revolution is always a revolution from one form of order to another. Moltmann's eschatology as a vision of perfect justice attainable within history drives people toward that goal. Yet there is little evidence in his thought of either what forms of order, or how specific forms of order, aid or hinder the search for justice.(141) Moltmann seemingly only adopts the anarchic side of the dialectic which Niebuhr developed.

Related to this, another critique of Political Theology's perspective on theology and order centers on the "option for the poor" that forms the target of its ethics. As we saw above, the essence of the Christian message is a message of freedom and emancipation. Consequently, this message is directed primarily to the poor and to others who suffer oppression. While this is a laudable contention, it neglects the necessary anticipation of the difficulties which will arise if and when the oppressed become the dominant, powerful group in society.(142) Niebuhr, using the development of Stalinist Communism as an example, explains that when this shift in power occurs, the group which has newly gained power is wont to continue understanding itself as those to whom the Christian message is directed and thus is also wont to create new forms of oppression out of its own ego-centrism. Moltmann's ethics, from the perspective of Christian Realism, does not possess the safeguards necessary to deal with those new forms of oppression perpetrated by those who have newly come into power "after the revolution".(143)

178

5.6: *Conclusion*

The creative interplay of Christian Realism and Political Theology carried out above reveals that the two perspectives can actually be understood to represent two moments in a practical theology. Niebuhr's perspective begins from human nature and derives what is possible from its relationship to that nature. This perspective maintains the sense of the impossible possibility of perfection of the world. Consequently, Niebuhr's theology is a word of caution that sinful pretension sometimes works against the search for liberation in society.

Moltmann's viewpoint is developed theologically from the perspective of the conjunction of God's history and human history. As such, it points to making the impossibilities of history possible through God's act of opening history to God's future. It provides a vision and an impetus to the concrete search for liberation in the world.

A theology which wishes to be practical needs a vision to urge on the transformation of the world. But it also needs a word of caution to prevent that vision from becoming so all encompassing that it loses touch with the necessity of dealing with a world which is sometimes in active opposition to the will of God. A dialogical understanding culled from Christian Realism and Political Theology can provide both aspects necessary for the creation of such a practical theology.

Notes to Chapter 5

1. Cf. CPP, 141-158; NDM,I, 53-4.

2. Cf. Vernard Eller, *Christian Anarchy: Jesus' Primacy over the Powers.* (Grand Rapids, Mich.: Eerdmans, 1987.) for an overview.

3. CPP, 144.

4. TH, 25.

5. The targets of Niebuhr's ethics were many, depending on the socio-political situation of the time in which he was writing. Thus, during World War Two, Nazi fascism occupied his pen. When looked at in an overall perspective, Niebuhr's Christian Realist thought contains a continuous antipathy to liberalistic views. Niebuhr could, however, appreciate certain benefits of Liberalism: it ended crude supernaturalism, it furthered the understanding of human rights, it maintained the hope that some of the chaos of life could be overcome. Cf. CPP, 193-4 and D.D. Williams, "Niebuhr and Liberalism", in RN, 278-280.

6. PSA, 17; RNP, 62f.

7. ICE, 270; CPP, 148.

8. CPP, 144.

9. ICE, 104.

10. CRPP, 106.

11. *Ibid.*, 6, 11-12, 104, 117-118, 123; FH, 53. This is part and parcel of Niebuhr's understanding of the modern view of history, Cf. FH, Chapter 2.

12. CPP, 193.

13. W. Rauschenbusch, *A Theology for the Social Gospel* (NY: Macmillan, 1917) pp. 141.

14. IAH, 12.

15. *Ibid.*, 2; CRPP, 37f.

16. *Reflections*, 48.

17. ICE, 6.

18. NDM,I, 316; CPP, 79, 193.

19. *Reflections*, 48. Cf. also CPP, 154-5.

20. For a detailed discussion of sin, Cf. H. Hofmann, *Theology of Reinhold Niebuhr* (NY: Scribners, 1956).

21. *Ibid.*, ; CRPP, 106.

22. ICE, 9.

23. CPP, 79, 141.

24. *Ibid.*, 105.

25. CPP, 151.

26. ICE, 11-12; CPP, 73,79, 193; NDM,I, 290.

27. MMIS, 3.

28. BT, 96.

29. MMIS, 83-111; SDH, 35-38.

30. ICE, 62; MMIS, 68; NDM,I, 295.

31. "Alternatives to Communism", *The New Republic*. 147/14 (Oct. 1, 1962) pp. 15-16.

32. CRPP, 34.

33. Radical Religion, 13/4 (Fall, 1948) p. 5.

34. *Ibid.*, 4.

35. CPP, 141, 145, 193; PSA, 33.

36. CRPP, 106-107.

37. *Ibid.*, 143.

38. NDM,II, 87; CRPP, 35.

39. CLCD, 183. Cf. also CLCD, 46; IAH, 3, 5, 165.

40. FH, 228; IAH, 165; CLCD, 46.

41. NDM,II, 111, 262.

42. NDM,I, 179; II, 252; LJ, 164; BT, 102.

43. NDM,II, 88; MMIS, 267; Cf. K. Lebacqz, *Six Theories of Justice.* (Minneapolis: Augsburg, 1986) p. 85.

44. ICE, ; NDM,II, 248. At the same time, however, Niebuhr maintained that justice did not provide its own norm. Rather, its norm lies in sacrificial love. Cf. ICE, 105, 106, 107, 117ff., 140; CRPP, 112.

45. Cf. A. Schlesinger's quote of Niebuhr in "Reinhold Niebuhr's Role in Political Thought", in RN, 213: "Religion is frequently a source of confusion in political life because it introduces absolutes into the realm of relative values." Cf. also, ICE, 23-24, 32.

46. ICE, 62-83.

47. LJ, 27; ICE, 39.

48. CPP, 10; MMIS, 3. This was the basis for Niebuhr's critique of pacifism. Cf. CPP, 1-32.

49. Cf. CRPP, 130-132.

50. NDM, II, 87.

51. NDM, II, 108; MMIS, 68; NDM,I, 295.

52. LJ, 49.

53. NDM, II, 254.

54. IAH, 5; CLCD, 174. Niebuhr's statement that a mere harmony of interests does not create justice must be kept in mind here to guard against the impression that Niebuhr believes that justice understood as harmony is the desired end of ethics. Cf. LJ, 32; MMIS, 238.

55. For a discussion of Niebuhr's use of the term *vitalities*, see above, Chapter 2.

56. CLCD, 49, 67; NDM,I.

57. MMIS, xii, xv; CLCD, 17.

58. CLCD, 174; Cf. also, IAH, 5.

59. *Ibid.*, 147.

60. *Ibid.*, 144.

61. *Ibid.*, 44. This is similar to Freud's view that the progress of civilization was to repress the id functions which cause conflict, while still allowing for their sublimated expression. For both Niebuhr and Freud, the development of society can be understood as an expression

of the "fallenness" of human nature and also as a means of ameliorating that fallenness. Cf. S. Freud, *Civilizations and Its Discontents*, trans., J. Strachey. (NY: Norton, 1961).

62. CLCD, xiii. In Niebuhr's perspective, government is only necessary because egoism creates conflicts which would make any social relations tenuous. Only democracy, however, places adequate checks upon the egoism of the rulers. It is precisely here that Niebuhr criticizes Hobbes. In Niebuhr's perspective, Hobbes' failure was that he was not realist enough. He recognized the role of egoistic self-interest in all political actors except in the rulers themselves. Cf. NDM,I, 25; CLCD, 45.

63. TPWW, 259.

64. CLCD, 174, 178; TPWW, 259.

65. "Can We Organize the World?", *Christianity and Crisis*, 23/1, (Feb. 2, 1953), p. 1.

66. Cf. CRPP, 15-31.

67. Probably fresh in Niebuhr's mind was the failure of previous examples of mutual trust such as the Hitler-Stalin Pact and Chamberlain's failure to see through Hitler's duplicity. Cf. CPP, 67.

68. Cf. CRPP, 22-26.

69. TH, 23, 25, 34.

70. FC, 42-45; TH, 243, 269.

71. TH, 25.

72. RRF, 175.

73. TH, 86, 102; RRF, 5, 17. This understanding of utopia differs from that of Niebuhr in that for Niebuhr u-topia means the imaginative construction of a set of circumstances that are totally divorced from the reality which presents itself in the present. Moltmann, following Bloch and Mannheim, contends that, in an eschatological perspective, Christianity announces a utopia of what has "not yet" been made real, rather than what *can not* be made real. It is, in effect, a *temporal* utopia rather than a *spatial* one. Cf. TH, 233 and E. Bloch, *Abschied von der Utopie* (Frankfurt a. M.: Suhrkamp, 1980), pp. 43-64; and K. Mannheim, *Ideology and Utopia* (NY: Harvest, 1936), pp. 193-263.

74. TH, 103.

75. *Ibid.*, 103.

76. *Ibid.*, 181.

77. HP, 171; TH, 106, 265.

78. TH, 279; RRF, 202; UZ, 155.

79. RRF, 7; FC, 47; TH, 86-87.

80. TH, 243, 267.

81. RRF, 159-162.

82. HP, 172, 175.

83. PS, 21-22.

84. *Ibid.*, 22.

85. PS, 35, 57; TH, 326.

86. PS, 83.

87. HP, 124.

88. *Ibid.*, 124.

89. GC, 241.

90. TK, 157ff.; GC, 234ff.

91. TK, 215.

92. *Ibid.*, 215.

93. *Ibid.*, 216.

94. *Ibid.*, 218.

95. TH, 338.

96. BT, 19; CLCD, 63.

97. J. Bennett, "Reinhold Niebuhr's Social Ethics", in RN, p. 103.

98. TH, 25.

99. Bennett, "Reinhold Niebuhr's Social Ethics", in RN, p. 103: "...the doctrine of man provides both limits and direction for social ethics. Those limits are themselves a direction. They steer us away from the effort to find absolute solutions...".

100. Cf. Niebuhr's quote on page 25, above.

101. The best example of this is Niebuhr's understanding of the horror of nuclear war in regard to the necessity of keeping the peace through a nuclear balance of terror. Cf. IAH, 1.

102. This too is a consequence of Niebuhr not taking into account the social construction of human nature. Only by understanding human nature as a compound of social and ontological elements does the political situation within which the individual finds himself or herself become relevant.

103. PS, 15-18, 20FF.

104. *Ibid.*, 35, 65, 83f.

105. This is also the critique of Liberation Theology over and against Political Theology. Cf. G. Gutierrez, *A Theology of Liberation* (Maryknoll, NY: Orbis, 1973), pp. 217-18; and Alfredo Fierro, *The Militant Gospel* (Maryknoll, NY: Orbis, 1977), pp. 263-264.

106. Cf. Earl Shaw, "Beyond Political Theology",in G. McLeod Bryan, (ed.), *Communities of Faith and Radical Discipleship*, (Macon, GA: Mercer, 1986) 33-67.

107. Supporting this is Moltmann's contention that anticipation within history does not involve planning, but involves the formation of goals. Cf. HP, 179.

108. Linked with the ideas of archy and anarchy is the function of government in the construction of the social order. Both Niebuhr and Moltmann understand government to be the primary way in which political society organizes itself. Cf. NDM,II, 269-284 and CCR, 18ff.

109. NDM,II, 284; CPP, 26; CLCD, 44.

110. NDM,II, 269; TPWW, 259.

111. MMIS, 6. Cf also MMIS, xi-xii, 18; CLCD, 48; IAH, 12.

112. CPP, 27.

113. CLCD, 181.

114. At the same time, Niebuhr sees a positive function in fanaticism in that it provides a vital source for social change. Cf. MMIS, 220, 221, 222, 230.

115. CPP, 80.

116. NDM,II, 71.

117. CPP, 15. Cf. NDM,II, 269.

118. CLCD, 46-7.

119. *Ibid.*, 178.

120. CLCD, 178.

121. RRF, 137.

122. *Ibid.*, 144.

123. *Ibid.*, 131.

124. *Ibid.*, 137.

125. Cf. CG, 320-321, 335f.

126. TH, 329. Cf. Boone, *Political Majesty*, 278-280.

127. Nowhere does Moltmann distinctly define what the justice inherent in the Kingdom of God really is. The closest he comes to defining it is in his understanding of the concept of *shalom*. According to Moltmann, *shalom* means not only the "salvation of the soul, individual rescue from the evil world, comfort for the troubled conscience, but also the realization of the eschatological *hope of justice*, the *humanizing* of man, the *socializing* of humanity, *peace* for all creation." Cf.TH, 329.

128. TH, 330.

129. TH, 103, 107-108, 330f.

130. CRPP, 119-146.

131. Cf.CPP, 27, 193; CRPP, 119. For a critique of this, see TH, 330, and R. Alves, *Tomorrow's Child: Imagination, Creativity and the Rebirth of Culture*, (NY: Harper and Row, 1972) p. 53.

132. Cf. TH, 25f.

133. This seems to be the heart of any realist perspective. Cf. D. Levy, *Realism* (NY: Humanities, 1981). This realist perspective can be understood as part and parcel of Niebuhr's shift of emphasis from his Marxist to Christian Realist period. Cf. above, Chapter One.

134. Cf. BT, 115: "Faith is always imperiled on the one side by despair and on the other side by optimism. Of these two enemies of faith, optimism is the more dangerous."

135. DCNR, 63-64: "Religion is easily tempted to...become oblivious to the inevitable compromise between its ideal and the brute facts of life."

136. DCNR, 78, 79,81; ICE, 103. It is important to note here that Niebuhr does not contend that one should be satisfied with a compromise: "The Church should be shrewd enough to see the compromise involved in every adjustment and be stubborn enough to make a new bid for victory after each partial defeat.", DCNR, 81.

137. TH, 328-9.

138. TH, 25.

139. The shift in Niebuhr's theological perspective which occurred in the 1930's further reflects the increasing interest in reaching a compromise form of theology. In Niebuhr's earliest works religious imagination performed a much more creative role in his political thought than it did in his later works. From a reading of R. Fox's biography of Niebuhr, *Reinhold Niebuhr: A Biography* (NY: Pantheon, 1985), it can be argued, I think, that the emphasis on religious imagination was central to his early thought because his audience was primarily those who suffered injustice. As his political insights became more important to the political leaders of his time, the emphasis of his theology shifted with his audience.

140. This is also the critique of Liberation Theology toward Political Theology. Cf. J. Miguez Bonino, *Toward a Christian Political Ethics*, (Phila.: Fortress, 1983).

141. Cf. T. Weber, "Beyond Political Theology: Toward a Constructive Theology of Politics", a paper delivered to the Consultation on Theology and Politics, in Washington D.C., April 15, 1978.

142. Moltmann was aware of this problem. Cf. RRF, 32. His theology, however, does not take adequate account of it.

143. Cf. NDM,II, 87, 166; CRPP, 35.

CHAPTER VI

CONCLUSION: CHRISTIAN REALISM, POLITICAL THEOLOGY AND THE CHRISTIAN HOPE

The previous analysis of Christian Realism and Political Theology has revealed two theological movements which developed out of and in response to different contexts and consequently emphasized different elements of the Christian message. For Niebuhr, the inability of optimistic Christian and secular liberalism adequately to face the totalitarianism of the Hitler and Stalinist regimes and the tensions of the Cold War, demanded a recognition of the elements of sin which accompany any advancement in human personal, social and political relations. He warned against the dangers of pride and the expansionistic desires which accompany it. Politically, he recommended a form of power politics which recognized the necessity of coercion in all political relations. He also urged caution in the transformation of government, based upon his understanding that greater justice is not always achieved through wholesale change. Rather, reform of the existing sociopolitical structures may be more conducive to the achievement of justice.

Moltmann's theology, on the other hand, developed within the context of directedness toward the future. Change and liberation became foci of cultural and political activity. Established structures were to be overthrown or at least transformed. In his theology, Moltmann emphasized those aspects of the Christian message which fueled an impetus for change. His eschatological viewpoint stressed the possibilities of the new rather than the resources for change already in existing structures.

Each of these perspective has implications for understanding the nature of Christian hope. Returning to the discussion which began this dissertation, both Niebuhr and Moltmann claim that their respective positions on hope are the most realistic. Niebuhr, for reasons delineated in the intermediate chapters of this work, maintains that a realistic perspective demands that one be cautious about the nature of one's hope for the transformation of society. Although the possibilities for greater justice and brotherhood are indeterminate, overly optimistic estimates of the possibilities for the attainment of justice, particularly absolute justice, lead to distorted and dangerous political judgments.

Moltmann, on the other hand, contends that in order for hope to be an effective force in life, it must look beyond the possibilities readily evident in the world and reach for the possibilities inherent in the openness of the future. Rather than focus on the dangers of overly optimistic estimates of hope, realistic hope, according to Moltmann, focuses on the dangers of underestimating the possibilities of change and transformation in the social world. For Moltmann, truncated visions of possibility in the world lead to despair or desperation and only operate to maintain the structures of injustice which have been established and ensconced in society.

The present sociopolitical situation, however, points to the inadequacies of both Niebuhr's and Moltmann's understandings of the realism of hope. In the twenty five years since Niebuhr wrote, many positive changes in the sociopolitical relations of the world have taken place which demand a new means of understanding human and political relations. American economic and political hegemony has declined, while Third World and European communities have increased in strength. Within the United States women and other minorities have made giant strides toward equality. And there has been a slow normalization of relations between the United States and the Soviet Union. While in one regard this validates Niebuhr's thesis that the effective balancing of power can create increased economic and social justice, once these balances are approximated, it may be more productive to develop more openness to possibilities of the new than Niebuhr allowed.

At the same time, while many of the hopes of the 1960's and early seventies have reached fruition or are well on the way to fulfillment, the optimism for greater justice which infused that era has been tempered by a recognition of the continual barriers to qualitative social change. The War on Poverty, if not lost, is in defensive retreat. The New Frontier, dependent as it was on new technology, has created a society in which technological interests have outweighed human and humane interests.(1) Moltmann's hope for the possibilities of qualitative increases in justice seems to be waylaid, if not disappointed.

The dilemma of a realistic contemporary theology, therefore, seems to be in walking the fine line between providing a vision for the development of future justice which does not become prematurely truncated through an underestimation of future possibilities and limning a future which can never be attained because the material grounds for its fulfillment are not present, and may never be present. For if the material conditions for fulfillment are not available, hope becomes unrealistically utopian.

It is at this point that a rapprochement between Niebuhr's Christian Realism and Moltmann's Political Theology may provide us with one means of walking that fine line. The remainder of this chapter attempts to draw certain conclusions about the shape of such a theology. It focuses again on the three components of any theology: the God-world relationship, view of history and anthropology.

As Gabriel Marcel has pointed out(2), hope has a subjective side which includes the prefigurement, imagining and picturing of new possibilities. At the same time, however, hope, if it is not to be sheer fantasy, needs to contain an objective side which includes the assessment of the material means for achieving the hoped for result. Of the two sides, the subjective seems to be primary. If hope has an all–encompassing vision, partial fulfillments are always possible in the world because the world will always contain the material means for some degree of fulfillment of that vision. If a vision is lacking or is too severely truncated, however, the material means of possible fulfillment in the world will not be completely recognized, much less come to fruition.

As we saw above, Moltmann primarily emphasizes the continuity and interpenetration of God and world in both causal and ontological senses. In so doing, Moltmann makes it possible to understand that *both* the subjective and objective bases for hope are grounded in the activity of God opening up creation to the future. For Moltmann, the revelation of God not only provides humans with a vision of possibility which surpasses that which can be developed by understanding the world apart from its interpenetration by God, but because God is in the world, the objective possibilities of hope are also given new form. In other words, God's presence in the world changes the material conditions for the fulfillment of hope.

Similarly, Moltmann's eschatological perspective on history begins by understanding human history within the horizon of God's history. Consequently, the possibilities of human history are not merely bounded by God's history, but are given new possibilities through God's history.

Niebuhr's understanding of the relative distinction between God and world causes him to reach a different understanding of the possibilities of the fulfillment of hope. Although Niebuhr does have an idea of God's providence acting in the world, he has a difficulty understanding God's activity in the world in a causal sense (apart from original creation). He also finds it somewhat difficult to conceive of the presence of the eternal in the temporal. While the revelation of God may enlighten the possibilities inherent in human history, it does little materially to increase the possibilities of history. Consequently, Niebuhr's vision of what is possible in the world is considerably more narrow than Moltmann's.(3)

These facts would suggest that the starting point for a contemporary theology should be similar to Moltmann's: based on its theological presuppositions, Moltmann's theology provides a more comprehensive foundation for hope than does Niebuhr's. By understanding hope in its widest perspective, it becomes possible to apprehend and make use of the material possibilities of hope which are open to human effort.

6.1: *The Strength of Moltmann's Theology*

As we have seen, Moltmann's theology attempts to bring the Christian message of freedom to actual manifestation under the conditions of existence. In developing this interest, Moltmann adopts a perspective which is based on the possibility of the appearance of the qualitatively new in the world because the power of the *Novum* of God's future creates a new, open future for humankind. For Moltmann, the future is *adventus*, the approach of a radically new situation, rather than *futurum*, an extension of what has occurred in the past.

The presence of the *Novum* in history has several meanings for Moltmann. In one sense, it is the presence and the power of the future in the present. It is God's involvement in the trials and sufferings of the world in such a way that God opens up possibilities of overcoming them. In another sense, the *Novum* is the prevenient grace of God operating within the world empowering those without power by countering the tendencies of the world which close off the future, creating enslavement, desperation and despair, through the activity of the Holy Spirit. Finally, The *Novum* makes past memories into "dangerous memories" which challenge the structures of the past and present with the possibilities of the future.

The result of this perspective is that it allows Moltmann's emphasis on transformation to take on its widest possible application. The future is disconnected from the past in a causative sense. Consequently, former structures of injustice can be overcome. Those who are involved in the quest for justice need not fall into despair because the "New" is always on the horizon, drawing people toward it. Rather than emphasize caution in the search for justice, Moltmann's perspective provides confidence and an impetus for that search. In the search itself, new possibilities will arise which could not be planned for or anticipated. Consequently, Moltmann's theology, with its emphasis on hope and the possibilities of the "New," serves the function of providing a means of and an impetus for looking beyond the present situation. It creates a necessary vision for overcoming the problems of the present. It demands that one not give in to despair and desperation, but act to create a new future based on the "New" offered to us by God.

6.2: *The Fundamental Weakness in Moltmann's Theology*

The greatest strength in Moltmann's theology, the *Novum*, also turns out to be its fundamental weakness. Moltmann's emphasis on the radically "New" does not take seriously enough the factors in the world and in the human constitution which make transformation difficult if not unlikely.

One of the reasons that this aspect remains underdeveloped in Moltmann's thought is that his focus on the future underestimates the degree to which the past is an active force which threatens both the present and the future. Moltmann (and Metz) understands the past as active in the sense of "dangerous memories" which call into question the partial fulfillments of the promised future of God and also prefigure the fulfillment which is to come. The past, however, is not merely the successive anticipations of future fulfillment. It is also not merely memories of what could be and should be. The past also contains memories which actively condition and limit the possibilities for fulfillment. In other words, the past is not only active as anticipation of the *adventus*, but is also active as *futurum*. By limiting his understanding of the future to *adventus*, Moltmann does not take adequate account of the forces in society which militate against the manifestation of the "New" in the world.

Moltmann's emphasis on *adventus* over *futurum* not only misses the negative aspects of *futurum*, it also neglects its positive aspects. The past is not only a restrictive force, but it can also be a source of creativity and novelty in the world.

A final difficulty with Moltmann's emphasis on The *Novum* is that his theology does not give us a means of distinguishing between what is "new" in the world, and thus dependent on the conditions already present in the world, and what is really "New" and dependent on God's activity in the world. In other words, Moltmann has not developed dialectically enough the subjective and objective sides of hope. The "New" must always be related to the "new". In his focus upon *adventus*, Moltmann peremptorily considers *futurum* in a negative sense, as inadequate and misleading. Without elements of *futurum*, however, God's *adventus* is never really connected fully with human history. God acts on history, opens up history, but really has no internal link to history. The "new" is never connected with the "New." Consequently, *adventus* is not a completely adequate way of describing the nature of history. It must be dialectically related to *futurum*.

It is here that Niebuhr's realism can be used as a means of both bolstering and providing objective checks on Moltmann's ever-enlarging hope.

6.3: *Moltmann and Niebuhr as Dialogue Partners*

As pointed out above, one of Niebuhr's strengths is that he recognizes the limits to liberation which are inherent in human existence itself. Where Moltmann understands the limits of liberation primarily in a structural sense, residing in sociopolitical structures, Niebuhr grounds those limits in human beings themselves.

The thrust of Niebuhr's anthropological argument is that human nature is not as mutable as Moltmann thinks. As John Bennett points out, the thrust of Niebuhr's work was to counter liberal optimism with an anthropology which grounded ambiguity in the human being itself.(4) Thus, for Niebuhr man is his own greatest problem.(5) Niebuhr then utilizes this idea of the ambiguity of human existence to develop a social theory and a view of history which emphasize the continued existence of moral ambiguity in all human endeavor. It is this problematic character of human nature, with its implications for social unrest and activity counter to the will of God, which Moltmann misses. By combining these two perspectives, a more adequate understanding of human existence can be developed. It roots the problematic character of human existence in both human nature and in society. It allows for a means of relating the individual aspects of human nature with the social realm. It takes into account the emphasis on sin which is so strongly represented in Protestant theology.

Niebuhr's detailed sociological analysis also provides a dialectical counterpart to Moltmann's understanding of society as basically open to change and transformation. Niebuhr points out how society is necessary for and aids in the complete realization of human potentialities. At the same time, he recognizes that inherent in the formation of *any* society there are factors (such as increased conflict of interest, egoism and a lack of moral control) which hinder the quest for justice.

This combined perspective allows for theology to recognize the extent of the problem facing its attempts at transformation. It disallows any idea of "easy grace" which underestimates the necessity for God's grace. At the same time, it emphasizes that God's grace is operative in the world and is transforming the world.

Finally, Niebuhr's theology provides a dialectical counterpart to Moltmann's theology in that it recognizes the creative aspects of *futurum*. While not totally adequate in itself, Niebuhr's understanding that the structures of reality already in place are not just negative, but also contain possibilities for transformation and change, provides insights which Moltmann's theology lacks. Niebuhr's emphasis on the vital aspects of human nature as they impact society to transform and shape it, when paired with Moltmann's understanding of the Novelty introduced by God's *adventus* enlarges the possibilities of transformation beyond that envisioned by either. Transformation has its source not only in God, but also within human history itself.

In conclusion, dialectically relating Jürgen Moltmann's theology with that of Reinhold Niebuhr can provide us with one means of developing a realistic theology which includes an adequate impetus and grounds for hope for the transformation of the world. Moltmann's emphasis on hope and transformation derived from a strong sense of the transforming activity of God in the world, of God opening the human future through his *adventus*, forms the starting point for this theology. Without this starting point, the quest for justice and transformation can be shortcircuited. This theology is deficient, however, if it does not include Niebuhr's recognition of the positive aspects of *futurum* along with the limiting factors which human nature, society and their combination counterpose to transformation.

Transformation is possible only if there is an adequate vision which drives the quest for justice forward. At the same time, however, transformation is only actual if it recognizes and takes seriously those factors which hinder its actualization. By combining the power of God's *adventus* with that of human *futurum*, the depth and breadth of the transformation possible in the world is given even more inclusive form. By understanding the intransigence of many elements of human existence to change and transformation demands a full understanding of God's grace operative in the world. Dialectically relating Moltmann's theology with Niebuhr's provides us with that fuller understanding.

Notes to Chapter 6

1. Cf. J. K. Galbraith, *The New Industrial State*, for a discussion of the role of technology in the social development of the twentieth century.

2. G. Marcel, *Homo Viator: Introduction to a Metaphysic of Hope*, tr. E. Craufurd. (NY: Harper and Row, 1962), p. 30.

3. Cf. Paul Lehmann, "Christology of Reinhold Niebuhr," in RN, 355 and D. D. Williams, "Niebuhr and Liberalism," in RN, 281.

4. J. Bennett, "Reinhold Niebuhr's Social Thought", in RN, p. 103.

5. NDM, I, 1-2.

BIBLIOGRAPHY

Works by Reinhold Niebuhr

"Alternatives to Communism", *The New Republic*, 147/14 (October 1, 1962).

Beyond Tragedy. NY: Scribners, 1937.

"Can We Organize the World", *Christianity and Crisis*, 23/1 (February 2, 1953).

"Christ the Hope of the World", *Religion in Life*, 23/3 (Summer, 1953).

The Children of Light and the Children of Darkness. NY: Scribners, 1944.

Christian Realism and Political Problems. NY: Scribners, 1953.

Christianity and Power Politics. NY: Scribners, 1940.

Does Civilization Need Religion. NY: Macmillan, 1927.

Essays in Applied Christianity. New York: Meridian, 1959.

Faith and History. NY: Scribners, 1951.

Faith and Politics. Edited by R. Stone. NY: G. Braziller, 1968.

An Interpretation of Christian Ethics. NY: Harper, 1935.

The Irony of American History. NY: Scribners, 1962.

Leaves from the Notebook of a Tamed Cynic. NY: World, 1957 (copyright, 1929).

Love and Justice. Edited by D.D. Robertson. NY: World, 1957.

Man's Nature and His Communities. NY: Scribners, 1965.

Moral Man and Immoral Society. NY: Scribners, 1932.

The Nature and Destiny of Man. 2 vols. NY: Scribners, 1941.

Pious and Secular America. NY: Scribners, 1958.

Reflections on the End of an Era. NY: Scribners, 1934.

"Revelation and the Meaning of History." Dudlean Lecture, Harvard University, (April 14, 1942).

The Self and the Dramas of History. NY: Scribners, 1955.

"Ten Years That Shook My World." *Christian Century* (April 26, 1939) pp. 542-546.

"The Theme of Evanston." *Religion in Life*, 23/3 (Summer, 1954) pp. 334-340.

"Theology and Political Thought in the Western World." *The Ecumenical Review*, 9/3 (April), pp. 253-62.

"Walter Rauschenbusch in Historical Perspective." *Religion in Life*, 27/4 (Fall, 1958) pp. 527-536.

Young Reinhold Niebuhr: His Early Writings. Edited by J. Chrystal. NY: Pilgrim, 1977.

Works About Reinhold Niebuhr

Alves, R. "Christian Realism: Ideology of the Establishment." *Christianity and Crisis*, 33, (1973) pp. 173-6.

Bennett, J. "Realism and Hope after Niebuhr." *Worldview* (May, 1972) pp. 4-14.

Brown, D. "Hope for the Human Future: Niebuhr, Whitehead and Utopian Expectation." *Iliff Review*, 32/3 (Fall, 1975), 3-18.

Carnell, E. *The Theology of Reinhold Niebuhr.* Grand Rapids, Mich.: Eerdmans, 1950.

Fox, R.B. *Reinhold Niebuhr: A Biography.* NY: Pantheon, 1985.

Gilkey, L. "Reinhold Niebuhr's Theology of History." *Journal of Religion*, LIV (October, 1974), pp. 360-86.

Griffin, D. "Whitehead and Niebuhr on God, Man and the World." *Journal of Religion*, 53/2 (April, 1973) 149-75.

Harland, Gordon. *The Thought of Reinhold Niebuhr*. NY: Oxford, 1960.

Harris, R., (ed.). *Reinhold Niebuhr and the Issues of Our Time*. Grand Rapids, Mich.: Eerdmans, 1986.

Hofmann, H. *The Theology of Reinhold Niebuhr*. Translated by L. Smith, NY: Scribners, 1956.

Kegley, C. and Bretall, R. *Reinhold Niebuhr: His Religious, Social and Political Thought*. NY: Pilgrim, 1984.

King, R.H. *The Omission of the Holy Spirit from Reinhold Niebuhr's Theology*. NY: Philosophical Library, 1964.

Lochman, J.M. "The Problem of Realism in Reinhold Niebuhr's Theology." *Scottish Journal of Theology*, 11, (1958) pp. 253-264.

McCann, D. *Christian Realism and Liberation Theology*. Maryknoll, NY: Orbis, 1982.

Patrick, D. "Opening Niebuhrian Thought to the Left." *Christianity and Crisis*, XXX (October 19, 1970), pp. 212-15.

Plaskow, J. *Sex, Sin and Grace: Women's Experience and The Theologies of Reinhold Niebuhr and Paul Tillich*. NY: University Press, 1980.

"Reinhold Niebuhr: A Symposium." *Union Seminary Quarterly Review*, XI (May, 1956), pp. 3-21.

Rutledge, D.W. "The Salvation of History: History and the End in Reinhold Niebuhr." *Perspectives in Religious Studies*, 8, (1981) pp. 122-33.

Sanderson, J.W. "Historical Fact or Symbol." *Westminster Theological Journal*, XX (May, 1958) pp. 158-69.

Shiba, C. *Transcendence and the Political* (Ph.D. Dissertation, Princeton Theological Seminary, 1983).

Stone, R. *Reinhold Niebuhr: Prophet to Politicians*. Washington D.C.: University Press, 1981.

Weber, T. "Niebuhr's Strategies of Justice." *Worldview*, XII (May, 1969), pp. 16-20.

Works by Jürgen Moltmann

"An Open Letter to José Míguez Bonino." *Christianity and Crisis*, (March 29, 1976) pp. 57-63.

The Church in the Power of the Spirit: A Contribution to Messianic Ecclesiology, Tr. M. Kohl. NY: Harper and Row, 1977.

"The Cross and Civil Religion", in Moltmann, *et al.*, *Religion and Political Society*. NY: Harper, 1974 pp. 9-47.

The Crucified God: The Cross of Christ as the Foundation and Criticism of Christian Theology, Tr. R.A. Wilson. NY: Harper and Row, 1974.

The Experiment Hope, Tr. M.D. Meeks. Philadelphia: Fortress, 1975.

The Future of Creation, Tr. M. Kohl. Philadelphia: Fortress, 1979.

God in Creation, Tr. M. Kohl. NY: Harper and Row, 1985.

Hope and Planning, Tr. M. Clarkson. London: SCM, 1971.

"The Liberation of Oppressors." *Journal of the Interdenominational Theological Center*, 6/2 (Spring, 1979) pp. 69-82.

Man: Christian Anthropology in the Conflicts of the Present, Tr. J. Sturdy. Philadelphia: Fortress, 1974.

On Human Dignity, Tr. M.D. Meeks. Philadelphia: Fortress, 1984.

Politische Theologie/Politische Ethik. Munich: Kaiser-Gruenewald, 1984.

Religion Revolution and the Future, Tr. M.D. Meeks. NY: Scribners, 1969.

Theology of Hope: On the Ground and the Implications of a Christian Eschatology. Tr. J. Leitch. NY: Harper and Row, 1964.

"Toward a Political Hermeneutic of the Gospel." *Union Seminary Quarterly Review*, 23/4. (Summer, 1968) 303-323.

The Trinity and the Kingdom, Tr. M. Kohl. NY: Harper and Row, 1981.

Umkehr der Zukunft. Munich: C. Kaiser, 1970.

Works on Jürgen Moltnmann

Bergmueller, A. (ed.). *Zum politischen Auftrag der christlichen Gemeinde*. (Gutersloh: Gerd Mohn, 1974)

Chopp, R. *The Praxis of Suffering*. Maryknoll, NY: Orbis, 1986.

Chapman, G. Clarke, Jr. "Moltmann's Vision of Man." *Anglican Theological Review*, 56/3 (July, 1974) pp. 310-30.

Deuser, H., *et al.* (ed.) *Gottes Zukunft/Zukunft der Welt: Zum 60. Geburtstag Jürgen Moltmanns*. Munich: C. Kaiser, 1986.

Fierro, A. *The Militant Gospel*. Maryknoll, NY: Orbis, 1977.

French, W. "Moltmann's Eschatology Naturalized." *Journal of Religion*, 68/1 (January, 1988), pp. 78-86.

McWilliams, W. *The Passion of God: Divine Suffering in Contemporary Protestant Theology*. Macon, GA: Mercer University, 1985.

Marsch, W.-D., *Diskussion über die "Theologie der Hoffnung" von Jürgen Moltmann*. Munich: C. Kaiser, 1967.

Meeks, M.D. *Origins of the Theology of Hope*. Philadelphia: Fortress, 1974.

Morse, C. *The Logic of Promise in Moltmann's Theology* Philadelphia: Fortress, 1979.

Niewiadomski, J. *Die Zweideutigkeit von Gott und Welt in Jürgen Moltmanns Theologien*. Innsbruk: Tyrolia, 1982.

Scott, D. "Ethics on a Trinitarian Basis: Moltmann's *The Crucified God*." *Anglican Theological Review*, 60/2 (April, 1978), pp. 166-79.

Weber, T. "Beyond Political Theology: Toward a Constructive Theology of Politics," an unpublished paper delivered to the Consultation on Theology and Politics in Washington D.C. (April 15, 1978.)

GENERAL

Alves, R. *Tomorrow's Child*. NY: Harper and Row, 1972.

Aquinas, Thomas. *Summa Theologica*, I, 93.

Augustine. *De Trinitatis*.

Barth, K. *Community, State and Church*. Gloucester, MA: P. Smith, 1968.

_____. *Church Dogmatics*, III/2. Edinburgh: T and T Clark, 1960.

_____. *Epistle to the Romans*. NY: Oxford, 1933.

Becker, E. *The Denial of Death*. NY: Free Press, 1973.

Bernstein, R. *Habermas and Modernity*. Cambridge, MA: MIT, 1985.

Bloch, E. *Abschied von der Utopie*. Frankfurt a.Main: Suhrkamp, 1980.

Boone, C.K. *The Concept of Political Majesty in the Thought of Reinhold Niebuhr and Jürgen Moltmann*. Ann Arbor, MI: University Microfilm, 1978.

Braaten, C. *The Future of God*. NY: Newman, 1970.

Braaten, C. and Jenson, R. *The Futurist Option*. NY: Harper and Row, 1970.

Bultmann, R. *Existence and Faith*. Tr. S. Ogden. NY: Meridian, 1960.

_____. *Jesus and the Word*. NY: Scribners, 1934.

_____. *Jesus Christ and Mythology*. NY: Scribners, 1958.

Burgmueller, W. and Weth, R. *Die Barmer Theologische Erklärung*. Neukirchen: Neukirchner, 1983.

Bury, J. *The Idea of Progress*. NY: Dover, 1932.

Carpenter, J.A. *Nature and Grace: Toward an Integral Perspective*. NY: Crossroads, 1988.

Dawson, C. *Progress and Religion*. NY: Doubleday, 1960.

Dillenberger, J. and Welch, C. *Protestant Christianity*. NY: Scribners, 1954.

Eller, V. *Christian Anarchy*. Grand Rapids, MI: Eerdmans, 1987.

Feil, E. and Weth, R. *Diskussion zur Theologie der Revolution*. Munich: C. Kaiser, 1970.

Fierro, A. *The Militant Gospel*. Maryknoll, NY: Orbis, 1977.

Fretheim, T. *The Suffering of God: An Old Testament Perspective*. Phila.: Fortress, 1984.

Gadamer, H. G., *Truth and Method*. NY: Crossroads, 1982.

Galbraith, John Kenneth. *The New Industrial State*. NY: Signet, 1967.

Gutierrez, G. *A Theology of Liberation*. Maryknoll: Orbis, 1973.

Harnack, Adolf von, *What is Christianity?* Gloucester, MA: Peter Smith, 1978.

Hebblethwaite, B. *The Christian Hope*. Grand Rapids, MI: Eerdmans, 1984.

Heilbroner, R. *An Inquiry into the Human Prospect*. NY: Norton, 1974.

Hobsbawm, E.J. *The Age of Revolution 1789-1848*. NY: Mentor, 1962.

Jüngel, E. *The Doctrine of the Trinity: God's Being is in Becoming*. Edinburgh: R. and R. Clark, 1976.

Käsemann, E. *New Testament Questions of Today*. Phila.: Fortress, 1982.

Kent, J. *The End of the Line?* Phila.: Fortress, 1982.

Kümmel, W. *The Theology of the New Testament*. Nashville: Abingdon, 1973.

Leiss, W. *The Domination of Nature*. Boston: Beacon, 1972.

206

Mannheim, K. *Ideology and Utopia*. NY: Harvest, 1936.

Marcuse, H. *One Dimensional Man*. Boston: Beacon, 1964.

McKnight, E. *What is Form Criticism?* Phila.: Fortress, 1969.

McWilliams, W. *The Passion of God: Divine Suffering in Contemporary Protestant Theology*. Macon, GA: Mercer University, 1985.

Metz, J.B. *Faith in History and Society*. NY: Seabury, 1980.

_____. *Zur Theologie der Welt*. Mainz: Mattias-Gruenewald, 1968.

_____. *Unterbrechungen*. Gutersloh: G. Mohn, 1981.

Miguez Bonino, J. *Toward a Christian Political Ethics*. Phila.: Fortress, 1983.

Montague, G.T. *The Holy Spirit: Growth of a Biblical Tradition*. NY: Paulist, 1976.

Pannenberg, W. *Theology of the Kingdom of God*. Phila.: Fortress, 1969.

Rauschenbusch, W. *A Theology for the Social Gospel*. Nashville: Abingdon, 1978.

Ritschl, A. *The Christian Doctrine of Justification and Reconciliation*. 3 vol. tr., H.R. Mackintosh and A.B. Macaulay. Edinburgh, 1900.

Robinson, J.M. *The Beginnings of Dialectical Theology*. 2 vol. Richmond, VA: John Knox, 1968.

Sanders, T. "The Theology of Liberation: Christian Utopianism". *Christianity and Crisis*, 33, (1973) pp. 167-73.

Schleiermacher, F. *The Christian Faith*. Phila.: Fortress, 1976.

Schmitt, C. *Politische Theologie*. Berlin: Duncker and Humblot, 1933.

Schweitzer, A. *The Quest of the Historical Jesus*. NY: Macmillan, 1968.

Tillich, P. *Systematic Theology*. 3 vol. Chicago: University of Chicago, 1951, 1957, 1963.

Toffler, A. *Future Shock*. London: Pan, 1970.

Tucker, R. (ed.) *The Marx-Engels Reader*. NY: Norton, 1978.

Veldhuis, R. *Realism vs. Utopianism: Reinhold Niebuhr's Christian Realism and the Relevance of Utopian Thought for Social Ethics*. Assen, Neth.: Van Gorcum, 1975.

Zahrnt, H. *Aufklärung durch Religion*. Munich: Piper, 1980.

Zimmerli, W. *Man and His Hope in the Old Testament*. London: SCM, 1971.

INDEX

DDS